THE SECOND CIVIL WAR

EXAMINING THE INDIAN DEMAND
FOR ETHNIC SOVEREIGNTY

T. David Price

[signature]

4-7-98

SECOND SOURCE, INCORPORATED
ST. PAUL PARK, MINNESOTA

The cover illustration is reproduced from the front page of *Harper's Weekly: A Journal of Civilization*, dated June 19, 1875. The illustration is by Thomas Nast, and represents Chief Spotted Tail and President Ulysses S. Grant. Color tinting was applied to the black and white print.

Published by Second Source Inc. St. Paul Park, Minnesota, 55071

ISBN 0-9663728-0-8

1st Paperback addition: March1998

1st Printing.

This book is dedicated to my wife and son. Special thanks is given to my mother, Marie, who taught me to persevere, and to my father, Thomas, who taught me to fish and hunt. I must also dedicate this book to Beatrice, as I promised 30 years ago.

CONTENTS

CHAPTER ONE

My Unequal Family

  In the afternoon of July 5, 1997, there was a family wedding in Superior Wisconsin. My cousin was marrying a beautiful Indian woman. It should have been a wedding like any other. I would drink too much, dance too much, and not remember anyone's name. The next morning I would wake up and regret that I asked some middle aged shirttail relation what her husband did for a living — twice in 5 minutes. But I had a different feeling this time, and it wasn't from the icebox mist that always comes off Lake Superior in the early morning. We were staying at the Barker's Island Inn, a trendy tourist motel on a small island sprinkled with relics of the pale lake's nautical past. A narrow bridge on the island's north edge ushered cars toward a whaleback freighter and steam dredge floating landlocked on the grass. They looked interesting but lonely, just the way the big lake always made me feel.

  This particular morning I hoisted my son onto my shoulders and we strolled the "elephant walk" past the downrigged salmon boats and reefed sailboats on the lee side of the island. He would be five in a month and still loved the view topside and the slow swaying gait of a big tusker. The sea gulls swooped and kittered overhead, stopping to flutter like tuxedoed humming birds when something looked edible. My son saw something on the water's edge and I swung him down gently on the rip-wrap. In 10 seconds, he had clamored down the jumble of rocks and plunged his foot deep in the clear water. It was time to go and have brunch, and if I saw Uncle George,[1] to apologize.

George was the father of the groom and a Methodist minister in Wisconsin. I knew George pretty well because we hunted deer on his farm near Richland Center. He is a distinguished looking man with a neat gray mustache who always looks like a minister, even when dressed in blaze orange and carrying a rifle. George speaks to you with his chin a little down or a little up. When it is down, he looks ready to say a prayer. When his chin is up and his eyelids are half closed you feel as if you need to confess something. George's chin was up when he appeared next to me at the wedding reception. I'd had a few beers and was lathered from an hour of waxing the dance floor. It must have been 11 p.m., and I'd made good on a promise to my wife not to utter the words "Indian treaty" to anyone, anyhow, anytime. I'd have made it too, easy, no sweat. The possibility had never occurred to me that the groom's father was going to ask me about my views on Indian treaty rights.

George had heard from his sister (my mother-in-law) about the anti-spearing demonstration I had staged at Mille Lacs Lake in Minnesota on April 10, 1997. George wanted to know why I opposed Indian treaty fishing. Specifically, did I have reasonable concerns or was I a racist? Even then, I might have kept my promise to my wife, but George cautioned that before I said anything he would provide a "simple" explanation of treaty rights.

For the last three years, I had been doing research on Indian sovereignty and treaty rights, so I was interested in his explanation. I knew treaty rights were a complex and confusing tangle of conflicting laws that had stymied the best legal minds. Now George was going to explain the whole mess to me in a few sentences. I knew that treaties could not be explained simply and that those who tried probably had not studied the subject to any extent. Almost everyone I met fell into this category. Few people have ever read an Indian treaty or know about major events in Indian history or policy, such as the Dawes Act or the Indian Reorganization Act of 1934. I had already discussed treaty issues with scores of people, including judges and lawyers who were involved in treaty law up to the level of the Supreme Court. I had also been to Washington D.C. less than a month earlier as the guest of the Citizens Equal Rights Alliance (CERA), a group consisting of both

Indians and non-Indians concerned about Indian issues.

As George began his explanation, I could sense the blood rushing toward my tongue, until it flexed inside my clenched jaws like a jogger stretching for a ten mile run. George was asking me point blank about treaty rights, and all promises to my wife were off.

George said that treaty rights were simply property rights, not privileges based on race. He confidently asked me to compare treaty rights to the easements he worked out with the man who had just purchased his farm. The man owned all the land, but George had an easement to hunt on the land for 10 years, just like the Indians had treaties to guarantee their hunting and fishing rights. It was exactly the same, he said, as explanations he had learned from some Indian friends of his. George did not know that I was already intimately familiar with this popular argument. In fact, I had written a rebuttal to it months earlier in response to an editorial with a similar theme, written by the D. J. Tice of the Saint Paul *Pioneer Press*. In his article, Tice claimed that treaty rights are simply property rights that do not change over time. He claimed, among other things, that Indians would (surely) not abuse these special rights, particularly against non-Indians who own land within reservations. He argues that "the likelihood of thousands of non-Indian Minnesotans being turned into defenseless subjects of the tribe is…highly debatable."[2] Tice said the real issue at stake is whether American traditions like property rights and contracts are being kept. He goes so far as to say that the American way does not always mean equal rights for everyone, implying that property rights have always given landowners special privileges that can be passed on to their offspring.

Uncle George's argument took on a similar logic, and when he finished his "simple" explanation, I began by talking about the Tice editorial and its claims. Though I had written a rebuttal as a "guest editor" to the *Pioneer Press* two days after the Tice editorial, the paper had never printed it. Now George was offering me the voice that the paper refused to let me air. It was an offer I couldn't refuse.

The treaty rights argument, I insisted, is not about property rights, it's about equal rights. Indian apologists would like to reduce the issue to property rights but to do so is an attempt to camouflage the real issues. I had been shocked to read in Tice's editorial that the American way is not always equal rights for everyone. Perhaps there is a revised edition of the Constitution that I'm not familiar with. Equal rights for everyone has always been the ideal of this country even though it has often failed miserably in practice. Throughout the history of the United States, there has always been some group (often composed mostly of White people) who have powerfully influenced or controlled public opinion for the purpose of subjecting another race, ethnic group, minority, or religious sect to blatant discrimination or oppression.

Perhaps the best known failure to live up to the American ideal of equality was the institution of slavery. In 1855, Lincoln wrote a letter to Joshua Speed which eloquently states convictions that equal rights should never be compromised, but were being willfully violated at the time:

> As a nation we began by declaring that 'all men are created equal.' We now practically read it 'all men are created equal, except negroes.' When the Knownothings get control, it will read 'all men are created equal except negroes and foreigners and Catholics.' When it comes to this, I shall prefer emigrating to some country where they make no pretense of loving liberty - to Russia, for instance, where despotism can be taken pure, without the base alloy of hypocrisy.[3]

Lincoln refused to bow to racist public opinion or to malleable courts. He was willing to go to war to preserve the sovereignty of the United States because he knew if the South seceded from the Union, he would have no power to use the Constitution to defend equal rights for everyone. Most people mistakenly think the Civil War was fought to end slavery, but that was a secondary cause for the war. The primary cause was the *question of sovereignty*. Lincoln realized the United States government would have no say about slavery if the Confederate States of America became a sovereign country.

The war that resulted cost the lives of more Americans than any other, including World War I and II, with casualties of approximately 650,000 men for both sides. Remember these men, this war, and

Abraham Lincoln's greatest achievement when thinking about whether the United States intended to share its sovereignty within its territory and jurisdiction. At Gettysburg, Lincoln states that the nation was "conceived in liberty, and dedicated to the proposition that all men are created equal."

As a result of the Civil War, two amendments were added to the U.S. Constitution. In 1866, the 13th Amendment made slavery illegal in the United States. The 14th Amendment of 1867 states, "Any person residing within the territory and jurisdiction of the United States is a United States Citizen. Within the territory and Jurisdiction of the United States, *all citizens shall be subject to the equal treatment of the law*" (emphasis added).[4] Unfortunately, constitutional law has proven to be a poor assurance that equal treatment would in fact prevail. Unequal treatment of Blacks continued in obvious ways for another 100 years under the doctrine of "separate but equal." Despite such egregious errors, however, few would dispute the good intentions of our equality-based laws. Yet, by knowingly circumventing these laws on behalf of a certain race, pro-Indian advocates thumb their noses at the foundation of the U.S. Constitution.

But let's return to my discussion with Uncle George. I told him the easements he had with the man who bought grandpa's farm from him were not the same as treaty rights. Indian treaties give special status to people based on race or ethnic origin. Suppose the hunting easement read, "I grant George or his descendants the right to hunt on the farm for ten years, unless any of the descendants are Jewish." Would that stand up in court? Or suppose you had a restaurant and you had a smoking and a non-smoking section. That would be constitutional because it is in the interest of public health to treat smokers and non-smokers differently, even though it might be an inconvenience. It would be quite a different matter, however, to have one section of the restaurant for Black, White, Asian, and Hispanic Americans and another for Indians. Property rights are not based on race, at least not anymore.

By the time I had said this, Uncle George was beginning to seem less sure of himself about property rights. He was, however, quite willing to continue. "Maybe property rights aren't the main issue about treaties, but treaties are hundreds of years old, solemn promises the government made and which the government has to keep. We owe the Indians something, after all we stole their land."

I asked him who the "we" was that stole the land from the Indians? It wasn't me or you, or our fathers or grandfathers. In the early years of the republic, the government bought some land from Indians and took the rest. The U.S. took 13 colonies from the British and the Southwest from Mexico. The government never apologized for the taking. To preserve southern culture, the Confederate States of America took the South, and the United States took it back, again without apology. For most of the course of human history, title to land existed by right of conquest. What nations could take and hold on to belonged to them. We can argue all night about whether the United States should have taken its land, but it won't matter. The Europeans brought the concept of land ownership to this country and now the land is all within the territory and jurisdiction of the U.S. government. The Civil War was fought to preserve the sovereignty of the federal government and that of the states. It was fought to ensure that one race would never again oppress another. We haven't always lived up to that ideal, but we have to try.

I agreed with Uncle George that the government owed Indians something, but we did not agree on what that "something" was. If the government owed Indians money for promises not kept, I reasoned it should pay up with interest. This is a task the government has been working on since the Indian Claims Commission was established on August 13, 1946. It was estimated at the time it would take 30 years to settle all the claims, but after 42 years, these claims still have not been settled.

Billions of dollars have been given to Indian tribes in the form of grants, court settlements and federal services; billions more have been funneled to tribes through exclusive casino rights granted by many states. Yet none of this will satisfy Indians. In addition to these concessions, they want much of their original territories in North America restored without any jurisdictional strings attached. I was sure of this based on my extensive research on Indian sovereignty, including such books as *Struggle for the Land*, written by prominent Indian author and university professor Ward Churchill.

I didn't mention it to George, but I thought that if America owed something to Indians, it also owed something to African-Americans. When we speak of the debt owed to Indians, we probably mean as much in a moral sense as in a treaty sense. If there is a moral debt to Indians, then there is an equal moral debt to African-Americans, even if they have no treaty to back up their claim. From the Indians, the U.S. took the land, from African-Americans, the U.S. took Africa. Blacks were taken *from* their land. African-Americans came from communal tribes, just as the Indians. We do not now propose to give Blacks an African-American homeland where they can make their own laws and rule themselves in the traditional African manner. We can give them liberty and equality, which itself is a prize most countries are incapable of providing. Nations must help the disadvantaged get an education, a job, and equal opportunity in every aspect of life. But governments must help people based on *need*, not race or ethnic origin.

In a utopian vision of the world, Indians want tribal jurisdiction over all current Indian lands without any interference from the American government or the U.S. Constitution. According to many tribal leaders and Indian sovereignty advocates, the balance of American soil currently not under Indian jurisdiction and taxation would be "rented" to the American people. Indians would live in sovereign nations with government-to-government relations with the United States. The "rent" for U.S. lands not under tribal jurisdiction would be paid to sovereign Indian nations in the form of free schools, medical care, roads, social security, welfare and other benefits associated with "special" American citizenship. The highest aspiration of the Indian sovereignty movement is to develop tribal utopias that are completely independent of the United States, while retaining access to the social and financial benefits of American citizenship.

Today, Indians have come a long way down the path to sovereign status and most of the gains have come since 1970. Three political protest events were instrumental in bringing about this change in Indian policy. In 1969, Indians occupied Alcatraz Island and controlled it for 19 months; in November 1972, they took over the Bureau of Indian Affairs building in Washington D.C.; and in February 1973, there was a 71-day stand-off at the Wounded Knee battlefield in South Dakota.

These protests occurred at a time when politicians were afraid of negative publicity associated with failing to help Indians. Indian acts of violence and terrorism were rewarded with cash payments and special Senate commissions that gave the protesters *carte blanche* to write their own Indian policy. Courts at the time were reluctant to convict Indians on any charge. In late 1975, court trials for Indians arrested in connection with the Wounded Knee occupation (including leaders such as Russell Means) had a conviction rate of about 7 percent.[5]

Out of the protest movement of the 1970s has come an Indian demand for sovereignty and the return of as much land as "White guilt" will allow. Indians say this is the only payment that will permit Indians to survive as a culture. The government has complied with these demands in many ways and the effects of this "payback" are beginning to impact large numbers of Americans — both Indian and non-Indian. I talked at length with Uncle George about numerous cases where civil rights of Indians and non-Indians were grossly violated but ultimately dismissed because of the tribal defense of sovereign immunity. Even when alleged offenses occurred on Indian-owned property located off Indian reservations (like casino corporate offices), sovereign immunity has been used as a defense to throw the case out of U.S. courts.

What Uncle George and newspaper editorialist D. J. Tice didn't realize is that treaty rights cover a lot more than fishing and hunting rights, and hundreds of thousands of Americans are potentially "defenseless subjects of the tribe" wherever Indian jurisdiction and immunity are allowed. Increasingly, that means not only on the reservation, but anywhere. The story of the Indian sovereignty movement is broad and complicated and can't be explained simply in a few minutes.

In the morning, I apologized to Uncle George for arguing with him for 45 minutes and said I hoped no one had overheard us (I'm sure people did). George was gracious and kind, and said it was all right, after all, he was the one who brought up the question. He said he didn't necessarily agree with all I had said, but he could see the issue wasn't as simple as he had thought. "I can see I'm going to have to rethink my liberal viewpoint a little," he said. Then he asked if I was going to be able to hunt with Michael and himself in the fall. Relieved, I said I hoped I could, but as it turned out, I was too busy writing a book.

CHAPTER TWO

Hunting and Gathering in the 21st Century

In the early 19th century, European settlers began to immigrate to North America in huge numbers. From 1830 to 1850 alone, the population nearly doubled from 12 million to 23 million people.[1] One of the influences that caused this mass migration was James Fenimore Cooper's *The Last of the Mohicans*, written in 1826. Cooper's success as a writer began with *The Pioneers* in 1823, when he introduced the world to the Leatherstocking Tales and adventurer Natty Bumppo. The series about the buckskin-clad frontiersman made Cooper world famous, and the stories created a nearly irresistible interest among Europeans about things American. *The Last of the Mohicans* was translated into many languages: German, French, Russian, Spanish, Italian, Egyptian and Persian, to name a few. Ironically, Cooper was one of the early conservationists in America. He disliked mass immigration and its effect on the Indians and the unspoiled wilderness. He had a strong dislike for the market hunting techniques practiced at the time. But the effect of Cooper's books was to introduce the idea of an endless pristine wilderness to the depressed masses in Europe. They came in a hoard, hungry for wilderness land, freedom and adventure.[2]

At this time, most of Europe was still ruled by kings and owned by barons, dukes and a hundred other forms of nobility. Religious intolerance was the rule almost everywhere. Societies were divided into rigid classes with little opportunity for most people to improve their position in life. Hunting and fishing were mostly the privilege of the kings and nobility. Most forests, streams and lakes were off limits to the common man, and severe punishment awaited those who dared to touch the king's game. In some cases, children were hanged for poaching a rabbit. Even today in England, trout streams and grouse moors are private property for the consumption of the rich. To fish one pays an exorbitant fee for access to a few yards of water for a day. But in the United States, we have always believed that all fish and game belong to all people equally. We don't talk much about it because it is so strongly ingrained that we take it for granted.

During the 1970s, I lived in Bellingham, Washington, in a town near Puget Sound and the Canadian border. I had a lot of fishing and skiing buddies across the border in Vancouver, British Columbia, and several of them were recent immigrants from Scotland.   Peter Ditchfield was one of them, an interesting character who knew a hundred pub songs like *Jack Duff, the Wild Colonial Boy*, and had a brogue as thick as Scottish Ale. One day we were fishing salmon on the Mamquam River just north of Vancouver. He told me how great it was that in Canada and "the States" we could just go to a river and fish. When he was a boy growing up in Scotland, only the rich could afford to fish, and it was one of the reasons he had immigrated. That day stuck in my mind: the name of the river, the scent of the riverbed, the sunshine glinting off a big rock at the end of a glass-like pool. My friend's words about American-style freedom from one who grew up under a different set of rules was also unforgettable. Here, lakes and rivers are in the public domain. I sat staring into the gin-clear water and wondered what it would be like to be a kid and watch someone else fishing on a sunny day, knowing you weren't in the right socio-economic class to participate.

Then came the *Boldt* decision in Washington State that divided fishing resources on the basis of race. On March 22, 1974, Judge George Boldt issued his famous decision giving 50 percent of the available fish resources to Indians fishing at the "usual and accustomed" fishing grounds and stations in Washington state. Boldt based his interpretation of treaty fishing rights on the short explanation of fishing and gathering rights contained in the Treaty of Medicine Creek. The part of the treaty pertaining to these rights is Article 3, shown on the next page.

TREATY WITH THE NISQUALLI, PUYALLUP, ETC., 1854

(Medicine Creek Treaty)

Articles of agreement and convention made and concluded on the she-nah-nam or Medicine Creek, in the Territory of Washington.

ARTICLE 3. The right of taking fish, at all the usual and accustomed grounds and stations, is further secured to said Indians **in common with** all citizens of the Territory, and of erecting temporary houses for the purpose of curing, together with the privilege of hunting, gathering roots and berries, and pasturing their horses on open and unclaimed lands: *Provided, however,* that they shall not take shellfish from any beds staked or cultivated by citizens, and that they shall alter all stallions not intended for breeding-horses, and shall keep up and confine the latter. (emphasis added) [3]

Those who are not familiar with the *Boldt* decision will wonder what part of the treaty talks about giving Indians 50 percent of the fish resources. Article 3 is the only part of the treaty that mentions fishing rights, and it says nothing about dividing fish resources according to race-based percentages. Furthermore, there is no 19th century precedent for doing so. Because treaty language is often very brief, however, the courts frequently assume there is something missing, and try to correct the problem by reading between the lines. This method of treaty interpretation was set up by the Supreme Court during the 1930s and 1940s when it established several rules by which treaties were to be interpreted. These rules are called the Canons of Treaty Construction:

1. Treaties are to be construed as the Indians who negotiated the treaty would have understood them.
2. Treaties are to be interpreted liberally to protect the Indians.
3. Ambiguities in treaty language are to be resolved in favor of the Indians.[4]

Given the fact that courts are expected to interpret treaties along these lines, it doesn't matter much what the treaty actually says. If non-Indians dispute a clause in a treaty, the courts will be biased in their interpretation toward the Indians. The Supreme Court sanctions this bias. It would be hard to find a better example of court-approved race preference since the time of the "Jim Crow" laws of the South. In fact, a treaty ruling regarding the Menominee Tribe of Wisconsin in 1968 established the precedent that if a treaty says nothing about hunting and fishing rights, the rights are said to exist in full force anyway.[5] By following this canon, the Supreme Court has given itself implicit permission to re-write Indian treaties, even though the treaty making process was ended by congressional law in 1871.

As I demonstrate in a later chapter, "Indian Treaties and Racial Segregation," treaties were often written by government agents in the field who were given a great deal of latitude. The brief nature of treaties is testimony to the lack of long-range planning in treaty making. This does not justify a racially biased interpretation, however. In general, treaties were written to help Indians make the transition from a hunting and gathering existence to that of full citizens, working side by side with other Americans.

The 1854 Treaty of Medicine Creek devotes two sentences to the question of Indian hunting, fishing, gathering, and oddly enough, castrating stallions. Judges tell us we must honor the solemn promises given in treaties. In the *Boldt* decision, the solemn promise was that the Indian had a right to fish "in common with" all citizens of the territory. Judge Boldt based his ruling on this three-word phrase, and he interprets the meaning of "in common with" as "sharing equally." Boldt said he used the dictionary definition of "in common with" to come to his conclusion. Boldt then made a leap of logic that many Americans have questioned ever since. He defined "sharing equally" to mean that Indians, who represent less than 1 percent of the population in most parts of America, are entitled to 50 percent of the fish resources on land Indians sold to the federal government. In the case of the Medicine Creek Treaty, this meant large parts of the state of Washington.

I believe Judge Boldt's decision to split available natural resources 50-50 between Indians and non-Indians is based on a misinterpretation. Ironically, this phrase is used again in Article 10 of the Medicine Creek Treaty to establish an agricultural and industrial school for tribes living in the Puget Sound district. It reads:

> The United States further agrees to establish at the general agency for the district of Puget's Sound, within one year from the ratification hereof, and to support, for a period of twenty years, an agricultural and industrial school, to be free to children of the said tribes and bands, *in common with* those of the other tribes of said district ... for the term of twenty years, to instruct the Indians in their respective occupations (emphasis added).[6]

Here are the same three words used again in the same treaty. Is it reasonable to interpret this second use of "in common with" to mean that one tribal group would have a right to *more* school access than any other group?

The Medicine Creek Treaty was written with nine tribal groups who lived within the Puget Sound district. The treaty says any other tribal groups in the district will share the district school facilities "in common with" the group that actually signed the treaty. If we suppose there are two additional tribal groups in the district who did not sign the treaty, is it reasonable to assume the treaty means 50 percent of the school resources would go to the non-treaty group of two tribes, and the other 50 percent of the resources would go to the nine tribal groups who signed the treaty? How could this fit the dictionary definition of "sharing equally"?

I don't believe the use of the phrase "in common with" in the Medicine Creek Treaty can be interpreted as meaning anything other than Indians have the same fishing rights in Washington state as all other citizens. Using the same interpretation of "in common with," all Indians in the Puget Sound School District should have an equal opportunity to go to school, regardless of which tribe actually signed a treaty 144 years ago. Judge Boldt and the Supreme Court appear to have it otherwise, with one definition of "in common with" for Indians, and another for non-Indians, based on the Court's Indian-biased rules of treaty interpretation. Unfortunately, such inconsistencies with treaty interpretation and application are common and have plagued Indian policy for the last hundred years.

In fact, since the *Boldt* decision, other treaties have been interpreted as if the phrase "in common with" were included in the treaty *even if the treaty doesn't contain the phrase*. Such a standard is being applied to the Chippewa Treaty of 1837, which is currently used by tribes in Minnesota and Wisconsin to claim half of the available fish resources in certain areas of Minnesota. The lakes from which the Indians want to spear and net fish are not on reservation lands, but on land sold to the government in this treaty. This treaty, like all of them I have researched, is very brief. Like many treaties written in the 1830s or later, it gives a 20-year time limit to Indian benefits (annuities) paid by the government, and indicates that Indians are to learn to become self-sufficient in the arts of civilization, such as farming, blacksmith work, and education during that time frame. In these respects, it is very similar to the Medicine Creek Treaty of 1854. With regard to Chippewa fishing and hunting, all privileges are mentioned in a single sentence in Article 5, totalling all of 38 words.

TREATY WITH THE CHIPPEWA, 1837

*Articles of a treaty made and concluded at St. Peters
(the confluence of the St. Peters and Mississippi rivers)
in the Territory of Wisconsin, between the United States
of America, by their commissioner, Henry Dodge, Governor
of said Territory, and the Chippewa nation of Indians, by
their chiefs and headmen.*

ARTICLE 1. The said Chippewa nation cede to the United States all that tract of country included within the following boundaries:

Beginning at the junction of the Crow Wing and Mississippi rivers, between twenty and thirty miles above where the Mississippi is crossed by the forty-sixth parallel of north latitude, and running thence to the north point of Lake St. Croix, one of the sources of the St. Croix river; thence to and along the dividing ridge between the waters of Lake Superior and those of the Mississippi, to the sources of the Ocha-sua-sepe a tributary of the Chippewa river; thence to a point on the Chippewa river, twenty miles below the outlet of Lake De Flambeau; thence to the junction of the Wisconsin and Pelican rivers; thence on an east course twenty-five miles; thence southerly, on a course parallel with that of the Wisconsin river, to the line dividing the territories of the Chippewas and Menmonies; thence to the Plover Portage; thence along the southern boundary of the Chippewa country, to the commencement of the boundary line dividing it form that of the Sioux, half a days march below the falls on the Chippewa river; at its junction with the Mississippi; and thence up the Mississippi to the place of beginning.

ARTICLE 2. In consideration of the cession aforesaid, the United States agree to make to the Chippewa nation, annually, for the term of twenty years, from the date of the ratification of this treaty, the following payments.

1. Nine thousand five hundred dollars, to be paid in money.
2. Nineteen thousand dollars, to be delivered in goods.
3. Three thousand dollars for establishing three black smiths shops, supporting the blacksmiths, and furnishing them with iron and steel.
4. One thousand dollars for farmers, and for supplying them and the Indians, with implements of labor, with grain or seed; and whatever else may be necessary to enable them to carry on their agricultural pursuits.
5. Two thousand dollars in provisions.
6. Five hundred dollars in tobacco.

The provisions and tobacco to be delivered at the same

time with the goods, and the money to be paid; which time or times, as well as the place or places where they are to be delivered, shall be fixed upon under the direction of the President of the United States.

The blacksmiths shops to be placed at such points in the Chippewa country as shall be designated by the Superintendent of Indian Affairs, or under his direction.

If at the expiration of one or more years the Indians should prefer to receive goods, instead of the nine thousand dollars agreed to be paid them in money, they shall be at liberty to do so. Or, should they conclude to appropriate a portion of that annuity to the establishment and support of a school or schools among them, this shall be granted them.

ARTICLE 3. The sum of one hundred thousand dollars shall be paid by the United States, to the half breeds of the Chippewa nation, under the direction of the president. It is the wish of the Indians that their two sub-agents Daniel P. Bushness, and Miles M. Vineyard, superintend the distribution of this money among their half breed relations.

ARTICLE 4. The sum of seventy thousand dollars shall be applied to the payment, by the United States, of certain claims against the Indians; of which amount twenty-eight thousand dollars shall, at their request, be paid to William A. Aitkin, twenty-five thousand to Lyman M. Warren, and the balance applied to the liquidation of other just demands against them - which they acknowledge to be the case with regard to that presented by Hercules L. Doussmand, for the sum of five thousand dollars; and they request that it be paid.

ARTICLE 5. The privilege of hunting, fishing, and gathering the wild rice, upon the lands, the rivers and the lakes included in the territory ceded, is guaranteed to the Indians, during the pleasure of the President of the United States (emphasis added).

ARTICLE 6. This treaty shall be obligatory from and after its ratification by the President and Senate of the United States. Done at St. Peters in the Territory of Wisconsin the twenty-ninth of July eighteen hundred and thirty-seven.

Henry Dodge, Commissioner.

From Leech Lake: Songa-ko-mig, or the Strong Ground.
Aish-ke-bo-ge-koshe, or Flat Mouth,   Chiefs
R-che-o-sau-ya, or the Elder Brother.   Wa-boo-jig, or the White Fisher,
                    Chiefs.   Ma-cou-da, or the Bear's Heart.

Pe-zhe-kins, the Young Buffalo,   Warriors
Ma-ghe-ga-bo, or La Trappe,   From St. Croix river:
O-be-gwa-dans, the Chief of the Earth,   Pe-zhe-ke, or the Buffalo,
Wa-bose, or the Rabbit,   Ka-be-ma-be, or the Wet Mouth.
Che-a-na-quod, or the Big Cloud.
                    Warriors   Pa-ga-we-we-wetung, Coming home
                                                        Hollowing
    From Gull lake and Swan river: Ya-banse, or the Young Buck,
Pa-goo-na-kee-zhig, or Hole in the Day,   Kis-ke-ta-wak, or the Cut Ear.
                                                        Warriors   7

The treaty demonstrates one thing very clearly: that Indians were no longer expected to subsist on traditional hunting and gathering methods, and the federal government would provide the skills and tools for Indians to learn alternative methods for daily subsistence. The debate over the morality of "forcing" Chippewa Indians into a new way of life has been debated for a century, but the reality of population changes renders the argument moot. Population increases in Minnesota would soon require Indians to adopt new ways or perish from starvation and stubbornness. From 1850 to 1857, the population increased by nearly 25-fold from 6,077 to 150,037.[8] Under such people-pressure, the land simply could not support traditional hunting and fishing-based subsistence for either Indians or non-Indians. Already by 1837, the Minnesota Sioux were facing starvation because game on ceded government territories had been overhunted. The treaty, then, was not seen by the government as the provision of permanent hunting and fishing privileges. Instead, the treaty was a time-limited intervention (20 years) whereby Indians would learn to support themselves by other means — hence the blacksmith equipment, farming implements and education — while temporarily retaining their hunting and fishing privileges at the time. Implicit in the treaty is the idea that hunting and fishing rights on the ceded lands were temporary. A single brief sentence gives Indians the privilege to hunt, fish and gather on the ceded territory, but the temporary nature of the grant is contained in the phrase "during the pleasure of the President." This grant was revoked by President Zachary Taylor in the treaty of 1850, at a time when subsistence hunting and fishing was becoming impractical.

The Chippewa Treaty also used the term "privilege" in connection with hunting and fishing. Some treaties use the word "right" instead of privilege. This is a critical legal distinction. If a right is revoked, the person losing the right must be compensated for the loss, as dictated by the 5th Amendment of the U.S. Constitution. When a privilege is revoked, no compensation is necessary. Framers of treaties such as the Chippewa Treaty of 1837 did not see treaties as a permanent grant of special privileges or government assistance to tribes. William Clark, who along with Lewis Cass negotiated many treaties with tribes in the trans-Mississippi region during the period around 1830, felt that treaties should not provide financial assistance for more than 20 years. Clark felt longer periods of government assistance did more harm than good. In the book *American Indian Treaties*, author Francis Prucha provides the following passage from Clark:

> In treaties concluded with the Kanzas and Osages, the annuities (government payments) are limited to twenty years; in the course of which time, the humane experiment now making by Government, to teach them to subsist themselves by the arts of civilized life, will have had a fair trial, and if it succeeds, they will need no further aid from the Federal government.[9]

Prucha is one of the foremost authorities on Indian treaties today. In explaining trends in treaty writing in the upper Mississippi River area from 1830 to 1850, he speaks of the common grant of temporary hunting privileges. "Many of the treaties provided for cession of portions of a tribe's lands to the United States and the concentration of the displaced Indians on remaining lands, with the privilege of hunting on the ceded lands *until they had been surveyed and sold to white settlers*" (emphasis added).[10]

One of the most common misconceptions about Indian treaties is the idea that treaties have been "broken" or "violated" when something changes regarding treaty-granted privileges. In fact, the Chippewa Treaty was clear in granting temporary hunting and fishing privileges, which have been legally revoked by congressional or presidential order five times since 1837, including twice this century.

President Taylor issued the first revocation in 1850. The second time was with the Chippewa Treaty of 1855, which made clear that "the laws of the United States and the territory of Minnesota shall be extended over the Chippewa Territory in Minnesota whenever the same may be ceded, and the same shall cease to be 'Indian Country.'"[11] During the treaty negotiations, Chief Hole-In-The-Day (who is also one of the signers of the 1837 treaty) stated flatly that maybe it was time for Indians to learn new skills and adapt to the new way of life that was evolving around the Indians:

> We want to change our habits and customs and live like the whites....You want us to work, to change our habits, and live like the whites, and I see the benefit of your advice, so do the Chiefs. It is very essential that the Indians shall be thrown on their own resources. The country is getting scarce of game, and we cannot get along without changing our habits. We have tried the old system, and found it wanting. We should therefore try a new one.[12]

In 1889, Congress approved the Nelson Act, which closed all Chippewa reservations in Minnesota except White Earth and Red Lake. During negotiations for the Nelson Act, U.S. Commissioner Henry Rice made it perfectly clear to Muh-eng-aunce, a member of the Mille Lacs Band, that hunting regulations off the reservation were the same for Indians as for all men. It could be done "during the season set apart for hunting; and wherever the white man may hunt, your young men will have the same right to do so."[13] In 1938, President Franklin D. Roosevelt reconfirmed the 1850 order of President Zachary Taylor to revoke the 1837 hunting and fishing privilege.

The final revocation of hunting and fishing privileges for Chippewa Indians was the result of legislation enacted in 1946, when the Indian Claims Commission was formed by Congress to make a final settlement of any outstanding Indian claims. Indians from the Chippewa bands filed claims alleging interference with their hunting and fishing privileges as well as asking for compensation for land ceded in 1837. In 1974, the Indians were awarded more than $9 million to settle the claim, though technically, the 1837 fishing rights did not require compensation since they were a privilege and not a right.[14]

Despite the repeated legal revocation of these privileges, Chippewa Indians continue to fight to have these privileges reinstated as rights circa-1837. Minnesota courts have helped this cause during the 1990s, overruling the five congressional and presidential orders and overstepping their legal jurisdiction in the process. *American Indian Law in a Nutshell* states, "If Congress expressly states that it is modifying a particular treaty, then the deed is done and the courts have no room to maneuver."[15] The court case of *Dalton v. Specter* confirmed this in 1994. This decision upheld the principle that when a congressional statute (treaty) gives the president the power to make decisions regarding changes in the statute, the courts cannot overrule the president.[16]

The court case regarding fishing and hunting privileges from the Chippewa Treaty of 1837 has been active since about 1992 and is now being appealed to the U.S. Supreme Court. Non-Indian landowners have been a part of this suit, along with the state of Minnesota. The landowner's attorney, Stephen Froehle, has filed a brief with the United States Court of Appeals alleging bias by the magistrate judge against the landowners. According to Froehle's court brief, when the magistrate judge was speaking with Froehle about the landowner's case, the judge said he "knew what was in the dark souls of my clients." Froehle states in his brief that, "This shocking statement was made without the Magistrate Judge ever having dealt with the Landowners. Any view of Landowner's motives or thoughts was pure speculation, reflecting the Magistrate Judge's bias toward those parties who opposed treaty claims."[17] The court proceedings were tape recorded, but when Froehle asked the court for a transcript of the tape the following day, the magistrate judge's office reported that the tape recorder didn't happen to be working at the time.

Froehle charges that the district court judge even admitted that she had formulated factual findings on the case before defendants (the White landowners) presented their evidence. On June 24, 1994, while the Mille Lacs Band of Chippewa was making its case on the 1837 treaty, but before the landowners had presented their case, presiding Judge Diana Murphy said:

> But assuming the court gives you some time to supplement your original filings, the closing arguments have the benefit of giving the court a preview, *because we already are working on our findings as we are going through the trial.* They obviously have to be adjusted because, as [you] hear more evidence, *you can change your view* on some aspects (emphasis added).[18]

Can Indian hunting and fishing rights be successfully challenged in court? It seems the lower courts have a built-in bias that precludes a fair hearing on any issue connected with a treaty. The court-dictated canons of treaty construction, mentioned earlier, stipulate that treaties are to be interpreted liberally in favor of the Indians. The case concerning the Mille Lacs 1837 Treaty is now being appealed to the U.S. Supreme Court. There is no guarantee the high court will hear the case, but Froehle believes the Supreme Court cannot ignore the long history of congressional and presidential orders that extinguished and paid for the treaty hunting and fishing privileges — that is, if it hears the case at all.

Public opinion might ultimately be the most serious impediment to a fair hearing on treaty issues. Legal experts as well as people on the street have picked up common misconceptions about treaties. One of these falsehoods is the idea that treaties were written using the phrase "as long as grass grows and water flows," thus promising that treaty agreements would never change. This phrase came into the common consciousness after it was used in the blockbuster Hollywood movie *Little Big Man* in 1970, starring Dustin Hoffman. In the movie, Indians talked about signing treaties with the government that contained this guarantee. According to treaty expert Francis Prucha, this phrase was never used in a treaty between Indians and the United States, but was used for treaties between the Confederate States of America and the Indians during the Civil War.[19] Thus, the phrase "as long as the grass grows and water flows" equals precisely four years, the duration of Indian treaties with the Confederacy during the Civil War.[20]

Another source of argument about treaty hunting and fishing privileges is whether these rules amount to preferences based on race. Indians insist that membership in a tribe is a *political*, rather than a race-based classification. The Indian Policy Review Commission of 1977 gives a clear definition of this claim of political status for Indians rather than as a racial or ethnic group. The commission says:

> The tribe's power to determine its own membership, that is, individual identity as Indian, has been repeatedly recognized by the courts; the power derives from the tribe's status as *a distinct political party*. The tribe's power over its own membership is the starting point for any discussion of Indian identity (emphasis added).[21]

This definition would seem to contrast markedly from the standard for tribal recognition of 25 percent Indian blood, or being able to trace ones ancestry to recognized tribal membership at the time of the Indian Reorganization Act of 1934. Some tribes have even tried to purify their bloodlines. The Cherokee Tribe of Oklahoma has openly stated its desire to have the descendents of Black slaves kicked out of the tribe. In the Indian Policy Review Commission Report of 1977, the tribe wrote this regarding the Black Cherokees:

> There are two specific problems facing the Five Civilized Tribes: (1) the reliance on the 1907 Dawes Commission rolls as the sole major determinant of tribal membership; and (2) the inclusion of the descendents of the freed slaves of the tribes, as a result of treaties made after the Civil War, on the tribal rolls.

> All descendents of those persons on the Dawes Commission

rolls are considered tribal members for purposes of voting in tribal elections and referendums, and distribution of judgment moneys. Therefore, *many persons of very little Indian blood are allowed to vote in tribal elections*, making decisions which may affect their lives not at all, while affecting Indians greatly.

The other membership problem plaguing the Indians of the Five Civilized Tribes is the inclusion of freedmen (former black slaves) bands. After the Civil War, the reconstruction treaties of the tribes said that they would provide lands for their freedmen. These freedmen were given allotments (land) which have long since passed into fee simple (private ownership) status. However, the descendants of these freedmen are considered tribal members because of the treaty provisions. It seems strange that the United States has violated almost every provision of those 1866 treaties, yet it holds the Five Civilized Tribes to their word. Again, these people do not identify as Indians, the Federal Government does not recognize them as Indians, yet they make decisions affecting Indians. Clearly, Congress should allow the tribes a method for restricting their membership to persons of Indian descent rather than imposing a Federal definition based on descendancy from the Dawes Commission rolls. The final irony of the situation is that, although the tribes must keep the descendents from the Dawes Commission rolls for tribal political purposes, the Bureau of Indian Affairs provides services only to tribal persons of one-quarter or more Indian blood (emphasis and parenthetical clarification added).[22]

As you can see from this passage, Indians from the Five Civilized Tribes (Cherokee, Choctaw, Chickasaw, Creek and Seminole tribes) don't want descendents of Black slaves in their tribe, nor people who have very little Indian blood. When the Five Civilized Tribes signed treaties with the Confederacy in the early 1860s, they were getting a guarantee to keep their Black slaves for as "long as grass grows and water flows." The subsequent reconstruction of the treaties by the United States in 1866 required the tribes to free their Black slaves and take them into the tribe. In 1977, the tribes went before Congress and unashamedly asked that the descendents of the slaves be kicked out of the tribe, since they no longer had a useful purpose. In the 1840s, the Cherokee of Oklahoma published their own newspaper called the *Cherokee Advocate*, whose motto was, "Our Rights, Our Country, Our Race." If Indians are simply a political party, they seem to be a very racist political party. The Five Civilized Tribes insist that the government honor solemn promises in Indian treaties, except the solemn promises the tribes don't like.

Some tribes have, in fact, waived the blood standard for membership in the tribe, which would lend credibility to the argument that tribes are politically based instead of race-based. With huge federal subsidies and casino revenues at stake, the chance of fraud increases, including indications that tribal memberships might be for sale. In *Killing the White Man's Indian*, author Fergus Bordewich reports;

> Since abolishing its blood quantum requirement in 1975, northern Michigan's Sault Ste. Marie Band of Chippewas has ballooned from 1,300 to 21,000 members and has earned a reputation, perhaps undeserved, for allegedly selling tribal membership and the valuable fishing rights that accompany it to fishermen who have little or no Indian blood.[23]

Other than the suspicious numbers, however, Bordewich offers no corroborating evidence. However, an unusual event in Minnesota provides additional fodder to charges that tribal membership is for sale. In June of 1997, a federal judge in Washington D.C. sentenced Herbert A. Becker, former head of the Justice Department's Indian affairs office, to home detention and a fine. While working for the government, Becker made appeals to the Bureau of Indian Affairs on behalf of two men, Patrick Welch and Charles Vig, who had been denied a share of the Shakopee Mdewakanton Dakota tribe's casino profits. The tribe pays each tribal member over 18 years of age about $50,000 per month, according to newspaper reports. Becker was able to get the Bureau of Indian Affairs to overturn rulings that the two men were ineligible for tribal casino payments. Becker was convicted of filing false government expense accounts and conflict of interest. Steven Bunnell, the Justice Department's Public Integrity unit prosecutor, argued that Becker should receive a jail term for the offenses because he had received payments of $60,000 each from Welch and Vig.[24]

Fish Stories

Few people question the Indian drive to reinstate resource-harvesting privileges as they experienced them hundreds of years ago. At some point, however, Indians and non-Indians alike need to question whether such attachment to the past has, in fact, hindered Indian inclusion in today's modern economy and prevented them from enjoying its full benefits. What's more, this blind attachment has quite possibly been a leading factor (if unintentional) in destroying much of their proud heritage, all because they refused to let go of subsistence methods that would have been eventually stripped regardless of any treaty by the sheer weight of immigration into the U.S. and its related demand on wild resources that Indians depended on for substinence. More than 160 years have passed since the 1837 Chippewa Treaty, far surpassing the initial 20-year time frame the treaty writers envisioned for Indians to develop a standard of living similar to that of the mainstream society.

Red Lake Reservation stands as a tribute to the failure of relying on hunting and gathering to support modern populations of Indians. The reservation had one of the largest and most prolific walleye pike fisheries in the world until Indian over-fishing forced the tribe to close the season in 1997. Red Lake itself covers about 275,000 acres, almost 430 square miles of water. The tribe has had control of the Indian fishery for 68 years. The lake once produced between 650,000 and 850,000 pounds of commercial fish per year, but over-fishing reduced the harvest to 50,000 pounds.

According to Bill Lawrence, a member of the Red Lake Band of Chippewa and editor of *The Native American Press*, there are currently about 4,000 Indian people living on or near the reservation.[25] During years when the walleye harvest on the reservation reached 850,000 pounds, the wholesale value of the catch was $1,275,000 if an average wholesale price of $1.50 per pound is used.[26]   Using the population figure of 4,000, the per capita commercial fishing income would be about $318 per person per year, assuming overhead costs were zero. The Minneapolis *Star Tribune* reported that the Indian population on or near the Red Lake Reservation in 1997 was about 8,100.[27] If we assume this higher figure is accurate, the per capita income would be $157 per person. Those who wrote the Chippewa Treaty of 1837 realized that hunting and gathering could not support Indian reservation populations 160 years ago. They were right then and still are today.

The Red Lake Reservation also had other income from natural resource harvests. Until recently, a fish processing plant employed 40 people. The tribe had significant timber resources, but over-harvest has cut sawmill production to half of what it was in recent years. The tribe also opened three casinos, but employment is only about 500 for all three, and only about 30 percent of the employees are Indian, despite efforts by the tribe to hire as many Indians as possible. One other major source of income for the tribe is federal funding. Tribal Chairman Bobby Whitefeather says federal grants for housing, education and health care are between $15 and $17 million per year.[28] In addition, the tribe gets huge tax breaks from local, state and federal government. Even with huge federal subsidies, tax breaks, revenues from three gambling casinos, and income from the dwindling natural resources on Red Lake Reservation, there is substantial poverty. Unemployment is currently about 65 percent. If Indians are to enjoy a standard of living similar to that of other Americans without massive federal assistance, they will need to have occupations as varied as those of other Americans and participate in a broad-based economy. Hunting, fishing and gathering of federal subsidies is not a long-term solution.

Today, many people believe spearing and netting fish is an integral part of the economic and social well-being of the Indians. In reality, spearing has dramatically hurt the fish base in many lakes, sapping future resources for Indians and non-Indians alike. In north central Wisconsin, the Chippewa Tribe has been spearing walleye pike during the spawning season since 1987. In the spring of 1997, I was sitting in a restaurant near the Lac Courte Oreilles Indian Reservation in the heart of the spearing territory. At the next table was a woman who worked for the Wisconsin Department of Natural Resources. I asked her if Indian spearing had any serious effect on walleye populations. "No," she said, "the news media has blown this all out of proportion. The Indians here only are allowed to take about 10 percent of the available fish, and the ones that are speared are mostly small males. The big females tend to stay in deeper water, so not many are taken. We monitor everything, to make sure the number of fish taken is correct."

This seemed highly reassuring until I looked at the sportsman catch quotas released later in the spring. Prior to Indian spearing, sports fishermen in that part of Wisconsin had been allowed five fish per day. After nine years of spearing, the catch had gone down to three. In 1997, the sports limit on most lakes was two, a 60 percent reduction in the limit in 10 years. All this from a 10 percent allotment to Indian spearing. Perhaps this shouldn't be particularly surprising. Anyone who reads the newspapers knows there are three kinds of math: the old math, the new math, and government math. That is how a 10 percent spearing harvest results in a 60 percent reduction in the sports harvest.

In Minnesota, when the Chippewa begin spearing and gill netting in Mille Lacs Lake and others in east central Minnesota in 1998, the Indian harvest will be phased in slowly. In Minnesota, the Indian harvest might reach 50 percent. Using government math, that figure does not paint a pretty picture. The Chippewa and the Minnesota Department of Natural Resources tell us the media has blown this out of proportion, and we have no need to worry. Indians are supposed to be much better conservationists than Whites. In Red Lake, as I have mentioned, the Indian harvest went from as high as 850,000 pounds per year to 50,000 pounds. The season was closed by the Indians in 1997, and ironically, they said this proved they were interested in conservation.

In October of 1997, there was an Indian symposium at University of St. Thomas in St. Paul, Minnesota. One of the featured speakers was Jim Genia, the solicitor general for the Mille Lacs Tribe. He provided some interesting statistics regarding fishing. The figures dropped in Wisconsin, according to Genia, because the sports fishermen used too much electronic fishing gear and caught too many fish. In Wisconsin lakes that were not speared, however, the bag limit for walleyes stayed at five as it has been for years. In Minnesota lakes, the sports catch limit for 1997 was six. Genia also said that 10 percent of the sports fishermen catch most of the available sports catch. Non-expert fishermen catch only one or two fish per outing, according to Genia. He claimed only the experts would be affected by reduced fish limits, since they are the only ones who regularly catch a limit of fish.[29]

This didn't seem logical, however. It seems reasonable that if the number of fish is reduced by half, those average fishermen who catch one or two fish, will catch zero or one. But then, I only learned the old math.

CHAPTER THREE

Reservation Rule

Preserving Indian cultural identity, its leaders say, requires that Indians have a special set of rights on top of those guaranteed to all Americans by the Constitution and the Bill of Rights. Unassuming Americans are mistaken, however, if they believe that special privileges given to Indians today are merely temporary stopgaps to help Indians achieve parity in American society. Indians are building quasi-sovereign and ethnically "stylized" homelands, and doing so with the help of tax exemptions, special government programs and business monopolies. Such "help" is not seen as a bridge into mainstream culture, but rather as a means to build a wall separating Indians from mainstream America. Once constructed, this wall will be difficult to tear down.

Within these Indian homelands, Indians want to be in charge of their own affairs, including the desire for their own governments, courts, and schools. They want to speak their own language and practice Indian religion. They would like to hunt, fish and gather in the manner of their grandfathers and grandmothers, and hope their grandchildren will be able to live the same way. There are numerous problems with this view of Indian culture, however. As I described in the previous chapter, hunting and fishing as a way of life is no longer practical anywhere in the continental U.S., no matter how romantic and nostalgic it might sound. It also undermines the rights of non-Indians owning land and living on reservations (detailed in later chapters of this book).

But the most overlooked problem regarding segregated tribal homelands is the fact that many Indians don't want to live in this

"Indian nationalist" type of environment. Indians are like other ethnic groups: some want to live one way, others in a completely different fashion. For example, not all Irish Catholic or English Protestant immigrants live in exactly the same way as other people from their "tribe." Even Amish people, who practice a more traditional lifestyle, vary greatly between sects in how they practice or live out their beliefs. Certainly they share common traditions, language, and cultural uniqueness, but people of the same heritage embrace and practice that culture in different ways. It is no different among Indians, particularly in light of the fact that there are over 500 different tribes in the U.S. today. Some want to live exactly as other Americans do, and have little interest in traditional Indian life.

This dilemma poses few problems for Indian leaders looking to create segregated homelands. Indians who want to live like other Americans can live off the reservation; those who want to be "traditional" in lifestyle can live on the reservation. Indians have a choice because they have "dual citizenship." Indians have American rights and privileges when on American soil, and different rights and privileges on Indian soil. This dual citizenship is not as innocuous as it might sound and has serious implications for Indians and non-Indians alike. But few people question the underlying logic of such a legal structure.

Somewhat ironically, Indians living on a reservation can find their civil rights severely limited by tribal constitutions which can arbitrarily mete out law and justice. Increasingly, reservations are becoming havens for influence peddling, where money from casinos can buy either favor and prosperity for those who go along with the system, or retribution and discrimination for those who buck tribal governance and the "proper" Indian way of life. On reservations, the U.S. Constitution has proved limited in its ability to intervene on behalf of Indian citizens whose human rights are either ignored or willfully violated by tribal constitutions.

Since the Nixon Administration ushered in the era of "self-determination" on Indian reservations in 1970, Indian leaders have gained much control over federal programs and money that is made available to reservations. In the 1990s, gambling casinos have come to reservations, bringing significant new revenue to tribes (although some more than others). What has resulted is nothing short of an Indian oligarchy that controls resources on reservations and distributes them in ways we often associate only with corrupt, third world governments. Such waste and corruption has resulted in further harm to the socio-economic and spiritual well-being of Indian tribes, as most are neither being helped to achieve economic parity with the rest of American society nor nurturing traditional Indian lifestyles.

To the Winner Go the Spoils

Darrell "Chip" Wadena was the chairman of the 22,000-member White Earth Band of the Chippewa (Anishinabe) Tribe in Northwest Minnesota for 20 years. For most of that time, he was also president of the Minnesota Chippewa Tribe which has about 50,000 members and consists of the White Earth, Fond du Lac, Grand Portage, Leech Lake, Mille Lacs, and Nett Lake bands. Wadena is proud of his achievements as chairman of the tribe, including meetings with Presidents Ronald Reagan and Bill Clinton at the White House, and negotiations with members of Congress on Indian land claims. Former U.S. Senator Rudy Boschwitz described Wadena as "a great voice of reason, a smart guy, a decent guy. He gets what he wants. He's a good politician."[1] Good, at least, in bringing federal programs and other spending home to his Chippewa Tribe.

Over the course of several years, Wadena was able to leverage federal money from different sources into development on the reservation. As more money came onto the reservation and more projects got built, so too grew Wadena's influence. But despite the influx of money, programs, and new facilities to reservations like White Earth, tribes remain dependent on the government for basic subsistence. Unemployment rates on reservations remain high, and the new wealth being created on reservations is often in the hands of a few, doled out surreptitiously to friends and political supporters.

In 1986, Wadena secured a land claims settlement against the federal government worth $17 million, $10.4 million of which was given to tribal members whose ancestors lost land in the early 20th century, and $6.6 million went to the tribal government for economic development, which helped finance the building of the Shooting Star Casino in 1992.[2] In 1995, the tribe used $5 million in profits from Shooting Star to construct a recreation center, complete with an Olympic-size pool. The federal government began construction of a $10 million Indian health clinic for the tribe in 1995, and provided additional funds for an aging K-12 school built in 1939 by the Federal Works Progress Administration. Currently, the White Earth Band is asking the Minnesota legislature to fund a new $10 million elementary school on the reservation, even though the reservation is exempt from property taxes normally used to build schools. The White Earth Band does not plan to use gambling revenues to build or operate its schools.[3]

In 1995, Shooting Star Casino employed 985 people, of whom about 60 percent were Indians. The average wage was $6.75 per hour, plus health insurance. In spite of the surge in casino employment, after two years of operation, the tribe's 1994 unemployment rate was still about 50 percent. According to a newspaper account, Wadena blamed this phenomenon partly on migration of Indians from metropolitan areas. "A lot of people move here to be unemployed," he said. "If they lived in Minneapolis and lost their job, they can move here and get by....Their income is next to nothing, but their rent is too."[4] Wadena didn't just get by though, he took home a salary of $258,000 in 1993.[5]

Members of the reservation complained that casino profits and federal revenues often end up in the pockets of tribal officials, but speaking publicly could jeopardize a person's job prospects. "You can't get a job at the casino unless you get Darrell Wadena's OK," one Indian, who didn't want to be named for fear of retribution, told a reporter. Another cautious Indian said she needed to remain anonymous because she was on a waiting list for tribal housing. "I don't want to lose that house because I'm not a full fledged supporter of 'Chippy.'"[6] Wadena himself adds credibility to these claims. In a 1989 interview reported by the paper, he said, "There's no question I lean toward people who support me for the key jobs. Politics are harsh. To the winner goes the spoils."[7]

The federal government pours approximately $500 million annually into reservation housing through Housing and Urban Development (HUD), but has failed for years to look at how the money is spent, according to a 1997 report by the *Seattle Times* on Indian housing abuses.[8] This would be consistent with the government policy of Indian self-determination which allows tribes great control over their internal affairs, including how they spend federal tax dollars. According to the report, Wadena put his friends and relatives in above-standard reservation housing. For example, one White Earth project involved $4.4 million in federal funding to build 50 reservation homes. The tribe completed only eight houses and partially finished 12 more with the money. Another $500,000 would be required to finish the 12 uncompleted homes.[9]

HUD officials knew for two years that Wadena was being investigated by the Justice Department for embezzling from the tribe's casino, the *Seattle Times* report noted, yet did not bother to check reservation housing practices. In 1992, whistle-blowers complained to HUD that Wadena's cronies were bumped to the front of housing waiting lists. HUD did nothing even after three HUD officials went to White Earth and confirmed the abuses. In September of 1996, HUD investigators finally arrived at White Earth offices for a serious investigation, but by then the federal money and many tribal records were gone. By this time, however, Chip Wadena had been convicted of 15 counts of conspiracy, bribery, money laundering, misapplication of tribal funds, and embezzlement.[10] Possibly embarrassed by the alleged abuses in cases such as Wadena's, a nationwide investigation is being conducted by HUD's inspector general into alleged housing abuses on reservations.[11]

In August 1995, a federal grand jury indicted Wadena, Secretary Treasurer Jerry Rawley, and Council Member Rick Clark on 56 counts. Charges included fixing elections, construction bid-rigging and taking hundreds of thousands of dollars from the tribe.[12] Wadena's lawyer, John Brink, said the tribal leader would challenge the government's ability to prosecute leaders of the semi-sovereign tribe. Brink explained Wadena's actions to the jury by saying Indian treaties and federal statutes allow for a restriction of competition on the reservation, so the actions did not constitute bid-rigging. Further, Brink argued "conflict of interest is not a crime" on a reservation.[13] Attorneys for the Indian defendants also complained that the government did not "understand the differences between Indian and non-Indian culture," arguing that the construction deal was simply a preference for an Indian contractor rather than bid-rigging.[14]

In connection with the election fraud indictments, Prosecution Attorney Jeanne Graham charged that half of the votes cast in a 1994 tribal election were suspect, telling jurors, "You will hear that dead people voted, that people actually voted at polls but an absentee ballot appeared in their name." But Defense Attorney Peter Wold told the jury that some of the election procedures at White Earth "don't exactly follow the rules." He said client Jerry Rawley turned in absentee votes, but these were sealed in envelopes, and Rawley didn't know any were fake. Attorneys for the defense dismissed charges of election fraud as little more than accusations from disgruntled tribal members who lost elections.[15]

Other charges for the three tribal officers included the allegation they set up a phony tribal fishing commission and paid themselves salaries of $65,000 to $75,000 per year. Wadena was charged with taking $10,000 from tribal funds to make a payment on his Cadillac. Ultimately, Wadena was found guilty on 15 of 15 counts, sentenced to more than four years in prison, and ordered to repay the tribe $635,000. Rawley was convicted of 17 of 18 counts, and Clark was found guilty guilty on 22 of 23 counts. Rawley and Clark also received substantial fines and prison time.[16]

In 1997, Wadena appealed his conviction from prison. His attorney, Daniel Gerdts, claimed Wadena was falsely convicted because a tribe's right of self-government precludes any U.S. government interference in reservation affairs. Gerdts compared Wadena's arrest to a *coup d'etat* of a foreign sovereign. By this reasoning, the federal government had no more right to prosecute the tribal leader than to arrest the Prime Minister of Canada. In rebuttal, U.S. Attorney Jeanne Graham said members of the White Earth Tribe were citizens of the United States as well as the band, and could not expect justice from the tribal government. She concluded that the federal government had to protect Indian citizens on the reservation because they were American citizens. "This is not about tribal autonomy. This is about violations of basic human rights," said Graham.[17]

Are Wadena, Rawley, and Clark just bad apples for which

government prosecutors have an easy cure, or is cronyism, corruption, and waste of government funds endemic to reservation life? Since the Indian self-determination era brought in by President Richard Nixon, the *modus operandi* for federal Indian programs has been to give tribes spending autonomy with little interference or oversight. Nixon said, "we must make it clear that Indians can become independent of federal control without being cut off from federal concern and support."[18]

Gambling profits have added millions more in unregulated funds for many tribes, and in most cases, no one but the tribal leadership is sure how much money is made and how it is spent. Most reservation Indians live in housing that is owned and controlled by the tribe. The tribal government can make a list of who gets a house and when, and also schedule needed repairs. Usually jobs in casinos, tribal administration and public works are also under the control of the tribal business committee. Does this result in fairness for the people involved? With little room for checks and balances, Indian leaders can easily say "trust me" without fear of great scrutiny.

Harold "Skip" Finn was one of the most trusted Indian leaders in the nation. A member of the Leech Lake Tribe, Finn was also a two-term Minnesota State senator and had served as the tribe's lawyer. In the 1980s, Finn helped the tribe start a self-insurance program because the tribe was having trouble getting insurance coverage. By the end of the decade, according to government indictments, he had cheated the tribe out of $1.1 million, and squandered the money on country club memberships and luxury items. In 1996, he was convicted on 12 of 12 counts, sentenced to five years in prison and given a $100,000 fine. Convicted with Finn in the scheme were Alfred "Tig" Pemberton, the tribal chairman, and Daniel Brown, the secretary-treasurer. At the sentencing hearing, Finn maintained his innocence and talked about a planned appeal.[19] As Yogi Berra once said, "It was déjà vu all over again."

Lawlessness pervades not only some tribal governments but the general reservation culture as well, evident from the fact that crime on reservations is soaring nationwide, due mainly to gang and drug activity. In 1996, the Royal Canadian Mounted Police arrested 170 people in a crackdown on smuggling over the U.S. border and seized $15 million in contraband. According to police sources, a significant part of the smuggled goods came through the Mohawk Indian Reservation of Akwesasne on the New York/Canada border.

The Justice Department reported that between 1994 and 1997 the number of reservation gangs doubled. Arizona is a prime example. On the Navajo Reservation alone there are reported to be 55 different gangs, while the Gila River Indian Community has 20, and the Salt River Pima-Maricopa Indian Community has 19. Two police officers were killed in separate incidents on the Navajo Reservation in two years. While homicide in the United States declined by 22 percent between 1992 and 1997, on reservations it increased by 87 percent.[20]

John Buckanaga, a tribal council member of the Minnesota White Earth Band noted in a newspaper article that arsonists have burned buildings and vehicles, and people have been threatened and beaten as a result of the growing drug market. Sadly, tribes are reluctant to divert casino revenue to deal with community problems like crime. Buckanaga said tribes would welcome more law enforcement money from the Justice Department on top of the $90 million provided by the Bureau of Indian Affairs for law enforcement on reservations.[21]

Indians expect the federal government to provide additional grant money — no strings attached — to deal with problems on reservations, while casino profits are preserved for other uses. For example, in 1996 the Leech Lake Tribe of Minnesota used $275,000 in casino profits for powwows, including paying the food and travel expenses for some participants. Tribal Chairman Eli Hunt estimates the tribe gets about $20 million per year from the federal government, yet the school's roof leaks and it is poorly heated. At the same time, the tribal newspaper reported that the two Leech Lake Casinos made $5.5 million in the 1995 fiscal year.[22]

Casino Culture

Casinos are seen by many people today as a panacea for the ills that have plagued reservations for a century. Indian leaders have speculated that the economic boost of casino profits, combined with Indian self-determination, will finally end dependence on the federal government. However, less than half of the nation's 550 or so federally recognized tribes own casinos, and a large share of gambling proceeds go to a fairly small number of Indians. For example, after examining 178 tribal casinos, the General Accounting Office estimated that eight casinos make 40 percent of all tribal gaming revenues in the nation, or about $2 billion. What's more, some of the largest casinos support tribes with very few members.[23]

At an Indian gaming conference at Harvard University in 1995, John Mohawk, a member of the Seneca Tribe in New York, talked about a "civil war" that erupted on his reservation over tribal politics and whether to build a gambling facility. During the disturbances, a good friend of his was shot and killed. The incident led Mohawk to question whether casinos are being built for the good of the tribe or to help a few members get rich.[24]

In Minnesota, Indians hold a casino monopoly and operate 18 casinos statewide. Approximately half of the state's 60,000 Indians live on or near reservations, and more than 80 percent of those on reservations live on just four Chippewa reservations (also called Ojibwe or Anishinabe): the Red Lake, Fond du Lac, Leech Lake, and White Earth reservations, each of which operates one or more casinos. The lure of casino jobs has apparently brought many Indians back to reservation areas, but ironically casinos have done little to improve overall unemployment. In 1991, before casino fever hit the state, there were about 10,600 able-bodied Indian workers living on or near reservations and the jobless figure for this group of Indians was 57 percent. By 1995, after the casino boom, that figure had risen to 15,500 able-bodied Indian workers, but the unemployment rate had only dropped to 54 percent. These jobless statistics are higher than actual unemployment figures because they include Indians who are not actively looking for work. If you don't count the people who have stopped looking for employment, figures were still a staggering 49 percent in 1991 and 43 percent in 1995, which is far greater than for the state as a whole.[25]

From an historical viewpoint, casinos have done little to change the landscape of employment on reservations. According to the Bureau of Indian Affairs, national unemployment for Indians in 1996 was 49 percent.[26] During the 1960s, the rate was about 40 percent, which means three decades of Indian self-determination has made no significant difference in Indian employment rates.[27]

To be sure, Minnesota casinos have produced many new jobs — 12,000 in all — but over 70 percent of these jobs are held by non-Indians. At the Fond du Lac Reservation, two-thirds of all Indian workers are not employed. Part of the reason is the sheer influx of Indians who have moved to the reservation to compete for a pool of jobs that has not grown as fast as the reservation's immigration rate. In 1991, about 3,300 Indians lived on or near the Fond du Lac Reservation; by 1995, the figure was nearly 6,700. The band runs Black Bear Casino near Cloquet and a casino in Duluth which employ a combined workforce of about 850 people, less than 300 of whom are Indians. Mike Himango, a tribe member and manager of Black Bear Casino, noted that although a lot of people moved back to the reservation in anticipation of casino jobs, many find the jobs unappealing. Some can't deal with casino patrons who can be demanding and rude. Others expect good wages ($9 or $10 and hour) for mostly low-skill jobs, but starting pay at Black Bear is $7 to $9, or minimum wage plus tips. Often entry-level jobs are on the night shift rather than 9 to 5.[28]

Himango also cited major problems with absenteeism caused by inadequate child care, transportation, and in some cases poor work ethic. According to Pam Omondson, a 39-year-old Black Bear dealer, "I've got relatives, they're young, in their 20's — they just don't want to work. A lot of times (my niece) couldn't find a baby sitter. A lot of times she gets into partying and doesn't want to come to work."[29]

Despite the boost provided by casino profits, social services are in poor shape on most reservations. The Indian education system, for one, is in shambles, with a 40 percent dropout rate among Minnesota Indian high school students, about four times the rate of other students. In addition, only about 15 percent of Indian high school graduates go to college, compared to 60 percent of non-Indians. Indians also have the lowest college graduation rate of any racial group.

The Fond du Lac Reservation badly needs a new high school, but it plans to wait up to five years for a government-funded school rather than using casino profits to build one. Currently, the tribe has about $30 million in savings. At present, students are housed in crumbling buildings considered health hazards (some classrooms had to be closed), but tribal members are willing to wait for the government to build a $9 million school. The band voted 3 to 1 to reject paying for the school from gaming profits. Tribal Chairman Robert "Sonny" Peacock said, "The U.S. has an obligation to Indian people, and I'm going to hold them to it. I'm not going to let them off the hook."[30]

Such a comment, however, ignores the millions of dollars already being spent by the federal government to educate Indians. According to an article on Indian education in the *Native American Press/Ojibwe News*, the Bureau of Indian Affairs (BIA) spends $17,000 per student per year on the Fond du Lac Reservation. Average spending per student in Minnesota public schools is less than half that amount. Looking at spending priorities, it seems tribal leaders view federal education dollars as merely another revenue stream, the article states, with education a secondary priority. Despite considerable BIA education funding, teachers often find themselves with virtually no books or supplies. On the Red Lake Reservation, only about 10 percent of students passed recent basic skills tests for reading and math, while the statewide average is 70 percent.[31]

Red Lake, in fact, is unique in many ways and demonstrates the many conflicts and contradictions evident on reservations. Red Lake is one of the few reservations nationwide that is still wholly intact as Indian land, having never been settled by Whites as part of the Dawes Act of 1887 (detailed elsewhere in this book). Encompassing a total of about 1,000 square miles, it is the size of Rhode Island. Today many tribes want non-Indian owned checkerboard lands on reservations returned to exclusive Indian ownership. To be self sufficient, tribal leaders say they need a large land base with abundant natural resources to support a traditional tribal economy. The Red Lake Reservation is such an intact reservation, with significant fish and timber resources. These resources have not provided an adequate standard of living for the growing tribal population, however, even with the help of huge federal subsidies.

As noted in the previous chapter, Red Lake has its own fishery (recently closed down due to over-fishing), a sawmill (whose employment base has been cut in half due to over-cutting) and three small casinos (one of which is in the town of Red Lake and caters almost exclusively to Indians).[32] Today, nearly 33 percent of Red Lake families are on welfare. The unemployment rate for the 8,100 Red Lake Indians living on or near the reservation is almost 65 percent. The Red Lake Reservation appears to be feeding upon itself, first over-harvesting its natural resources, then trying to find scarce gambling dollars in the pockets of its own tribal members. Red Lake is proof that isolation can harm the long-term economic stability of tribes even if they have significant natural resources and land.

Compounding this problem is the fact that money generated on the reservation often makes it into only a few select pockets. According to the *Native American Press*, tribal council members often hold multiple positions with a tribe, each of which comes with a separate paycheck. The newspaper article notes:

> Their family members are also given plum positions, resulting in an inordinate number of the highest paying jobs on reservations being controlled by a few families in power. Most tribally-operated casinos are stuffed with tribal council members and their family members, friends, and political supporters.[33]

Where is it Written?

Another anomaly of reservations is a persistent abuse of freedom of speech rights that most non-Indians take for granted. Bill Lawrence, editor of the *Native American Press*, has considerable experience in dealing with tribes intent on censoring the media. Lawrence is a former industrial development specialist for the Red Lake Reservation. He proposed a development plan for the reservation that included private enterprises and tribal-owned businesses such as a liquor store, golf course, airport, motel, and water and power associations. His economic development philosophy was to increase the number of reservation employers and encourage individuals and independent corporations of tribal people to establish enterprises on the reservation. His ideal was to have tribal people earning and spending — exchanging goods and services and sharing economic risks — on the reservation as a way of reducing dependencies on off-reservation businesses and government institutions.[34] Red Lake tribal officials were not so keen on such plans, so Lawrence left the reservation.

In a personal interview in February 1998, Lawrence told of sending one of his reporters to cover a meeting of the Minnesota Chippewa Tribal Executive Committee on October 22, 1997. These meetings had been open to the press for years, according to Lawrence, but on this day, the *Native American Press* reporter was allegedly not welcome. The meeting was scheduled to start at 11:30 a.m., but reporter Jeff Armstrong was arrested before the meeting started and taken to the county jail in Milaca, Minnesota. He was released only after the meeting ended. Lawrence said he may file suit on the matter, alleging a violation of civil rights.[35]

Other accounts support this idea that tribal councils can be very secretive about their proceedings. Robin Powell, an Indian woman, went to work for the Turtle Mountain Band of Chippewa in North Dakota. In 1993, while still working on a master's degree in journalism, Powell got an offer from the tribal chairman to become editor of the tribal paper. At first, things went well, but she ran into trouble when she tried to do a story about several reservation murders. Apparently, one of the victims was a housewife who had gone to tribal court to get protection from a violent spouse. Instead of getting help, the judge allegedly laughed at the woman and sent her away. Soon the spouse murdered the woman, her sister, and an uncle. Powell tried to investigate the story, but found that although everyone knew what happened, no one was willing to talk. The reservation was pervaded with a sense of fear. It was a way of life.[36]

When Powell tried to collect material for a story, she soon began to see that tribal politics was a big part of the problem. Powell asked the police and courts for statistics on drunken driving. Officials of the band who had kept tribal operations secret for years refused, telling the journalist, "Where is it written that you have a right to know anything?" When Powell tried to publish the minutes of council meetings, the council also refused. After repeated requests, the frustrated editor began to print blank spaces in the paper with the caption, "This spaced is reserved for the tribal minutes." After eight months on the job she was fired. Tribal Chairman Richard "Jiggers" LaFramboise sent a letter of dismissal to Powell, stating, "It is very disturbing to find people who are thinking they are professional and only have hidden agendas including manifestations of political grandeur."[37]

Lack of accountability and secrecy is the hallmark of most reservation tribal councils. In an effort to develop a more open form of government, Vince Hill, Solita E. Reum, and Irene Wade Benjamin started the Mille Lacs Anishinabe People's Party (MAPP) in April of 1994 on the Mille Lacs Reservation in Central Minnesota. Vince Hill, the president of MAPP, said he believed the organization was the first-ever grass roots political party on the Mille Lacs Reservation.[38] According to a position paper, some of the objectives of the new organization were to monitor tribal books and casino accounts by a certified public accountant, allow tribal members a bigger share of casino profits (currently members only receive a $500 check as a Christmas bonus), and use casino profits to increase services such as school anti-drug programs, shelters for abused children, and more foster homes.

Hill, Reum, and Benjamin were all living and working on the reservation when they started MAPP. The organization immediately attracted a lot of interest both on the reservation and among urban Indians because it represented a break with the entrenched bureaucracy. It also attracted the attention of Tribal Chief Exectuive Marge Anderson, who came to their first meeting at the reservation's community center and told the organization it was meeting illegally. Hill objected to Anderson's attempt to prevent MAPP from meeting on the reservation, and cited freedom of speech and assembly guarantees in the tribal constitution and the Minnesota Chippewa Constitution. Anderson agreed the group could meet if they first posted public notices in places such as the Tribal Government Center and Health Care Center. Vince maintains the group did post its future meetings, but the posters had a habit of disappearing.

They met for a second time in May and were able to get a candidate for the office of tribal secretary-treasurer on the ballot for the June 1994 elections. Among eight candidates, the MAPP candidate lost by only 29 votes. MAPP was somewhat suspicious of this loss, especially with regard to urban Indian absentee voters. (Though urban

Indians can't hold office, they have the right to vote in tribal elections.) MAPP believes there was considerable urban support for the MAPP candidate, but according to MAPP documents, absentee voters did not get ballots in time to vote in the election, and the urban polling location was not open on election day.

By August of 1994, MAPP was notified verbally and in writing that it could no longer meet on the reservation, according to Hill. In reaction to this ban, a MAPP position paper says:

> Restricting MAPP's assembly would be understandable if MAPP were supporting violent overthrow of tribal government. But MAPP advocates democracy, dialogue, and accountability. That's exactly what the tribal government is afraid of. They know that if people really had their say, the current leaders would no longer be in power.[39]

MAPP lodged a complaint with the tribe in September of 1994, citing violations of freedom of speech and assembly. Hill said the group was able to get a court hearing in October, and the MAPP people decided to act as their own attorney because Indians historically have handled disputes in a non-confrontational manner. The tribal judge, however, was confrontational and told them they didn't present the case properly.[40]

MAPP asked for another hearing with a non-local tribal judge. The hearing took place in December under Judge Dee Fairbanks from the Leech Lake Reservation. Hill claims Fairbanks is a friend of Marge Anderson, the tribal chief executive who had restricted MAPP from the beginning. Fairbanks dismissed the case in 15 minutes, citing MAPP's failure to post notice of their meetings. Feeling that they had exhausted the "non-confrontational" avenue, MAPP hired a lawyer to draft a formal complaint. In a final ruling in May of 1996, Tribal Judge Tad Johnson also ruled against MAPP, stating that unless they could show a pattern of discrimination, the court wouldn't protect the right of MAPP to assemble.

The trial was the culmination of a rash of political retributions against MAPP members, according to Hill. In June of 1994, just after

MAPP was formed, Hill resigned his post as director of social services for the reservation and moved to Minneapolis because, in part, things began to get uncomfortable as a result of his involvement in politics. Solita Reum, MAPP's secretary-treasurer, and her husband Al had their casino jobs terminated, according to Hill. Irene Benjamin, described by Hill as the most vocal member of the political party, and her husband Larry were evicted from the Chemical Dependency Half-way House where they were caretakers. Larry Benjamin, who at 61 had lived on the reservation all his life, also lost his job with the school system. Having no place to live, Benjamin and his wife were forced to move from the reservation. People were still interested in political changes on the reservation, Hill said, but didn't know how anything could be accomplished. When MAPP members saw what happened to their leadership, MAPP grew dormant.

According to Hill, Mille Lacs Reservation is becoming quite prosperous, and tribal dissidents fear losing services. He claims that if you are in the right family or know the right leaders, you have free housing, free utilities, and free government commodity food. In other words, keep your mouth shut and the tribe will make sure it's full. According to MAPP, "Living on the Mille Lacs Reservation is literally like living under the oppression of a third world dictatorship."[41]

How Indian reservations got to this point in their evolution is a long, winding story, one that is detailed in part in the following chapters. Suffice it to note that when Congress ushered in the era of self-determination in the 1970s, they intended to create a governance structure and a way of life for Indians that is dramatically different than the reality on reservations today.

CHAPTER FOUR

Indian Treaties and Racial Segregation

Sovereign: The supreme, absolute, and uncontrollable power by which any independent state is governed; supreme political authority; paramount control of the constitution and frame of government and its administration; the international independence of a state, combined with the power of regulating its internal affairs without foreign dictation; the power to do everything in a state without accountability, to make laws, to execute and apply them, to impose and collect taxes and levy contributions, to make war and peace, to from treaties of alliance or of commerce with foreign nations, and the like.
- Black's Law Dictionary, 5th Edition, 1979

Though there are few comprehensive sources that look at the history of Indian treaty making, Indian leaders today believe there is but one interpretation of the intent and purpose of Indian treaties. According to Indian interpretation, treaties forever guarantee recognition of tribes as sovereign nations and also protect their trust status with the federal government. In recent years, sovereignty has been interpreted to mean tribes would have the right to territorially govern reservation and trust lands under tribal constitutions using their own ethnic court systems.

Under this scenario, Indian tribes win while non-Indians lose (particularly those owning property within reservation boundaries).

For starters, non-Indian property owners would be subject to the jurisdiction of Indian courts if they live in Indian country. The civil rights of non-Indians can be abused because the constitutional rights they hold as American citizens are essentially suspended when on tribal lands and are replaced with "rights" as described by tribal constitutions. What's more, some tribes are beginning to tax non-Indian residents of reservations as part of tribal claims of sovereignty.

By the same token, tribal lands, homes and businesses are exempt from most local, state and federal taxes, and to add injury to insult, tribal members are eligible for government benefits of education, health care, and social welfare. Trust benefits for Indians may also include some privileges not available to other Americans, including the right to harvest up to 50 percent of available wildlife resources in large parts of some states, even though the harvest would take place outside Indian-held lands.

How we got to this point lies largely in the interpretation of treaties between the U.S. federal government and various Indian tribes. While acknowledging the ill-treatment of Indian tribes over many years, the interpretation of treaties has, nonetheless, been totally biased in favor of Indian tribes to the point of constitutional heresy. This has given special rights and privileges to a people who today comprise less than 1 percent of the American population, while the rights and fair treatment of the other 99 percent of Americans are jeopardized. Because of reforms brought about by the Indian Reorganization Act of 1934, which allowed tribes to develop their own constitutions, and the Nixon-era policy of Indian self-determination, tribes have been given the opportunity to write their own body of law. To wit, Indians have taken full advantage by giving themselves certain advantages over other ethnic and political groups and by providing legal protection through a court system administered by the tribes themselves.

Imagine the license to operate a conglomerate of ethnic businesses exempt from many tax liabilities and without competition from anyone else. Protect this ethnic empire with an in-house court system, hired and fired according to the whim of the business committee or the ethnic leaders. Use the claim of sovereign immunity to avoid legal liabilities whenever it is expedient, and claim racism and cultural genocide if anyone objects.

The real issue at stake, however, is whether the current interpretation of Indian treaties is consistent with what the United States intended during the years of treaty making with tribes. Are ethnic courts, tribal business monopolies, and natural resource quotas based on race compatible with the U.S. Constitution? Are pro-Indian treaty interpretations necessary to protect tribal cultures? Was this the point of the treaties themselves? A look at the history of Indian treaties sheds some interesting light on these questions and yields some facts that many Indian advocates might easily overlook or dismiss altogether.

The Beginning of Treaty Making

The United States inherited the Indian treaty process from the British and continued to modify it to suit changing political realities for 90 years, from 1778 and 1868. In all, there are 367 ratified Indian treaties.[1]

In the beginning of treaty making, colonial leaders hoped to gain the help or neutrality of tribes who historically sided with the British. Southern Indian tribes had strong ties with the Spanish, who formed another potential source of trouble for American colonies. The Revolutionary War with Great Britain posed a serious risk for the 13 loosely united colonies, because both Great Britain and Indian tribes had a stake in the defeat of American colonies.

Official U.S. policy toward Indian tribes was first established by the Continental Congress during the American Revolution. Individual states also made war on tribes and held treaty ceremonies with them. These early treaties were not contracts in the sense that we have come to view them today. During the Revolutionary War (1775 to 1783), only the Delaware Treaty of 1778 was actually written up as a document. In these early times, to "treaty" simply meant talking about differing viewpoints and grievances between the two parties. This was a continuation of 200 years of British practice. The "treaty" process resulted in the forgiving of past injuries, expressions of friendship, and promises of future cooperation. When dealing with the Iroquois and other northern tribes, expressions of agreement were confirmed by the exchange of wampum by the tribes and gifts of trade goods from the government. Formal written agreements were not considered essential to the process.

By the time the United States declared its independence from Britain, Indian tribes had become very dependent on trade goods. Tribes possessing firearms, swords, axes, cooking utensils, cloth and other manufactured items had a tremendous advantage over those who did not. Trade goods and gifts were an integral part of treaty negotiations from the beginning. The loyalty of particular chiefs or headmen was often secured with special gifts such as silver medals or other ornaments. Treaty negotiations often were held at forts and included displays of American military might, calculated to influence the negotiations.[2]

A problem during the early years of the American Revolution was whether individual states or the federal government alone should hold negotiations with tribes. As early as 1754, Benjamin Franklin had proposed that the president-general of the colonies should regulate Indian trade, have the power to declare war or peace with tribes, and provide for the purchase of Indian lands not within colonial boundaries.[3] The idea of federal congressional control of Indian affairs was drafted in 1776 for the Articles of Confederation, but advocates for states rights succeeded in having the language modified to give states some power to act independently.

The Articles of Confederation, ratified in 1781, established the first "official" policy toward Indians. It states that Congress "shall have the sole and exclusive right and power of...regulating the trade and managing all affairs with the Indians, (who are) not members of any of the states, provided that the legislative right of any State within its own limits be not infringed or violated."[4] This appears to give exclusive power to the Congress, but the ambiguity introduced by announcing that the rights of a state within its territory shall not be infringed left room for broad interpretations of the law. This is a dilemma that remains unresolved to this day.

In the early years of the American republic, there were important reasons for not letting states make Indian treaties. Had the states been able to control Indian affairs, they might have used the opportu-

to declare war, make peace and sign treaties. That could have quickly destroyed the ability of the federal government to exercise sovereignty over both Indian tribes and individual states, a condition that could have caused trouble for the young republic. To protect its status as the absolute sovereign, the federal government began to issue written treaties with tribes to ensure that states or individuals could not enter into treaties on their own.[5]

Many people today believe that federal policy has gradually stripped Indian tribes of their sovereign status over the past 200 years. This is false because Indians never had sovereign status nor were they ever accorded special legal considerations during negotiations. Whether you agree with the morality of it or not, the fact of the matter is that once the United States won its independence from Britain, the U.S. federal government held plenary, or absolute, power over Indian tribes by right of sheer force, just as the many different tribes controlled the land previously for hundreds of years.

Judge R. A. Randall of the Minnesota Court of Appeals has done extensive study of the legal concept of Indian sovereignty in the course of writing opinions on important Indian legal cases. He argues that the U.S. had two chances to confer true sovereignty upon Indians: first, when Columbus landed and second, at the beginning of the westward expansion. "The first missed opportunity was not our fault," according to Randall. "The second was."[6]

Randall believes Columbus had the first opportunity when Europeans initially came in contact with the new world. Columbus, steered awry by a cloudy sextant, believed he had found India and was now going to trade. Had he gone ashore and found that he was on the wrong side of the Earth, Randall asserts, "he could have ordered his crew back onto the ship and said, 'Come on boys, this is somebody else's land. We are turning around and going back to our home. We will tell other Europeans to stay in Europe.'"[7] Of course, he did not do that.

The second opportunity to confer true sovereignty on all Indian tribes came at the beginning of the westward expansion. The Mississippi River provided an easy and firm demarcation as a possible border between the states and Indian country. But Randall notes:

Like all other discussion concerning Indian rights, it did not translate into action. We could have recognized the Mississippi as our national border....Then, whatever the Indian tribes did west of the Mississippi would have been their own business. They could have continued to roam free in small bands, or organized into counties, regions, or provinces. In other words, they would have had the same options citizens of Mexico and Canada have.[8]

But the founders of the U.S. chose not to limit the western border at the Mississippi River.

When the Revolutionary War ended in 1783, Congress was eager to settle any problems with Indian tribes that might have interfered with the peace process. Treaty negotiations with the Indians were necessary for several reasons. With the defeat of the British and their Indian allies, the tribes essentially became conquered nations themselves, conferring authority and the spoils to the U.S. federal government. White settlements required more land, and new boundaries needed to be negotiated with the tribes. From 1783 to 1788, the federal government developed the basic tenants by which Indian treaties were negotiated: tribes must consider themselves to be under the protection of the United States; they were not to form alliances with any foreign power, nor with any state or individual of any state; and Congress would have exclusive power to regulate commerce with Indians and to manage Indian affairs as they saw fit.[9]

Six treaties were written from 1783 to 1788 and contained numerous references to the lack of Indian sovereignty. The Treaty of Fort McIntosh, ratified in 1785 between the U.S. and the Wyandot, Delaware, Chippewa and Ottawa Tribes, stipulates that the tribes are acknowledged "to be under the protection of the United States and no other sovereign whatsoever."[10] The treaty with the Shawnee in 1786 stated, "The Shawnee acknowledged the United States to be 'the sole and absolute sovereigns' of all territory ceded to it by Great Britain; the United States granted peace to the Shawnee Nation and received the Indians into its friendship and protection and 'allotted' lands to them within specified boundaries."[11] Though "Indian Nation" was used in

Indian treaties such as this one, it was a matter of convention rather than one of reality. "Nation" was commonly used to refer to Indian tribes as an entity, while not conferring actual nation status nor giving tribes the right of sovereignty.

Sovereign power was officially conferred to the federal government once the United States Constitution was ratified in 1788 by the required nine states. Indians have argued that some passages in the Constitution give tribes sovereignty equal to that of the states, but Article 4, Section 3 of the Constitution makes it clear that states are not expected to share governmental power within state boundaries. It reads, "New States may be admitted by the Congress into this Union; but no new State shall be formed or erected within the Jurisdiction of any other State...without the Consent of the Legislatures of the States concerned as well as of the Congress." Currently, there are 557 tribes that claim sovereign status in the United States. However, until state legislatures and Congress see fit to admit these tribes as new states within the union, they are no more sovereign in a truly legal sense than the average American declaring his or her home and backyard a newly sovereign nation.

The dilemma of having a state within a state has persisted to the present day because Indian tribes *claim* they possess "original sovereignty" that predates the U.S. Constitution. But the British, Spanish and French also were sovereign in U.S. territory before the Constitution. Their sovereignty, like that of the Indians, was extinguished by war or purchase of land. War also took the southwest from Mexico, and subsequently extinguished Mexican sovereignty over this land.

In stark contrast to those who believe the treaties gave Indian tribes sovereignty, the treaties actually *extinguished* Indian sovereignty as a matter of concession, and the treaties state this matter-of-factly. Present interpretations of Indian treaties ignore the written language of treaties, choosing instead to define treaties as Indians *wish* they had been written. But early treaty making with Indians created a problem that has yet to be resolved, namely the quasi-sovereign status of Indian tribes. Both the federal government and Indian tribes had an interest (though unflattering in both cases) in maintaining a separate, homogenous, place-based identity for Indian tribes. The problem was post-poned to some extent while there were vast territories beyond the boundaries of established states where Indians could be relocated. But eventually all of these territories would become states and jurisdiction-al problems would become acute. This led to the creation of permanent reservations whereby the government put Indians on neatly defined tracts of land so westward expansion could continue unfettered.

While both Indian treaties and the Constitution state the U.S. government's sovereignty and authority over Indian tribes, neither did much to define how Indian affairs should be regulated. The question of Indian affairs was given scant attention in the Constitution. Section 8 of Article 1 of the Constitution states, "The Congress shall have power…(to) regulate Commerce with foreign Nations, and among the several States, and with the Indian Tribes." This trailing phrase does not go a long way in explaining how tribes might fit into the govern-mental system of the United States.[12]

Treaties were meant to fill in some of the "regulatory details" left out of the Constitution and provide legal footholds for the land rush westward. The period around 1800 was significant for the welfare of the United States, and indirectly for Indians as well. The steadily increasing population caused a constant demand for more land. Threats from French, British and Spanish interests also fueled the quest for land, and there was concern about securing the eastern bank of the Mississippi as a natural border for the growing United States.[13] At the same time, increasing pressure on Indian hunting territories was mak-ing it very difficult for tribes to survive by hunting and gathering.

These colliding factors made treaties attractive for both parties, though possibly more so for the U.S. government who stood to gain considerable territory. In fact, the idea of assimilating Indians into mainstream society was the intent from the beginning of treaty making. Treaties not only offered trade goods, but seed, farm implements, domestic animals, horse-operated milling machinery and blacksmith tools. Some treaties also provided instructors to teach Indians the arts of European-style civilization. The increasing dependence of Indians on manufactured goods and the decline of the fur trade because of over-harvest meant Indians often had to pay for trade items by selling land. This became a vicious cycle, soon leading to the impoverishment of many tribes.[14]

For leaders of early America, this led to an inescapable conclusion. Either Indians must be acculturated to the ways of American-defined civilization (self-sufficient farmers or tradesmen), or they must continually be pushed further west. These solutions often were pursued simultaneously by treaty negotiation.

The federal government sought to improve interactions between Whites and Indians on the frontier by passing Trade and Intercourse Acts in 1790, 1793, 1796, 1802 and 1834. Not all tribes had treaty relationships with the United States, and treaties could not be relied upon to address every problem in otherwise lawless territory. The laws were the beginning of frontier law that could be changed rapidly to reflect experience and reality. These Acts, starting with the Ordinance of 1786, required licenses for those engaged in Indian trade, and provided punishment for crimes committed against Indians. The laws also enforced the idea that persons or states could not purchase lands from Indians, except under the treaty-making authority of the United States. It was hoped that these Acts would help to keep traders honest and fair in dealings with Indians, keep immigrants from encroaching on Indian lands, and lessen the chances of hostility between the two groups.[15] Another purpose of these laws was to keep Indians from trading with the British, French and Spanish.

The War of 1812 between the Americans and British had a profound effect on Indian affairs in the United States. Many Indians again joined forces with the British, and during the war, it was uncertain whether the lands south of the Great Lakes would belong to the British Crown. When the war ended, the United States was much more secure in its domination of lands east of the Mississippi River. Prior to the war, Thomas Jefferson had hoped the Indians could be easily assimilated into American society. The wilderness was fast disappearing before the advances of civilization, and Indians could be expected to give up the uncertainties of the hunter's existence for the obvious benefits of farming and industry. "While they are learning to do better on less land," Jefferson noted, "our increasing numbers will be calling for more land, and thus a coincidence of interests will produced between those who have lands to spare, and want of other necessaries, and those who have such necessaries to spare, and want lands."[16]

After the War of 1812, treaties were written in an increasingly dominant manner. With the loss of the British alliance, Indian tribes would never again pose a significant military threat to the United States. Many prominent statesmen began to call for an end to treaty making with tribes, but the process would continue for more than 50 years. In 1817, Andrew Jackson became the first leader of national standing to suggest that writing treaties with Indian tribes was "an absurdity" that couldn't be reconciled with the American form of government. In a letter to President Monroe, Jackson said Congress should treat Indians as it did "regular" American citizens. Congress could take care of Indian needs and determine the boundaries of Indian territory. When the interests of the United States demanded the use of any part of Indian lands, the government could take it by the exercise of eminent domain and provide compensation to Indians as it would any other American.[17]

In 1820, Jackson was appointed treaty commissioner, and he promptly complained to Secretary of War John Calhoun that he had "determined never to have anything to do again with Indian Treaties." Calhoun replied, "I entirely concur with you that it is perfectly absurd to hold treaties with those within our limits, as they neither are or can be independent of our government."[18]

Despite such rhetoric, 94 treaties were written during Jackson's two terms in office, and in May of 1830 Congress approved an act to begin "voluntary" removal of Indian tribes to areas west of the Mississippi. The precipitating event was the writing of a constitution by the Cherokee Tribe in Georgia, whereby the tribe declared itself a separate nation not subject to the jurisdiction of Georgia courts. For the first time in our history this caused a serious debate in Congress about future Indian policy. As civilization began to encroach on Indian territory, the inevitable conflicts that arose led to two possible solutions; one was to assimilate Indians into society, the other was to simply push the Indians further west. The Cherokee constitution created a new dilemma. Instead of assimilating, the tribe formed what was essentially an independent Indian state within the state of Georgia. To the residents and politicians of the state of Georgia, this was unacceptable. It was also unconstitutional.

The solution to this dilemma came in the form of a measure called removal policy which solved the problem of state jurisdiction over tribes by simply moving Indians out of state territories. Indian lands east of the Mississippi River would be exchanged for lands west of the great river. Removal policy was based on a mistaken perception by the American government and people of the early 19th century. Indians were to be moved west of the Mississippi because this part of the country was largely wilderness with a sparse population. It had taken more than 300 years (1500 to 1800) for immigrant society to begin to approach the shores of the great river which conveniently divided East from West. People of the time believed it would take an even longer time for the new civilization to reach the West Coast because of the greater distance involved and the difficulty of the terrain.

By the time civilization overtook the western lands, it was believed Indians would have already learned the arts of civilization, and assimilation would be accomplished without a problem. Few people of the early 1800s could have possibly imagined the settlement to the West Coast would be accomplished in only 50 years. As such, policy makers were unaware that reservations would be formed under flawed assumptions about westward settlement.

Andrew Jackson and the Georgia Cherokee

In the South, a number of tribes had adopted White men's ways. By the early 1800s, members of the Cherokee Tribe in Georgia had gone a long way toward American assimilation. They had developed plantation lands, purchased Black slaves to work them, and developed industry including a printing press and a distillery. Cherokees historically used Indian slaves also, but had given up the practice by the time of the American Revolution. Cherokee slave owners generally owned small numbers of slaves, but a few had more than 50, and a half-breed named Joseph Vann had 110. Other slave-owning southern tribes were the Choctaws, Chicasaws, Creeks, and Seminoles, who along with the Cherokee were known as the Five Civilized Tribes.[19]

There were other examples of Indian assimilation as well. The Cherokee had developed a written form of their language as early as 1821 and had 18 schools by 1825 with a combined enrollment of 314 students. Many received a Christian education, and students were sent to colleges in New England for advanced education. John Ross, perhaps the most influential Cherokee of the time, was elected chief in 1828 and was one of the principle authors of the Cherokee Constitution. Ross had fair skin, blue eyes, red hair and was seven-eighths Scottish. A good deal of intermarrying occurred between Whites and the Cherokee Tribe. In 1824, the tribal census showed 220 Whites were married to Indian spouses, in addition to many half-breeds.[20]

Andrew Jackson was elected president the same year (1828) John Ross was made chief of the Cherokee. These leaders would disagree completely on the status of tribes within the American states, and their argument would lead to important Supreme Court rulings. Georgia passed a law in 1828 declaring the laws of the Cherokee Constitution null and void as of June 1, 1830. Under the guidance of John Ross, the Cherokees fought the case to the Supreme Court, which produced the most famous ruling on Indian treaties in U.S. history. The 1831 ruling by Justice John Marshall in *Cherokee Nation v. State of Georgia* denied an injunction against Georgia by the Cherokee Tribe. The court pronounced the Cherokee a "domestic dependent nation" rather than a foreign state. Because the Cherokee Tribe was a domestic affair, the Marshall court ruled that it did not have jurisdiction in the case.[21]

Cherokee Nation v. State of Georgia demonstrated the folly of regarding tribes as sovereign nations. It states:

Though the Indians are acknowledged to have unquestionable, and, heretofore, unquestioned right to the lands they occupy until that right until that right be extinguished by a voluntary cession to our government, yet it may well be doubted whether those tribes which reside within the acknowledged boundaries of the United States can, with strict accuracy, be denominated foreign nations. They may, more correctly be denominated domestic dependent nations. They occupy a territory to which we assert a title independent of their will, which must take effect when their right of possession ceases. Meanwhile they are in a state of pupilage. Their relation to the United States resembles that of a ward to his guardian.

They look to our government for protection; rely upon its kindness and its power; appeal to it for relief to their wants; and address the President as their great father. They and their country are considered by foreign nations, as well as by ourselves, as being so completely under the sovereignty and dominion of the United States, that any attempt to acquire their lands, or to form political connection with them, would be considered by all as an invasion of our territory, and an act of hostility.

In 1830, Georgia passed a law requiring Whites living in Cherokee country to swear an oath of allegiance to the state and be licensed by the governor. Two missionaries defied the order and were sentenced to prison. The case went to the Supreme Court and the state of Georgia was overturned with the Court finding the federal government alone had jurisdiction on the Cherokee lands.[22]

Jackson used the treaty process to sidestep the question of state jurisdiction on Indian lands. If there were no tribes in Eastern states, there would be no need to spar with the Supreme Court over jurisdictional issues. Using treaties to remove the Indians, Jackson succeeded in relocating the Creeks, Choctaws and Chickasaws by 1833. In 1833, the Seminoles signed a treaty to move west, after having first sent a delegation to inspect the new lands. But after signing, they changed their minds and refused to leave Florida. The impasse resulted in the Second Seminole War which sputtered from 1835 until 1842.[23] By then, all but a few had been killed or removed to Indian lands.

In 1835, the last Cherokees residing in Georgia signed a treaty for $5 million to resettle in Oklahoma. Continuing disputes delayed the removal until the spring of 1838 and then bad summer weather caused further delays. As a result, the Indians were caught in winter at the end of the journey.[24]

Sixteen thousand Indians and their Black slaves made the journey remembered today as the "Trail of Tears." Many died of dysentery during the journey and in temporary camps in Oklahoma, although there is much dispute as to exactly how many died. Most authors accept the figure of 4,000, which was reported by Dr. Butler, a physician who accompanied one of 13 Indian groups led by John Ross. Two thousand of these deaths were said to have occurred on the trail, and two thousand at the Oklahoma camps. Records kept by Cherokee leader John Ross, however, indicate that of the 13,149 Indians who accompanied him, 424 died en route, with an equal number dying in temporary camps. Thus, the number of deaths occurring as a result of the migration is about 800 from one source or 4,000 from another. Doctor Butler, who reports the figure of 4,000, was one of the missionaries sent to prison for defying the 1830 Georgia law requiring Whites living in Cherokee territory to swear an oath of allegiance to the state. As such, he might not have been an impartial observer.[25]

The only recourse for Indians not wanting to be relocated was to become American citizens. As early as 1817, removal treaties had allowed Cherokees to exchange lands in Georgia for lands in Arkansas. Those who did not wish to move were given 640 acres of land (one square mile) and allowed to become American citizens. In 1828, a removal treaty had been signed with part of the Cherokee Tribe, and they became known as the Old Settlers, or Western Cherokee Tribe.[26]

As these events show, Indian policy was a haphazard process. When the Georgia Cherokee began to form an independent state within the state of Georgia, the government reacted by removing the tribe. At the same time, Indians who wanted to become citizens and individual landowners like other Americans were occasionally allowed to do so. In general, Whites saw that Indians would need to learn the ways of mainstream American culture in order to survive and prosper, but they were not sure how long the "civilizing" process would take. Some thought 20 years would be enough, while others thought the process would take generations.[27] In general, it was poorly understood exactly how Indians would transition from nomadic hunting to a new, American-style agrarian or urban lifestyle.

Indians were less sure than other Americans about the supposed benefits of American culture, but they were very eager to adopt trade goods such as firearms, traps, axes, tools, cooking utensils, blankets and horses. These items created a surge in prosperity as long as there were sufficient game and fur-bearing animals in Indian territory. The increased efficiency and mobility in hunting and warfare soon made Indians who possessed firearms and horses wealthy by tribal standards. However, the combined pressure on game stocks from increased numbers of immigrants and Indians in the West soon destroyed this short-lived prosperity.[2] For non-Indians, the solution to this problem was for Indians to become farmers. The idea of taking up a farming existence was not appealing to many Indians, however, as they preferred the free life of the hunter and did not understand the need to change.

In 1837, the eastern bands of Sioux sold their land east of the Mississippi River in Wisconsin. They were allowed to hunt on the ceded lands, but Indian agent Lawrence Taliaferro reported that Indians soon came to Fort Snelling, Minnesota to plead for quick payment of government annuities (treaty payments in cash and goods). The Indians had found no game on the ceded lands and were on the verge of starvation on their Minnesota reservations.[29] By 1849, the territory that was to become Minnesota contained a population of less than 4,000 non-Indians, but swelled to 150,037 just eight years later. Under these circumstances, subsistence hunting was no longer practical.[30]

While it is easy to detect racist tendencies in Indian policies throughout the 19th century, it is important to look at these events from the perspective of the time. Indian policy most often reflected what people of the time believed were reasonable and humane solutions to problems between two vastly different cultures. In the 1800s, most people were farmers, and it was believed that Indians would begin to learn the ways of civilization (as Americans defined it, at least) by first becoming farmers, receiving an education (which couldn't be accomplished until they learned to speak English), adopting Christianity, cutting their long hair, and trading their beads and buckskin for traditional American clothing.

To many 19th century bureaucrats, leaders and churchmen, Indian people could only be saved by destroying their culture. Assimilation meant adopting American speech, industry, dress and religion while stamping out Indian languages, religion, dress and culture. The 19th century concept of assimilation differs markedly from today's concept of integration which means accepting groups into a mainstream culture while maintaining cultural traditions and nuances within individual racial or ethnic groups. In contrast, assimilation in the 1800s meant accepting people into the mainstream only if they were willing to look and act like White Christians. Today, we would regard this as a White supremacist view, but during the time of treaty writing, it was considered to be the essence of civilization.

By the 1850s, the concept of removal no longer made sense as the southwestern and western states of Texas, California, Arizona, Nevada, Utah, Wyoming, Colorado and part of New Mexico were brought under U.S. control. A treaty with the British in 1846 set the northern boundary at the 49th parallel and Oregon became a state by 1859. In the war with Mexico (1846-1848), the U.S. gained another 1,193,061 square miles of land (about 740,000,000 acres). The federal government paid Mexico $18,250,00 for the lands earned in war, or about two and a half cents an acre.[31] In 1850, the concept of an American republic stretching to the West Coast was a reality.

At this point, treaties also took on a new form, as the idea of assimilation overcame the push for removal. Indian territory was by then surrounded by American civilization, and many felt it was only a matter of time before Indians would adopt similar lifestyles. It was at this point in history that the dreaded reservation system came into being. Indian country was carved into ever smaller "reserves" where Indians could live during the period of acculturation to civilization. These reserves were seen as a temporary sanctuary where Indians would be segregated from White settlers while education, religious indoctrination and technical instruction prepared Indians for entry into American society.[32]

During this period, members of Indian tribes were admitted to the United States as citizens in significant numbers. The first tribe to do so were the Wyandots in 1855. The Potawatomi became citizens in 1861 and the Kickapoos in 1862.[33] Once they became citizens, their relationship to the U.S. changed. The Wyandot Treaty of 1855 is unequivocal in its language regarding the rights of Indians once they became citizens:

Article 1. The Wyandot Indians having become sufficiently advanced in civilization, and being desirous of becoming citizens, it is hereby agreed and stipulated, that their organization, and their relations with the United States as an Indian tribe shall be dissolved and terminated on the ratification of this agreement...and after the date of such ratification, the said Wyandot Indians, each and every one of them...shall be deemed...to be citizens of the United States, to all intents and purposes; and shall be entitled to all the rights, privileges, and immunities of such citizens; and shall in all respects be subject to the laws of the United States, and of the Territory of Kansas in the same manner as other citizens of said Territory; and the jurisdiction of the United States and of said territory, shall be extended over the Wyandot country in the same manner as over other parts of said territory.[34]

This treaty of 1855 anticipated the 14th Amendment of the Constitution, which become law in 1868. Both documents guarantee citizenship and the equal treatment of the law. It is no coincidence that the last Indian treaty ever written was ratified in 1868. After the 14th Amendment, treaties were obsolete, because nations do not make treaties with their own citizens. But equality is not accomplished simply by passing a new law. For one, all Indians would not receive full citizenship until 1924. In other cases, the benefits of citizenship were squandered when Indians were awkwardly thrust into different lifestyles. For example, many Wyandots, suddenly owners of their own land, sold it and lapsed into poverty. Indians had grown accustomed to being wards of the government, and had become dependent on annuities. Indians would not become prosperous by the magic of U.S. citizenship. What's more, racism would not disappear suddenly because of a new law.

The Civil War also had an effect on treaty policy. Some Indian tribes would choose sides in the war, though many remained neutral. Of those who fought, the majority — 6,435 — sided with the Confederacy. These soldiers were mainly from the Five Civilized Tribes: the Cherokee, Choctaws, Chickasaws, Creeks and Seminoles.[35]

Removal policy had relocated most members of these tribes to Oklahoma. As they had done in Georgia, many Cherokee were more interested in their own nationalism than in taking sides in the war. William Ross, a nephew of tribal leader John Ross, published the *Cherokee Advocate*, a tribal newspaper printed in English and Cherokee. The newspaper's motto was "Our Rights, Our Country, Our Race."[36] Theirs was not a "melting pot" philosophy. The Cherokee had done very well in Oklahoma territory. By 1860, their population was 20,000 and they owned 300,000 head of livestock and 4,000 Black slaves.[37] The Cherokee were divided in their allegiance. John Ross was the leader of one Cherokee faction. Although a slave owner, he sympathized with the North, but hoped the tribe would remain neutral. A rival Cherokee faction, the Ridge Party, led by Stand Waitie, was adamantly pro-Confederacy. John Ross gave in and signed a treaty with the Confederacy in 1861. The Five Civilized Tribes all signed treaties with the Confederacy, as did the Osages and Comanches.[38]

John Ross was convinced the war would divide the United States and the Confederacy permanently.[39] The South offered attractive treaty terms to the Indians. Slavery would be continued, and tribes were promised the "undisturbed use" of their lands "as long as grass grows and water flows."[40] A popular misconception among Indians even today is that this phrase is contained in many U.S. treaties. In fact, it has become a sort of mantra among some Indian activists today. But the phrase was only used in Confederate treaties. Confederate treaties promised Indians their lands would not be "included within the bounds of any State or Territory." Treaty clauses also required the return of stolen slaves and horses to their rightful owners.[41] While Confederate treaties appear to give Indians more autonomy than those of the North, this was an illusion. The treaties borrowed the language of the U.S. Supreme Court and referred to Indians as "wards" of the Confederate government.[42] The government extended criminal jurisdiction over the tribes and made rules regarding tribal membership.[43]

Stand Waitie, of the Ridge Party, became a general in the Confederate Army. He lost an important battle with the Union cavalry at the Battle of Cabin Creek in July of 1863. The Confederacy was soon defeated in Indian territory. In September 1863, the South lost its key outpost of Fort Smith.[44] The Cherokee repudiated its treaty with the Confederacy in that year and abolished slavery within weeks of Lincoln's Emancipation Proclamation.[45] But Stand Waitie and his faction continued to fight for the Confederacy. He was promoted to brigadier general in 1864 and began to fight against the Cherokee of the Keetoowah Society, which adamantly opposed slavery. Raids and counter raids laid waste to homes and farms in Cherokee country.[46]

Indians of the Iroquois Six Nations Confederacy, on the other hand, volunteered by the hundreds to join the Union Army with major contingents coming from New York and Wisconsin. Iroquois leaders rose to high rank in the Union Army. Ely S. Parker, a Seneca from New York, had studied law and engineering before the war and served in the New York state militia in 1853 as captain of engineers. Parker knew Ulysses S. Grant before the war broke out, and during the war he served as assistant adjutant general, secretary, and division engineer for Grant. By the end of the war, he had risen to the level of brigadier general and had great influence, assisting Grant in writing the articles of surrender signed by Robert E. Lee at Appomattox in 1865.[47]

Reconstruction treaties signed by the Five Civilized Tribes and others who had sided with the Confederacy ended slavery among the southern tribes and required the freed slaves to be accepted into the tribes. Slavery was also common among the tribes of the Pacific Northwest, but the slaves were Indians captured from rival tribes. These slaves were mostly women and children, and they were used to do much of the routine work around tribal villages.[48] The 1854 Treaty of Medicine Creek, written for tribes in Washington state, specifically prohibits the practice of slavery. Article 11 states, "The said tribes and bands agree to free all slaves now held by them, and not to purchase or acquire others hereafter."[49]

During and immediately after the Civil War, some U.S. treaties offered citizenship to tribes, placing them under the same state jurisdiction as all non-Indians. The treaty with the Ottawa Tribe of 1862 stipulates that "each and every one of them, shall be deemed and declared to be citizens of the United States…and shall be entitled to all the rights, privileges and immunities of such citizens, and shall, in all respects, be subject to the laws of the United States, and of the State or

States thereof in which they may reside."[50] The treaty also stipulated that the federal trust relationship would be dissolved with the tribe after 5 years. A treaty with the Seneca and Shawnee of 1867 allowed Indians of the tribe to choose between remaining with the tribe or becoming citizens.[51] Those who became citizens however, would "have no further rights in the tribe." The last Indian treaty was written in 1868 with the Nez Perce Tribe. Officially, treaty making was ended by Congress in 1871.

In 1868, the 14th Amendment to the Constitution was ratified, extending citizenship to Blacks. Giving citizenship to Indians was fiercely debated, with many feeling Indians should become citizens as well. Those opposed generally fell into two groups: one contending that letting Blacks become citizens was a mistake that didn't need repeating, while the others felt Indians would simply be manipulated by Whites intent on swindling Indians out of their land. As usual with Indian policy, the government couldn't make up its collective mind whether to make Indians citizens or not. Many people felt there should be some demonstration of competency before Indians could become citizens, so schemes were developed by which Indians would gradually be given citizenship. The Dawes Act of 1887 allowed many Indians to attain citizenship as well as individual ownership of land. In 1901, members of the Five Civilized Tribes were given citizenship. By 1906, there were 166,000 Indian citizens. The census of 1890 had listed 248,253 Indian residents in the U.S. Thus, by the beginning of the 20th century, just over half of the Indian population were citizens, typical of Indian policies that did everything by half-measure. Later, approximately 17,000 Indians were made citizens when Indian veterans returned from World War I.[52] All other Indians were granted citizenship in 1924 by congressional act.

Racism and paternalism no doubt played a great part in the refusal to apply the 14th Amendment to Indians. Just as Jim Crow laws were enacted in the 1880s to segregate Blacks, American courts acted to keep Indians in their place on the reservation. In the case of *Elk v. Wilkins* in 1884, a federal circuit court ruled that an Indian who tried to vote in an Omaha, Nebraska election was not protected by the 14th Amendment and therefore couldn't vote. Ironically, this was done when the professed aim of Indian policy was to prepare Indians for entry into mainstream civilization.[53] Condescension toward Indians as a race is apparent in a circuit court ruling of 1912 which stated that if a person had one-eighth Indian blood, it would "substantially handicap them in the struggle for existence."[54] The Supreme Court voiced similar attitudes about Indians when in 1876, in *United States v. Joseph*, the court declared that the Pueblos of New Mexico should not be treated as an Indian tribe because they were industrious, intelligent, Christian and agricultural. This made them "superior to all but a few of the civilized tribes of the country." The court reversed itself in the 1913 case of *United States v. Sandoval*, however, and decided that federal guardianship of Pueblos was appropriate because of reports of "drunkenness, debauchery, dancing, and communal living." The court declared the Pueblos *were* Indians after all.[55]

Ironic? Absurd? Yes, federal policy toward Indians was all this and more. It has gone on for so long, in fact, that a fundamental shift has taken place. For most of U.S. history, Indians were denied constitutional rights because of White supremacy. Today both Indian and non-Indian people are denied constitutional rights on reservations because of Indian supremacy. We haven't abolished racism; it's just been recycled.

Treaties and International Law

Central to arguments upholding Indian treaty rights is the idea that these treaties are instruments of international law. For this reason, Indians believe treaties can never be changed or abolished without Indian consent. At the Senate Hearing on Indian Sovereign Immunity in 1996, Jessie Taken Alive, chairman of the Standing Rock Sioux Tribe of South Dakota, testified about the Indian desire to elevate treaty issues to international status. Taken Alive said, "(L)et's find an international court system to hear issues between indigenous nations of North America and the United States of America."[56] However, as mentioned earlier, the legal status of Indian tribes in the United States was settled in 1831 in the Supreme Court decision of *Cherokee Nation v. the State of Georgia*, where the court ruled Indian tribes were not foreign nations according to the Constitution. Ownership of American land was settled in an earlier case, *Johnson v. McIntosh* in 1823, when the court ruled that the United States held title to the land within its territorial boundaries and "had the exclusive right to extinguish the Indian title of occupancy either by purchase or by conquest."[57]

The treaty relationship between Indian tribes and the United States is unique, since tribal lands technically belong to the United States and are under its jurisdiction. This situation is further complicated by the fact that all Indians are American citizens with every right guaranteed to other Americans. To suggest that treaty issues are international law and should be handled in international courts rather than U.S. courts is to deny the whole of American history. In the *Cherokee Nation* ruling, Justice Marshall described Indian nations as best he could, "The relation of the Indians to the United States is marked by peculiar and cardinal distinctions which exist nowhere else."[58]

The legal limbo created in the 1800s when tribes were designated domestic dependent nations led to many abuses of the treaty system. Because Indians were not citizens, their legal status was uncertain. While tribes were not designated foreign nations, their treatment reveals a callousness that would not have been shown American citizens. In this sense, Indians were treated as if they were foreign, and international law would indeed allow such treatment.

The apartheid status of Indian tribes and the slavery of African-Americans resulted from a perception of these groups as unqualified to assume the rights of citizenship. Although these two groups were unquestionably American, they were not citizens. African-American slaves were considered "property," and Indians were designated as "wards." By the time of the Civil War, these problems could no longer be ignored. Great efforts have since been made to change American law, and there have been successes and failures. To regulate Indian/United States relations according to the whims of 19th century treaties is to continue one of the great failures in American law. Although Indian treaties cannot be reasonably or accurately regarded as international, other types of treaties are. If Indian treaties are seen as *comparable* to international treaties, it is instructive to look at international law regarding treaties. Indians see treaties as unchangeable over time. Other laws change, but Indians wish treaties to be interpreted today as if nothing had changed since the treaties were written. Are international treaties unchangeable? Obviously not. Treaties, like other contracts, are written to take into account a fixed set of circumstances. When these circumstances change, the treaty becomes obsolete. According to *International Law: Cases and Materials* by William Bishop, "It is a well established principle of international law, *rebus sic stantibus*, that a treaty ceases to be binding when the basic conditions upon which it was founded have essentially changed. Suspension of the convention in such circumstances is the unquestioned right of a state adversely affected by such essential change."[59]

Certainly, the basic circumstances of legal reality in the United States have changed dramatically since treaties were written. The Civil War, the 14th Amendment, the Citizenship Act of 1929, and the Civil Rights Act are not minor adjustments in the landscape of American law; these principles and precedents are the substance of American rights and responsibilities today. Indians demand these rights as American citizens and then say they are also exempt from the whole of American law, claiming the defense of tribal sovereign immunity.

Indian leaders express the mistaken view that tribes are the legal equals of states. Indian testimony to the Senate American Indian Policy Review Commission of 1977 stated this belief:

All Indian reservations within a State are islands where the laws of the state cannot reach. Those Islands are governed by the institutions of the tribes. To put it another way, the laws of Arizona have no effect for most purposes in New Mexico or Utah. Absent express federal legislation, the laws of Arizona have no effect for most purposes on the Papago and Navajo reservations.[60]

This view of tribal sovereignty would appear to violate the constitutional ban (Article IV, Section 3) on forming a state within the jurisdiction of another state.

In fact, Indian treaties are not immune to changes in government policy. The Supreme Court case of *Lone Wolf v. Hichcock* in 1903 specifically addressed the question of whether Indian treaties could be modified to suit changing circumstances:

> The power exists to abrogate the provisions in an Indian treaty…When, therefore, treaties were entered into between the United States and a tribe of Indians it was never doubted that the power to abrogate existed in Congress, and that in a contingency such power might be availed of from considerations of governmental policy, particularly if consistent with perfect good faith towards the Indians.[61]

The Supreme Court also addressed the question of whether new laws, such as the 14th Amendment, apply to Indian treaties. In the case of *Ward v. Race House* in 1896, the court said it is elementary "that a treaty may supersede a prior act of Congress, and an act of Congress may supersede a prior treaty."[62] The court decision cited the example of a case in which Congress passed a law imposing a tax on tobacco, and although this conflicted with a clause in a treaty with the Cherokees, the new tax law was *paramount* to the treaty.[63] If a tobacco tax is a sufficiently important aspect of government policy that it can override a treaty, isn't the 14th Amendment also? What could be a better example of "good faith" toward Indians than equal treatment of the laws?

These court precedents are unequivocal proof that treaties are subject to revision when there are significant changes in government policy or laws. The period from the Civil War to the present is filled with examples of changes in law and policy aimed at ending segregation, racism and discrimination. Indian treaties, whether viewed as comparable to international law or domestic law, cannot escape revision when the circumstances under which they were written no longer exist. "Law follows reality and experience," according to Senator Lloyd Meeds of the Indian Policy Review Commission.[64] Today we wouldn't honor an international treaty about whaling that was written in the time of sailing ships. Reality and experience teach us that whales must be protected by a different set of rules today. Treaties become obsolete and are discarded.

Indian treaties have become almost mythological creatures, often talked about but seldom ever seen or read. Many commonly held views about treaties are false. Perhaps the most common misconception about Indian treaties is that the United States treacherously broke every one. Even judges believe this misconception. In one of his court opinions on Indian sovereignty, Judge R. A. Randall of the Minnesota Court of Appeals says, "I know of no major treaty that we have not broken."[65]   Vine Deloria Jr., the famous lawyer, writer and Indian activist repeats the broken treaty refrain in his book *Custer Died for Your Sins*. "America has yet to keep one Indian treaty or agreement despite the fact that the United States signed over four hundred such treaties and agreements with Indian Tribes."[66] But this is a one-sided view that is often used to induce "White guilt." In *American Indian Treaties*, author Francis Prucha correctly points out that treaties were regularly broken by *both* sides:

> There certainly are well-confirmed cases in which the federal government failed to live up to the stipulations of the treaties, just as there are cases in which the Indian signatories 'broke' the treaties. Neither the United States nor the Indian tribes were able to control the actions of their subjects, as aggressive white settlers moved illegally into lands reserved for the Indians and as young Indian warriors continued their raids on white settlements after the chiefs had agreed to permanent peace.[67]

It must be remembered that after treaties were negotiated in the field, they were often changed or rejected by the Senate, and Congress could be glacially slow in appropriating treaty funds. Treaty making was a haphazard process, often failing to meet *any* of its objectives. New treaties were written to correct past wrongs, usually adding another layer of paternalism and bureaucracy. But Indians often play the "choose-the-best-treaty game." Indians now pick through the pile of treaties and try to find the one with the most utopian promise. According to Prucha, "It is not proper to maintain, as some Indian groups have done, that an initial treaty is absolute and that any subsequent treaty, agreement, or statute that changes its provisions is an illegal abrogation of the original treaty."[68]

There are many instances by which the treaty contracts between the U.S. and the many different Indian tribes have been either legally modified or nullified. Some treaties were voided by the outbreak of hostilities between the treaty parties. Other treaties became obsolete when a new treaty was written for the tribe, superseding the older one. Indian tribes who signed treaties with the Confederate States voided previous treaties signed with the United States. These are well-recognized circumstances by which treaties usually become null and void. Voided treaties cannot be resurrected, especially since the treaty making process was officially ended by law in 1871. Finally, Indian treaties became obsolete when Indians became citizens of the United States.

While it has taken too long to get to this point in American history, Indian culture and prosperity can best be protected by the U.S. Constitution. Since the Civil Rights Act of 1964, protection of the cultural values and habits of diverse peoples has been truly possible in the United States. It is ironic that precisely at the time when American law and mainstream American values were beginning to embrace the concept of cultural diversity, Indians were beginning their radical movement to permanently segregate themselves on American Indian reservations. A second irony is that tribal constitutional governments, established under the Indian Reorganization Act (IRA) of 1934, are in many ways the antithesis of the traditional tribal governments they replaced. It might very well be that IRA-style tribal governments have done more to destroy traditional Indian culture in the last century than anything since the forced indoctrination of Christianity on reservations.

INDIAN POLICY 1868-1964

ALLOTMENT OF INDIAN LANDS 1887
THE INDIAN REORGANIZATION ACT 1934
TERMINATION POLICY 1953

Once treaty making was officially discontinued by the United States in 1871, federal policy continued to evolve in important ways. The discontinuance of ill-fated treaties was a major step forward in addressing Indians as people of the United States and not as some muddled, quasi-sovereign entity. However, federal policy over the next 100 years or so would continue to lack fundamental consistency and a workable method for solving problems concerning Indian reservations. As a result, federal policy continued to be a failure for both the Indians and the American system of government

After the abolition of treaty making, there would be three landmark laws passed by Congress roughly three decades apart from each other that would have a major impact on Indian affairs throughout the country. In essence, these laws would light the fire of discontent in Indian leaders to finally rebel in civil protest in the 1960s and 1970s, eventually leading to an Indian policy commission that set in motion the state of affairs being hotly debated today. These three laws were: the Dawes Act of 1887 which allotted land to individual Indians and gave these landowners citizenship rights, the Indian Reorganization Act of 1934 which gave Indians a constitutional type of government, and the Termination Policy of 1953 which sought to assimilate Indians into mainstream society.

The Dawes Act of 1887

With the end of the Civil War came the 13th Amendment and the end of slavery, and later the 14th Amendment which made all people within the territory and jurisdiction of the United States a citizen, subject to the equal treatment of the law. These amendments were aimed at ending racial oppression and discrimination in the United

States, but they were only a beginning. Mainstream society was reluctant to share political power or the benefits of civilization with anyone who was not White and Christian.

The argument about whether to keep Indians segregated on reservations or give them citizenship and push them quickly into mainstream society was hotly debated after the Civil War. Ultimately, both groups felt the Indians should be Christianized, educated and trained for work or enterprise. The question debated was how long the transition would take and by what means it would be accomplished. According to Brian Dippie in *The Vanishing American*, one school of thought favored allotment of lands to Indian families as the surest and quickest path to civilization. Individuals would own land like other Americans, rather than living a communal existence with the tribe. They would become civilized in a decade or two by learning to help themselves. Opposed to this view were groups that felt the civilizing process was evolutionary. This group saw Indians as childlike (or barbarous) and thought it would take generations for Indians to slowly learn the cultural nuances of civilization. Indians must be concentrated and protected on reservations during this acculturation process, because moving them into society too fast would simply destroy them.

The allotment philosophy was less complex than the evolutionist view. Those who favored allotment felt that private property was the key element in the civilization process. Once Indians owned their land as individuals, they would quickly learn farming, and by gradual steps would branch out into other occupations as well. Allotment would also free up much reservation land that was considered to be surplus. Indian farmers would not need more than 160 acres, the same amount of land White homesteaders received under the Homestead Act of 1862.[69] It was also believed that when Indians owned their land in fee simple (private ownership) White settlers would accept the validity of Indian ownership and stop encroaching on Indian lands. Another attractive benefit of allotment would be Indian self-sufficiency, which meant the government would no longer have to provide financial support.[70]

The evolutionists believed this philosophy was hopelessly naïve. A publication called *Catholic World* gave a concise definition of the evolutionist viewpoint in 1886.

Man's mental grasp is very finite. And he must acquire knowledge by degrees. The Indian in many respects is but a child, and in this development must be treated accordingly. And yet his ill advised well-wishers would have trained and developed him into a full-blown civilized American citizen whilst at present the bud is still in embryo.[71]

An evolutionist named Lewis Morgan outlined a system for helping Indians climb the steps of civilization. According to Morgan, science had discovered a series of "ethnical periods" through which man must pass on the journey to civilization. Some Indians were more steps away from civilization than others and would take longer to civilize.[72]

For plains tribes who were used to hunting buffalo on horseback, Morgan thought cattle herding could be introduced. More settled tribes with less "steps" to climb could be persuaded to create reservation factories to produce fabrics, pottery, and other goods for American markets. Morgan chaffed at the idea of quickly allotting reservation lands. He said Indians "have the skulls and brains of barbarians, and must grow towards civilization as all mankind have done...by a progressive experience."[73]

The allotment faction was able to get a bill introduced into Congress in 1881, but the measure failed to win approval. Questions of when and how Indians would become citizens caused much debate. Finally, a bill introduced by Henry Dawes was made law in 1887. The Dawes Act allowed each head of an Indian household 160 acres of land, 80 acres for children over 18 and orphans, and 40 acres for each minor child. Where lands were suitable only for grazing, the allotment amounts were doubled. Indians were allowed to pick their own parcels from within the reservation. Once allotted, land was held in trust by the government for 25 years (or more if deemed necessary for the benefit of the Indian), after which time title was given in fee simple. With ownership came the grant of citizenship.

When land had been allotted for every member of the tribe, surplus reservation land was sold to White settlers. The proceeds of such sales were held for the tribe and used for education and other reservation development. As such, the Dawes Act of 1887 opened up many reservations to settlement by non-Indians for the first time, resulting in non-contiguous, "checkerboard" ownership of land within many reservations which still exists today. Checkerboard ownership also came about when individual Indians sold their land once they had ownership rights.

As with treaties granting citizenship, the Dawes Act stipulated, "Upon the completion of said allotments...each and every member of the respective bands or tribes of Indians to whom allotments have been made shall have the benefit of and be subject to the laws, both civil and criminal, of the State or Territory in which they may reside." The Dawes Act prevented any territory from passing or enforcing any law that did not guarantee Indian citizens the equal treatment of the law.[74] For the second time, Congress placed Indians who became citizens under the jurisdiction of the states in which they lived.

The Dawes Act failed in its purpose of making Indians into self-sufficient farmers and citizens. As its critics suggested, the premises under which it was written were hopelessly naïve. While the law proposed to make Indians into farmers, it did not adequately address two questions. First, lands slated for allotment were not always suitable in size and quality to support a family in an agrarian lifestyle. Arid western lands were often unsuitable for farming on a small scale. Second, many Indians did not want to be farmers, and those who were interested in farming faced a steep learning curve and short time frame to master the complex skills and knowledge necessary to be successful in farming.[75] Had untrained White men been chosen randomly to take up a farming lifestyle, without regard for inclination or aptitude for farming, the failure rate would no doubt have been similar.[76] Racist stereotyping also was apparent in the attitudes of those who framed Indian policy, believing that Indians were only suited for farming or trades. Long before the Dawes Act, Indians were employed as statesmen, engineers, generals and doctors.

Unable or uninterested in farming their lands, many Indians simply leased the lands out to White men and learned nothing about farming in the 25 years their land was held in trust.[77] Once they owned their land, many Indians sold out and soon were destitute. During the height of the Depression in 1934, approximately 100,000 Indians were landless out of an Indian population of 327,958.[78] (Not that losing land was unusual during the Depression. Many non-Indians also lost their land during the Depression, of course, including my grandfather.)

The Indian Reorganization Act of 1934

By the 1920s, a movement to reform Indian policy was beginning to take shape, championed by an idealistic New York social worker named John Collier. Collier was a romantic and fell in love with the Pueblo Indian culture he discovered in the western splendor of Taos, New Mexico. For the transplanted New Yorker, this was the perfect antidote for the crowded industrialist drudgery of the East Coast.[79] Taos was a mecca for artists, writers and free thinkers. The Pueblo cause was also taken up by people like Carl Sandburg, D.H. Lawrence, and Zane Grey. A new social philosophy had been emerging around the turn of the century called "cultural relativism." A leading anthropologist of the time, Franz Boas, proposed that if "the mental processes among primitives and civilized are essentially the same," the view cannot be maintained that the present races of man stand on different stages of the evolutionary series.[80]

The theory was a revelation for Collier who saw that the Pueblo culture of New Mexico was being destroyed by those who sought to "help" the Indians ascend the steps of civilization. Collier devoted the rest of his life to saving the tribal culture and religion. The abuses of the civil rights of the Pueblo people were appalling, including 1st Amendment violations of free speech and religion. Among the abuses Collier noted were prohibition of Indian religious ceremonies, speaking native languages and wearing long hair. In addition, Indians were forced to attend Christian church services and boarding schools.[81]

Collier was named commissioner of Indian Affairs in 1933 at the height of the Great Depression, and developed the ideas for the Indian Reorganization Act of 1934, often called "The Indian New Deal." As commissioner, Collier immediately attacked the rights violations he saw on the reservations where many Indians were subject to the jurisdiction of the notoriously corrupt Courts of Indian Offenses.

Judges were appointed by reservation superintendents and "acted as a prosecuting attorney, justice, jury, constable, and jailer."[82] Superintendents also could hire and fire the judges at will, obstructing justice to suit their own whim.

Collier immediately reformed this system, requiring judges to be approved by Indians living on the reservation, and replacing the Code of Indian Offenses with rules formulated with input from the tribes. Reforms were aimed at protecting Indian rights consistent with the Bill of Rights and the U.S. Constitution. Past rules had often been used to suppress native culture. Forced attendance at boarding school religious services was also prohibited, a move that prompted missionaries to brand Collier a "devil worshiper." Another cornerstone of Collier's philosophy was to preserve the Indian land base, so he placed a moratorium on competency certificates that allowed Indians to sell allotted lands.[83]

The Indian Reorganization Act (IRA) of 1934 had four major goals:

1. Preservation of tribal lands. No more lands are to be allotted to individual Indians. Lands deemed to be surplus are to be restored to tribal ownership. The government will provide funds yearly to acquire additional land for reservations, whether such lands are within reservation boundaries or not.

2. Tribes may charter tax-exempt business corporations to promote economic development and manage tribal properties. The government will provide revolving loan funds to promote development.

3. Educational loans shall be provided to promote Indian education. Tribal members will receive preference in hiring for any jobs related to the administration or services provided to the tribe. This will be done without regard to civil-service laws.

4. Tribes may develop their own tribal constitutions and bylaws, and employ their own legal council. The goal is to develop Indian leaders who can effectively run tribal

organizations and corporations with a minimum of governmental interference.[84]

In his annual report of 1934, Collier touted the benefits of his IRA reforms. Condemning the allotment process as "50 years of individualization" delivered with ever-increasing paternalism and arbitrary rule, he believed his reforms would revive the shattered morale of Indians who had been taught to believe in their racial inferiority. He cautioned that the *"awakening of the racial spirit must be sustained*, if the rehabilitation of the Indian people is to be successfully carried through". Collier had complete faith in the Indian capacity for self-sufficiency. "In the past they have managed their own affairs effectively whenever there was no white interference for selfish ends. They can do it again under present conditions with the aid of modern organization methods."[85]

Collier's IRA reforms represented perhaps the first time Congress recognized the legitimacy and uniqueness of Indian culture and religion and its need for constitutional protection. In spite of his self-conscious efforts to promote Indian self-determination, however, Collier's reforms were ultimately just one more heavy-handed attempt by a powerful bureaucrat to show Indians what was best for them whether or not they liked it or believed in it. In fact, many Indians did not want to live in the tribal utopia Collier envisioned.

Governments sanctioned by the IRA were not based on traditional forms of Indian government. In fact, when the initial version of the bill was written, no Indians were consulted. When meetings were finally held on reservations to explain the new legislation, the Navajos replied that their tribal council did not need improvement. Many tribes traditionally ruled themselves by consensus; the concept of majority rule by a highly structured government was foreign to their cultural heritage. The Comanches had allotted much of their land and feared for the right of individual ownership. Christian Indians were afraid of the return of native religions.[86]

Under the IRA, tribes were allowed and encouraged to draft their own constitutions which would become the first law of the land on reservations. Ironically, many of Collier's pre-IRA reforms were aimed at protecting Indians' rights as guaranteed by the U.S. Constitution, but many Indians lost these basic rights when the new tribal constitutions were written, and abuses of Indian civil rights began soon after the new tribal governments were formed.

When the Rosebud Sioux Tribal Council encountered opposition to its reservation policies, it passed ordinances prohibiting political gatherings by its opponents. Although this violated the right of free speech and assembly, the tribal council ruled that the Bill of Rights did not apply on the reservation. At Collier's beloved Taos Pueblo, Tribal Police Officer Antonio Mirabel closed down a peyote ceremony and arrested the participants. Mirabel acted as prosecutor, judge and jury, and fined the defendants after finding them guilty. During the trial, one of the defendants, Geronimo Gomez, questioned Mirabel's authority to operate in such a fashion. Mirabel fined Gomez $225, but the defendant was unable to pay. Mirabel then confiscated 300 acres of Gomez's farmland. In addition, several Indians were jailed for witchcraft. In spite of efforts by Collier and other federal officials, the tribal council refused to change its policies, leading to years of abuse of the tribe's religious freedom.[87]

At the time of the Indian New Deal reforms, tribal governments did not have to guarantee the 5th Amendment right of due process nor the 14th Amendment right of equal treatment of the law. Tribal courts were not bound to recognize state certified attorneys, and some courts required non-Indian attorneys to establish affiliation with an Indian attorney before they could appear in court. Other tribes were able to exclude non-Indian attorneys by requiring a native language, such as Navajo, to be used in court.[88]

Collier was ruthless in his efforts to help the Indians help themselves. When tribes with traditional consensus-based or elder-based governments resisted IRA reforms or refused to approve tribal constitutions, the Bureau of Indian Affairs would penalize them by withholding information about government programs or denying benefits given to more cooperative tribes. Collier actively tried to crush Indian resistance to his ideal. He felt that only "modern" tribal governments could produce needed changes on reservations.[89] Although the IRA was implemented to replace the Bureau of Indian Affairs' bureaucracy with tribal self-government, many things remained the same on reservations. Crooked courts and corrupt officials did not disappear. Rather, because the U.S. Constitution was not applied on the reservation, corruption flourished. The difference was that White government corruption was replaced with Indian government corruption.

Felix S. Cohen was instrumental in developing guidelines for drafting tribal constitutions under the Indian Reorganization Act of 1934. Cohen later wrote the *Handbook of Federal Indian Law* in 1941 for the federal government and was considered one of the foremost scholars and lawyers in the field of Indian law. He was assistant solicitor to the Department of the Interior from 1933 to 1948 and later taught at Yale Law School. Along with Collier, Felix Cohen played a huge part in shaping federal policies aimed at keeping reservation Indians permanently segregated. In 1949, Cohen wrote an article for *The American Indian* entitled "Indian Self-government." Cohen's assessment of the virtues of self-government might seem a little strange today. He wrote:

> Not all who speak of self-government mean the same thing by the term. Therefore let me say at the onset that by self-government I mean that form of government in which decisions are made not by the people who are wisest, or ablest, or closest to some throne in Washington or in Heaven, but, rather by people who are most directly affected by the decisions. I think if we conceive of self-government in these matter-of-fact terms, we may avoid some confusion. Let us admit that self-government includes graft, corruption, and the making of decisions by inexpert minds. Certainly these are features of self-government in White cities and counties, and so we ought not be scared out of our wits if somebody jumps up in the middle of a discussion of Indian self-government and shouts 'graft' or 'corruption.'[90]

Cohen believed corruption was acceptable on reservations as long as it was *Indian* corruption. He accused people who found fault in Indian reservations and who believed in assimilation of simply engaging in "double-talk." According to Cohen:

There are two answers to this double-talk: One is to deny the clichés and to insist that there is nothing wrong about having a state within a state; that, in fact, this is the whole substance of American federalism and tolerance. We may go on to say that the right of people to segregate themselves and to mix with their own kind and their own friends, is a part of the right, of privacy and liberty, and that the enjoyment of this right, the right to be different, is one of the most valuable parts of the American way of life. We may say further that it is not the business of the Indian Bureau or of any other federal agency to integrate Indians or Jews or Catholics or Negroes or Holy Rollers or Jehovah's Witnesses into the rest of the population as a solution of the Indian, Jewish, Negro, or Catholic problem, or any other problem; but that it is the duty of the federal government to respect the right of any group to be different so long as it does not violate the criminal law.[91]

Cohen says the other cure for double-talk is to reject the "tyranny of words" and rely on facts to teach us about the virtues of Indian self-government. It is our "egocentric predicament," Cohen proposes, that makes us think we always know what is best for the Indian. Rather, he says, we can help the Indians more if we allow them to make their own mistakes and also their own success.[92]

When Cohen wrote his essay on Indian self-government in 1949, segregation was the law of the land. At the time, Jim Crow laws were common in the South, laws that mandated "separate but equal" treatment for Blacks and Whites. In practice, this meant separate restrooms, lunch counters, bus seats and schools. Because Cohen lived during the time of legal segregation of Blacks, it is perhaps understandable that he would view Indian segregation as normal, even good. But the government of the United States was soon to decide that segregation was wrong and should be outlawed. Cohen died in 1953, just before the landmark Supreme Court case of *Brown v. the Board of Education* which made segregation illegal in 1954. The decision not only made segregation in Black schools illegal, but meant that American society could not segregate Jews, Catholics, Holy Rollers *or Indians*.

In the 19th century, the justification for removing Indians to western reservations was based on the idea that Indians were either barbarous or simple-minded, perhaps both, and would need many generations of learning the ways of civilization before they could enter society as equals to Europeans. A similar justification was used to separate Blacks and Whites in South Africa, under a system called apartheid. In the Afrikaner vocabulary, apartheid literally means "apartness" of the races. In South Africa, this policy began with "Whites only" facilities and railroad coaches. Eventually, apartheid was expanded by the Natives (Urban Areas) Act which made segregation the official policy of the government. Under this law, Black "homelands" were created. Blacks could enter White areas only to work, not to visit or to live.

Under a law called the Natives Land Act, areas in South Africa designated for Blacks were called "reserves," and Blacks could not lease, buy, or live in other parts of the country. Blacks comprised about 65 percent of the population and were forced to live on 7 percent of the land (about 22 million acres). The act was designed to create parallel institutions and forms of government for Blacks and Whites — South Africa's version of "separate but equal."

This segregation did not preserve Black culture or prosperity, however. Black farms collapsed; poverty, crime, and infant mortality increased. Culture and tradition disappeared as missionaries took over education. The Black "reserves" were also subjected to taxation without representation.[93] While there are significant differences between Black reserves in South Africa and Indian reservations in the United States, there are also many parallels. Neither institution was developed solely for the good of the native population, though there was plenty of rhetoric that proclaimed the benefits of segregation. In both cases, the near destruction of culture was accomplished by prejudice that isolated native populations and suppressed their civil rights, causing the "homelands" to lapse into crime, poverty and economic collapse. Thus, peoples separated from mainstream society did not keep pace with prosperity and development; they remained a permanent underclass.

The "Indian New Deal" through the IRA was an attempt to create a kind of apartheid in America, with parallel governmental powers adapted to Indian tribal homelands. Indians were originally pushed onto reservations as an exercise of White supremacy. The formation of new constitutions on the reservations may appear to have solved the Indian problem, but in reality it merely transformed White supremacy into Indian supremacy.

Today, large parts of Indian reservations are "Indians only" where non-tribal people may work (as in tribal casinos) but cannot live or own land. Non-Indians on the checkerboard (mixed ownership) part of reservations are not allowed to vote or hold office in tribal governments, but are often taxed and regulated without their consent.

The civil rights of Indians and non-Indians were never adequately protected under IRA tribal constitutions and economic prosperity remained illusive. Graft and corruption continued unabated on reservations.[94] By the late 1940s, the failures of the Indian New Deal were becoming apparent and a new group of reformers were beginning to agitate for change.

Termination Policy and Public Law 280 (1953)

After two decades, the shortcomings of the Indian Reorganization Act (IRA) of 1934 were obvious, and a new movement was afoot to once again attempt to get a handle on Indian affairs. In 1953, a policy to terminate tribes reversed the IRA mandate for Indian segregation and self-governance and officially returned federal policy toward Indians to one of assimilation.

Termination was the brainchild of Dillon S. Meyer who was appointed commissioner of Indian Affairs in May, 1950. Earlier, Meyer was the director of the War Relocation Authority, an innocuous name for the agency that oversaw the forced internment of Japanese-Americans during World War II. Meyer's job was one he disliked; he took a dim view of the dehumanizing detention camps which some felt were a war-time necessity. Meyer felt the termination of the Japanese camps at the war's end was a relief, and he was eager to apply the same methods to Indian reservations which he saw as another kind of concentration camp.[95]

Meyer's philosophy was eagerly taken up by Congress.   To

many it seemed incongruous to oppose communism in the rest of the world while supporting what seemed a similar style of government on Indian reservations. The deplorable state of reservation education, health services and economic conditions were another reason to end Indian dependency on government welfare. Debate in Congress for a time focused on repealing the Indian Reorganization Act of 1934, but eventually both houses settled on Joint Resolution 108, now popularly known as Termination Policy.[96] The stated purpose of the legislation was to make Indians "subject to the same laws and entitled to the same privileges and responsibilities as are applicable to other citizens of the United States, to end their status as wards of the United States, and to grant them all of the rights and prerogatives pertaining to American citizenship."[97]

In short, termination meant the end of both the federal trust relationship with Indians and tribal quasi-sovereignty. Tribes and reservation lands would also be subject to the same taxes other Americans paid. The Bureau of Indian Affairs (BIA) would be dismantled — a prospect that appealed to both Indians and non-Indians — and its functions would be replaced by state and local governments. The idea of terminating the federal trust relationship was not new. When the BIA was set up in 1834, it was assumed the "Indian problem" would soon be solved and the agency would no longer be needed. The aim of Collier's 1934 Indian Reorganization Act was a different vision of termination. Collier's was a gradualist approach; when Indian tribes became self-sufficient they would no longer need BIA assistance.[98]

There was nothing gradual about Termination Policy. Resolution 108 stated that termination would be carried out as rapidly as possible. Initial plans called for terminating some tribes immediately, a second group of tribes in 10 years, and others in 50. When the process began, however, the Department of the Interior estimated the process could be completed in five years.[99]

To complete the emancipation of tribes from the federal trust relationship, several other policy changes were necessary. In 1946, the Indian Claims Commission was set up to settle old land disputes and other injuries caused by government practices. Public Law 280 was enacted in 1953 to extend state criminal and civil jurisdiction over

Indian reservations. In 1955, the Public Health Service assumed jurisdiction over Indian health administration in an effort to improve sub-standard conditions on reservations.[100] Finally, a relocation program was started to encourage Indians to move to urban areas where better employment opportunities were available.[101]

In spite of 20 years of IRA-based reforms, reservation conditions in the mid-1950s were still appalling. Compared to the general American population, the Indian infant death rate was two to seven times higher, and tuberculosis rates were an astonishing five to 28 times higher. Fifty percent of Indian deaths were caused by curable diseases like pneumonia, infant diarrhea and influenza. Alcoholism and suicide also took a heavy toll. The life expectancy of Indian males was 36 — a full 25 years lower than the White male average at the time. In the Navajo tribe, males had an average life expectancy of 20, and for the Papago tribe of Arizona it was 17.[102]

Government termination and relocation programs had a two-fold aim: improving conditions on reservations and reducing unemployment by encouraging migration to urban areas. Large numbers of Indians did move to cities during this time, but World War II was responsible for much of the exodus. The war caused a considerable reduction in government services and programs for reservations, as well as a related increase in war-time manufacturing jobs, causing many able-bodied men and women to leave reservations. During the war, approximately 50 percent of Indian men joined the army or worked in defense industries. Many returning veterans had new skills and the benefits of the GI bill for education and housing. By the late 1960s, nearly half of all Indians (a few hundred thousand) lived in urban areas. The vast majority of Indians had urbanized voluntarily or out of necessity, rather than as a result of a government program.[103]

Termination Policy was never carried out on a large scale and completely lost momentum in a few years. Joint Resolution 108 mentioned 13 tribes slated for termination in 10 states. Approximately 11,500 Indians were eventually terminated with the biggest number, 3,270, coming from the Menominee Tribe in Wisconsin who owned 233,000 acres of land, much of it forest. They owned a sawmill and a power plant and were considered one of the more prosperous tribes.

The tribal assets in land, timber, and business enterprise were placed under the control of a corporation of which the tribal members were shareholders. The tribe's land became Menominee County, and since they owned it, they were the only taxpayer. Unable to meet tax and other obligations, the tribal corporation was forced to sell assets to non-Indians and many members of the tribe ended up on welfare.[104]

Like other government programs designed to help Indians, Termination Policy was a failure. The biggest failure was in its attempt to reduce the number of Indians who were wards of the government. When termination was started in 1953, there were 179 federally recognized tribes.[105] Today, in 1998, there are 557. Well under a million Indians were wards of the government in the 1950s; now the number is nearly two million.[106] Large government expenditures for reservation poverty programs have done little to reduce problems, and the last 30 years of the government trust relationship has not significantly changed reservation poverty. In 1968, eight percent of Office of Economic Opportunity spending was used for Indian programs, yet Indians were less than one percent of the population. High school drop out rates in 1968 were around 60 percent, and unemployment figures were about 40 percent. On the Pine Ridge Reservation of South Dakota, the unemployment rate hit 95 percent during parts of that year.[107]

In 1997, the Saint Paul *Pioneer Press* reported nationwide unemployment for Indian reservations at 49 percent. Pine Ridge Reservation had an unemployment rate of about 80 percent. At the same time, the national unemployment rate for non-Indians was less than 5 percent. In South Dakota, where Indians comprise about 10 percent of the population, 3,047 of the 5,746 families on welfare were Indian families.[108] The Pine Ridge Reservation alone had 1,081 families on welfare.[109] Tribal segregation has created levels of unemployment resembling those of third world countries — or worse. Welfare is as much a part of Indian culture today as buffalo hunting was a century ago.

Indian activists insist that Termination Policy is one of the worst government policies of the 20th century. It was an ill-conceived policy and did a great deal of harm. But termination only affected 11,500 Indians, less than two percent of the Indian population. The real culprit is the Indian Reorganization Act, which has been the dominating force in reservation policy for the last 60 years. If there continues to be problems on reservations today, the apartheid-inducing IRA must be blamed for the lion's share.

Termination Policy was implemented without proper funding or any significant forethought. Its basic premise was foolish and naïve, as most tribes in 1953 possessed neither the expertise nor the economic power to compete in an unprotected environment. As it had for many decades, Termination Policy was another example of federal Indian policy that fluctuated between the extremes of smothering paternalism and absolute *laissez-faire*. Relocation programs of the 1950s provided a one-way bus ticket to a city ghetto, complete with a month's free rent and a few dollars for expenses with no training and no education. Add racism, a fact of life for minorities in that era, and it should not be surprising that many ended up destitute. Public Law 280 allowed state jurisdiction on reservations, but states often did not provide funds for law enforcement or court systems, leaving reservations without law and order.[110] Termination and relocation were a recipe for disaster that coalesced in a predictable manner. Uneducated minorities cut loose in a racist society are not likely to rise to the top of the economic hierarchy.

The Civil Rights Act of 1964 is the best Indian policy the United States has developed. It outlaws segregation and discrimination on the basis of race, color, religion, sex, or national origin. If combined with a workable economic and educational program, it will prove to be much more valuable for Indians than 367 treaties that contain no such guarantees.

At about the time the Civil Rights Act was being implemented in the early 1960s, the radicalism of the Indian sovereignty movement was beginning to change the way Indians viewed mainstream society. Indian radicalism appeared to be a part of the civil rights movement, but its goals were completely different. Indian leaders began to build a wall around reservation life that would permanently separate Indians from other Americans. The wall was called Indian sovereignty. This happened just as the law was finally breaking down the walls that prevented American minorities from fully participating in the benefits of American citizenship.

CHAPTER FIVE

70s Activism

The Rock

Every year millions of tourists flock to San Francisco to look at three of the most famous landmarks in America: the Golden Gate Bridge, Fisherman's Wharf, and Alcatraz Island. Alcatraz can be seen easily from Fisherman's Wharf, a mile and a quarter across the unswimmable water. The island congers up images of America's most dangerous and colorful criminals like the Bird Man of Alcatraz and Al Capone. On November 20, 1969, it became famous for another reason, a takeover by 89 young Indians intent on making history. For the next 19 months, Indian activists held on to "the Rock," an inhospitable and desolate island in the center of one of the world's most beautiful cities.

The takeover of Alcatraz marked the start of three and a half years of Indian activism that often turned violent. During this time, Indians were involved in a number of demonstrations that virtually shut down small towns and intimidated Whites into making obscene concessions to Indians. Indians discovered they could take over government property and destroy it with little fear of reprisal. Over and over the government proved it would give in, rewarding Indians with what they asked for. From November 1969 through May 1973, Indians also found that the worldwide press was sympathetic to their cause. This activism lead to an important federal commission on Indian affairs which set in motion the Indian sovereignty crusade with which the nation is currently besieged.

The seeds for this activism were planted by Termination Policy which threatened to assimilate all Indian tribes into mainstream

America, starting in the 1950s.   But maybe more importantly, termination motivated young Indian activists like Clyde Warrior to fight back with a crusade of their own.   Their crusade boiled at a low temperature for years, as various Indian organizations battled each other over the mission and means for greater Indian sovereignty.   By 1969, the crusade boiled over in civil protest, and three major events — the occupation of Alcatraz, the takeover of the Bureau of Indian Affairs, and the stand-off at Wounded Knee — would profoundly change the way the federal government treated Indians as a race and culture.

Behind these protests were a handful of Indian leaders, each with unique skills to cultivate Indian unrest. It might be said that within the Indian sovereignty movement, Clyde Warrior was the angry spark, Hank Adams the savvy negotiator, Vine Deloria Jr. the brains, and Russell Means the angry raised fist. Each played an important role in motivating many disparate Indian tribes to unite as a race against the federal government.

Much of the early revolutionary rhetoric can be traced to Clyde Warrior, a Ponca Indian born near Ponca City, Oklahoma in 1939. He was raised by his grandparents who spoke Ponca and still practiced the traditional way of life, living in clans and extended families, and celebrating the old ways in dance and ceremony. Clyde Warrior was one of the best Indian singers and dancers of his time. As a teenager in the late 1950s, Warrior attended many powwows and tribal dances and earned the right to wear honored traditional garb while he performed. Warrior even worked a stint at Disneyland, but his temperament was not suited to performing for tourists in an amusement park; he wanted more.[1]

His predilection for the stage made him a natural for the political arena as well. In the late 1950s, at the age of 20, he got his first taste of government and institutional attitudes about Indians. A summer college program at the University of Colorado in Boulder introduced him to Bureau of Indian Affairs administrators, anthropologists and Indian experts who taught about the political, social and economic realities of American Indians. Immediately, Warrior began to develop his own political philosophy that bristled at the idea of Indians changing their lifestyle in order to fit into American society. In an essay, "What I Would like My Community to Look Like in Ten Years," he argued that although Indians needed education, technical training, and economic aid for development, the programs would do no good unless Indians took pride in themselves as Indians.[2] He believed that assimilation would be the undoing of Indian culture and identity. He was convinced that the policy of termination was the vehicle of Indian destruction.

Warrior's first political experience came in 1960 when he ran for the presidency of the Southwest Regional Indian Youth Council. His opponent gave a speech stressing the standard ideals of the day — the need for education and professionalism. Then, Warrior strode up to the podium and rolled up his sleeves. Gesturing to his bared arms, he delivered what might be the shortest speech in political campaign history. "This is all I have to offer," said the young revolutionary. "The sewage of Europe does not flow through these veins." Warrior won by a landslide, a mandate for blood purity and rage over education and professionalism — clearly a new direction for the Indian movement.[3]

The dissident character of Warrior carried him in 1961 to conferences on Indian affairs in Chicago and later Gallop, New Mexico where participants formed the National Indian Youth Council (NIYC) and made Warrior one of the leaders. The NIYC represented a major addition to Indian's political visibility because it was only the second such group of national standing. The other was the National Congress of American Indians (NCAI), a relatively conservative group that was formed in 1944 in Denver, Colorado. The NCAI was the Indian conduit to Congress, allowing Indians to lobby the House and Senate directly rather than dealing exclusively with the Bureau of Indian Affairs and the Department of the Interior.[4] The Youth Council represented a return to traditional methods of Indian interaction. Whereas the National Council held conventions in big cities and lobbied Congress, the youths began to hold meetings on the reservations. Every Youth Council meeting included traditional tribal songs and drum ceremonies, something for which Clyde had superb talent and an encyclopedic memory.

In 1963, Warrior managed to connect with Marlon Brando after the actor had completed a civil rights march in Washington with Martin Luther King Jr.   Brando recommended that the Indians hook up with the Black protest movement, but most Indian activists preferred the idea of going their own way.[5]   It is worth noting that the Black civil rights movement had a completely different goal than the Indians. Blacks wanted to be fully integrated into society, whereas Indians wanted the option to remain segregated, integrating only on their own terms, if at all. Most non-Indians and government officials at the time were unaware of this critical difference during the activist days of the 1960s and 1970s, and most Americans still fail to understand this basic fact.

In spite of the different philosophical approach, Clyde Warrior adopted the most basic premise from the 1960s civil rights movement and instilled it into the Indian movement: civil protest was a much more effective tool to forward Indians' goals than were education and meetings with bureaucrats. He understood that civil protest was the only useful lever to overturn the federal policy of termination.

During this time, Warrior met another young Indian who was more interested in action than education. His name was Hank Adams, an Assiniboine/Sioux who lived on the Quinalt Reservation in Washington state. The reservation is located on the Pacific Ocean almost straight west of Seattle and had been the scene of decades of argument between the State Department of Natural Resources and the Indians. The tribes wanted to net fish according to 19th century treaties. Hank's activism started in 1958 when Public Law 280 began to take effect in Washington state. Public Law 280 allowed state jurisdiction on Indian reservations which interfered with Indian fishing. Adams was able to convince Marlon Brando to take part in a "fish-in" in March of 1964.[6] Brando tried to get arrested twice, first on a river near Tacoma, where he was soon released because of his movie star status, then on the Quinalt Reservation with Hank Adams. The rising Indian Youth leader and movie star were unable to find any game wardens, however, and Brando had to settle for catching pneumonia instead of a pair of handcuffs.

The effect of Brando's non-arrest was to catapult the National Indian Youth Council into the national news, making Clyde Warrior and Hank Adams celebrities among Indians. The general public, however, would soon forget the young Indian activists. Warrior continued to work within the NIYC but seldom found it radical enough.   In frustration, he resigned from the organization but was immediately offered the position of president. Though Indians often found him abrasive, his ideas were compelling — best summed up by his belief that Indians needed autonomy in everything. "Programs must be Indian creations, Indian choices, Indian experiences."[7] Basically, Warrior believed that Indians were never free but always subject to the whims of federal bureaucrats and the tribal officials they had in their pocket.

Warrior divided Indians into five types: the "white nosers" who integrated into mainstream society, "hoods or slobs" who lived up to society's negative image of Indians, "jokers" who made fools of themselves in order to be accepted among non-Indians, "ultra-pseudo Indians" who acted out the image of popular Indian stereotypes, and finally the "angry young nationalist" who rejected American society. It was the last group that best fit Warrior's image of the ideal Indian.[8] Oddly enough, this champion of Indian nationalism and independence still wanted federal programs but simply with no bureaucratic strings attached.

In 1966, speaking before a White audience, he spoke of a coming alliance between educated young Indians and older traditionalists also favoring Indian nationalism. He warned that some towns in the U.S. had "better look out" when the two groups finally got together, a prediction that would later come true.[9] Clyde Warrior never got further than being the inspiration and role model for the Indian revolution that would soon flare up in America, however. His seething disdain for mainstream society was matched by one other fault, an uncontrollable and legendary thirst for alcohol. Within two years, the radical leader of the NIYC was dead of liver failure at the age of 28.[10] It would be up to Hank Adams and other Indian nationalists to bring the fiery youth movement into the mainstream of Indian thought. Foremost among this new breed of Indian men were Vine Deloria Jr. and Russell Means.

In 1964, Vine Deloria Jr., a Standing Rock Sioux, was elected executive director of the conservative National Congress of American Indians (NCAI). Deloria held the post for four years, encouraging the young radicals to challenge the old guard at the NCAI. Unlike Hank Adams, who dropped out of college to become an Indian activist,

Deloria was the son of a Sioux missionary and was educated at some of the finest schools in the country including an East coast prep school, college and even a seminary. Eventually, he became a professor of law and history at the University of Colorado and took a very scholarly approach to the question of Indian nationalism.[11] A prolific writer, Deloria wrote a bestseller in 1969 on his first attempt, the acclaimed *Custer Died for Your Sins*. His books provided the philosophical, legal and religious underpinnings for much of what the radicals were trying to accomplish. Deloria was often at work behind the scenes at events that captured national headlines.

Along with fishing and hunting rights, an early obsession of Indian activists was a desire to recover Indian lands lost to American immigrant civilization. Alcatraz Island became the unifying symbol of a plan to recover land using old treaties as the justification. More than one attempt was made to occupy the island, the first occurring in 1964. Russell Means, his father Walter, and about 40 other Indians claimed Alcatraz Island under the surplus federal land clause of the 1868 Fort Laramie Treaty with the Sioux. The treaty, Indians believed, contained a clause that promised the Sioux the right to claim federal land or buildings that were abandoned as compensation for land the Sioux had lost.[12]

The problem with this assertion — which most Indians still believe today — is that *no such clause exists in the treaty*. In his 1974 book *Behind The Trail of Broken Treaties*, the well-read Professor Vine Deloria Jr. himself acknowledges this fact. He states:

> The Indian activist movement degenerated into sporadic landings on federal property, accompanied by the demand that the property be turned over to them immediately under the provisions of the Sioux and Arapaho Treaty of 1868. *No one could ever find the provision which allowed this restoration, but the restoration was demanded anyway*[13] (emphasis added).

Unfortunately, the truth hasn't stopped Indians from using this fictitious legal right as justification for action and continues to appear in popular literature by Indian authors. The book *Like a Hurricane* by Paul Smith and Robert Warrior, written in 1996 about Indian activism of the 1970s, continues to assert that the 1868 Sioux Treaty has a surplus land clause.

A Minnesota Chippewa named Adam Nordwall (who now uses the name Adam Fortunate Eagle) also took part in the first attempt to claim Alcatraz in 1964, the same year Deloria was elected executive director of the NCAI and Hank Adams and Marlon Brando were chasing game wardens in Washington. Although it was looked upon primarily as a publicity stunt at the time, Nordwall was impressed by the press coverage the occupation got in Oakland and San Francisco papers. It was an event that the large urban Indian community would not soon forget.[14]

Nordwall moved to California in 1951 and became a successful businessman. He owned an exterminating business and had good connections in town. Nordwall helped create an organization in Oakland called the United Bay Area Council of American Indian Affairs, which was primarily a social club for helping Indians adjust to city life. By 1969, the council was thinking of formally applying to the government so Alcatraz could be used as a community center for Indians. By then other groups were also vying for the site, so the Indians decided simply taking it might be the only way to get control of the island. Nordwall's Indian council wasn't the only group thinking about a forced takeover, however. Indian student activists were also talking about occupying the abandoned federal site.[15]

A chance meeting between Nordwall and Richard Oakes, a leader of student activists, occurred at a Halloween party at the home of Tim Findley, a reporter for the San Francisco *Chronicle*. When Nordwall told Findley that he had a big story and wanted publicity, the journalist suggested he come to the party and tell everyone since most of the guests were from the press.[16]

Oakes was a student of Native American Studies, a new program at San Francisco State in 1969. He was a Mohawk from the St. Regis Reserve in New York. Upon coming to San Francisco, his first job was bartending at a place that catered to an Indian clientele. It was here that Oakes learned of the problems in urban Indian communities, and the occupation of Alcatraz seemed like one way to help.[17] With similar goals, Nordwall and Oakes decided to join forces.

Nordwall planned to invade Alcatraz on November 9, 1969. He arranged five charter boats for the crossing and invited local news crews. Nordall arrived in his best powwow outfit, but none of the boats showed up. Oakes had the students stall the reporters by reading a proclamation prepared for the landing while Nordwall frantically looked for a boat. Conveniently, a beautiful three-masted schooner complete with cannon was just casting off, and Nordwall managed to talk the Canadian skipper into a ride to the island. The boat provided a newsworthy sight for the assembled press, but the captain refused to land on the island so Oakes and three others jumped from the boat as it neared the island and swam toward the shore against the strong current. Within an hour, the Coast Guard returned them all to the dock, but Oakes would not give up. Later that night, he and 13 others returned to Alcatraz by boat and spent the night. By morning, they returned to the mainland, but the student leader was determined to repeat the attempt on November 20, this time under his own planning and with a larger group of students.[18] The final successful landing was accomplished in the pre-dawn hours by 89 activists who neglected to bring adequate food or clothing to the damp, inhospitable 17-acre island. The obsession to reclaim the island did not include elaborate plans for holding the island once the Indians landed. Alcatraz could hardly have been a worse choice for an extended occupation since it was completely isolated from the mainland by treacherous ocean currents. There was no water or power on the island, save for the lighthouse that still operated there.

Thus, one of the great events in the history of the Indian sovereignty movement happened by chance as much as anything else. It was however, the culminating event that Clyde Warrior, gone then for almost a year, had so precisely predicted. Within 10 days, the young radicals would have the attention of the world and the national Indian leadership. Even more astonishing would be the fact that 89 unorganized student occupiers would almost immediately begin communicating directly with the White House Administration of President Richard M. Nixon and gain the sympathies of the world.

The Indian students were breaking a number of laws by occupying the island, including trespassing and destruction of government property. The abandoned and crumbling buildings were also danger-ous, eventually causing one death during the occupation. Federal offi-cials had every right to remove the Indian activists from the island, but did not, and the resulting occupation would last 19 months. Federal officials were prepared to remove the activists quickly, giving them 24 hours to leave the island peacefully or have U.S. marshals remove them by force. There were no reports that the students were armed, but the West Coast GSA administrator was concerned that the U.S. marshals would get involved in a violent confrontation. Against the orders of the GSA director, the eviction was put on hold. The stalemate would prob-ably not have lasted an hour without resolution, but the White House decided to handle the matter itself.[19]

As he would demonstrate time and time again in different polit-ical arenas during his presidency, Richard Nixon was more concerned with his political career than any pressing need to uphold the law. A critical flaw in the Nixon plan was the fact that he and his staff com-pletely misunderstood the real agenda of the Indian movement. Indians wanted power and sovereignty as Indians; they did not want to be "equal Americans." Nixon also had an agenda. The Vietnam War and the civil rights and feminist movements were a constant source of baf-flement to Nixon, and he hoped for some sort of domestic policy coup that would lessen the impact of his other failures. The Indian occupa-tion of Alcatraz could prove to be another messy problem, or if handled correctly, might be one bright spot in the dismal domestic landscape. With deft handling of the affair, the president might be able to help the Indians and improve his political image at the same time.

Like any "good" bureaucracy, a federal task force of top cabi-net officials was formed and the Alcatraz occupation became a matter of national importance rather than a simple trespass.[20] The government began to negotiate a settlement through Indian moderator Grace Thorpe, daughter of Olympic star Jim Thorpe, and provided amenities like candy, cigarettes, a water barge and ambulance service to the island. The ambulance service was necessary because the protesters frequently injured themselves in the crumbling prison buildings.

The Indians originally wanted title to the land, and necessities such as medical supplies and a generator, but as negotiations drug on, demands became more outlandish including a cultural center, college, and environmental research lab. The government negotiators estimated it would cost $8 million just to make the island livable and far more to add any other improvements, so the meetings ended with no agreements. Nonetheless, a sense of optimism pervaded the early days of the occupation.[21] For Thanksgiving, the grounds were filled with happy revelers and turkeys were catered free by Bratskeller's, a local restaurant. The festivities included Indian drums, rock and roll, and a contingent of press. Movie stars and sympathetic Whites began to show up in the following days including Jonathan Winters and Anthony Quinn. The mayor of San Francisco, Joseph Alioto, gave a press conference upon returning from a European trip in December and told of the tremendous interest Alcatraz generated in Europe.[22]

After three weeks, donations of food, clothing and money were pouring in. Twenty-eight teepees were donated to the occupiers, and the Creedence Clearwater Revival band provided a boat. A benefit music concert was given at Standord University on December 18, featuring Cree folk singer Buffy Sainte-Marie. Nordwall was the emcee for the concert and told about Indian goals. He proclaimed, "We call ourselves out there the Indians of All Tribes. That is pretty significant. This is one of the first pan-Indian movements in this country."[23] Nordwall also read a proclamation prepared by the occupiers listing the future plans for the site. There would be a center of Native American studies, a museum, and an Indian training school that would provide technical training and sell arts and crafts. In addition an Indian center of ecology would do research and build a desalinization plant for making fresh water from the sea.

These high ideals would soon be overshadowed by a lack of leadership and purpose on the island. As the occupation wore on, the island became a disgusting mess of garbage and non-functioning toilets amidst the crumbling squalor of the abandoned buildings.[24] The bleakness of early winter was in stark contrast to the jubilation everyone felt at the beginning of the takeover. Pot smoking was endemic, and the nationwide publicity began to attract a bad element from places like the Mission District of San Francisco, where hoodlums and drug pushers mingled with drunks, the homeless and the hopeless.[25] By Christmas time, "the island became a truly wild place, a strange combination of a constant powwow and a street fight."[26]

Violence and chaos became an increasing problem, and the Indian security force for the island was a major part of the problem. In a lampoon of the Bureau of Indian Affairs, security people dubbed themselves the Bureau of Caucasian Affairs. Soon the group had special jackets and called themselves the Thunderbirds.[27] The Thunderbirds became notorious for their heavy-handed tactics. The book *Like a Hurricane* reports, "For some in the Thunderbird security force, the agenda was bootlegging liquor and trashing residents who criticized the leadership or who asked too many questions about finances."[28]

Infighting among the occupiers began to creep in as well. As the island settled into mayhem, Richard Oakes began spending more time away from the island, despite the fact that he had brought his wife and kids to the island to live in the abandoned buildings. Other Indians began to resent Oakes' penchant for grabbing the spotlight and playing politician in San Francisco. They felt that he should share the deprivations with those on Alcatraz, but he was often gone for days or weeks. There were also fears that he was using some funds donated to the protest for his own use. Amid the rising tensions and problems, Oakes lost his 12-year-old daughter, Yvonne, who slipped from a railing and fell three stories to the concrete in early January. Rumors flew about the cause of the tragedy. Oakes' secretary was more familiar than most with the situation. She lived in the building where Yvonne fell and her children were familiar with the girl. She claimed that Richard and Anne Oakes often left their five children alone when they left the island. There were also reports that the children were sniffing glue when the tragedy occurred.[29]

After seven weeks, local people were beginning to see the occupation as unbridled lawlessness rather than high political drama. Tim Findley, the *Chronicle* reporter who had helped Nordwall and Oakes gain important press coverage in November, wrote a devastating account of the occupation in early January. By coincidence, the two-part series ended on the day Yvonne Oakes died of severe head injuries. Findley wrote about the beatings perpetrated by the Thunderbirds and the drunken excesses of the protesters. He compared the Alcatraz occupation force to the brutal society established in the novel *Lord of the Flies*, where fictional children degenerate in the absence of parents and civilization. Because Findley had always written sympathetically about Indians, the article dealt a powerful blow to the credibility of the occupation.[30]

When local press coverage continued to point out problems on the island, Indians banned reporters unless they guaranteed favorable stories. By that time, however, the national media had become interested in Alcatraz. *Look* magazine did a feature entitled, "The Uprising That Worked." Merv Griffith did a talk show about the occupation, and Hank Adams used his considerable public relations skill to secure a $10,000 grant for the occupation from the Episcopal Church in New York.[31] As a result, the protest continued in spite of the problems. Ironically, many of the protesters were college students participating in Equal Opportunity programs approved by Congress at the urging of the National Indian Youth Council. Some collected scholarship money while protesting.[32]

After fruitless January negotiations, federal officials spent two months trying to find a way to bridge the gap between the Indians and the government. The head of the National Council of Indian Opportunity spent days talking with Indian leaders, student protesters, the GSA and several other government organizations in hope of finding a workable solution. By March, federal officials appeared acquiescent and went so far as to propose razing the crumbling prison buildings and replacing them with a cultural center and Indian museum. The island would belong to the U.S. Park Service but would be controlled by an Indian board of directors and have a largely Indian staff. Hovercraft would ferry passengers from several bay area locations, and profits would be used to maintain and improve the center. The federal government would pay millions to complete the construction and involve Indians in the planning committee to insure a satisfactory result. This was their best offer. What the White House and its negotiators did not comprehend was the Indians did not want a culture center or a museum. That was mere window dressing. *Indian occupiers wanted title to the land; they wanted control*. The Indians would settle for nothing less.[33]

Vine Deloria Jr. visited Alcatraz in the early days of the occupation and wrote an article for *The New York Times* magazine on March 8, 1970. Deloria distilled the essence of Alcatraz activism in a few lines stating, "At the present time everyone is watching how mainstream America will handle the issues of pollution, poverty, crime and racism when it does not fundamentally understand these issues. Knowing the importance of tribal survival, Indian people are seeking more and more of sovereignty, the great political technique of the open council."

Deloria felt the key to cultural health was tribal unity and fortitude. In a conversation with an old Papago Indian in 1965, Deloria had been told the Indian people were like an old mountain they could see in the distance. The Spanish dominated Indians for 300 years, and the Mexicans ruled them for a century. Both eventually left. The elder told Deloria, "Americans have been here only about 80 years. They, too, will vanish but the Papagos and the mountain will always be here." Deloria states flatly, "It just seems to a lot of Indians that this continent was a lot better off when we were running it."[34] This was the message of Alcatraz.

In spite of Deloria's hope for a utopian Indian society, things began to unravel on the island. Don Carroll, the government caretaker for the island, reported that a group led by Richard Oakes had attempted to break into the lighthouse, and about 50 firearms had been stockpiled on the island. To underscore their anger, some of the protesters beat Carroll's dog, which later had to be put to sleep. There were also rumors of a thousand people coming to the island on Memorial Day and blowing up the lighthouse. Indians told Carroll that Nixon must give a televised speech about the island, giving the occupiers some credibility. It was hoped that the caretaker could get the message through to government officials at the GSA who could relate the demand to the White House. On Memorial Day, the mood on the island was tense, but far fewer people than expected showed up. At a press conference, Stella Leach threatened that the government would create another Wounded Knee if they tried to remove the protesters. There was no response from Washington.[35]

On June 1, 1970, spectacular fires burned on Alcatraz, severely damaging four historic buildings and raging for hours. Numerous small blazes had occurred in the past because fire was the main source of heat and light for the invaders, but this conflagration involved separate buildings. Obviously the fires had been set. John Trudel, a protester who hosted a radio program, "Radio Free Alcatraz," blamed the fires on outsiders who wanted to discredit the Indians, but given the history of the occupation, his accusations were given little credibility.[36] In July, the Los Angeles *Herald Examiner* wrote an unfavorable article on the occupation titled "The Dream Is Over." Trudel's wife wrote an angry response, saying the fires did not hurt any people or cause a tragedy. It was tragic that Yvonne Oakes had died, she said, but American Indians lived lives filled with tragedy, and the purpose of the Alcatraz occupation was to prevent a tragic future for Indians. She ended the letter with the news that she had given birth to a beautiful boy on Alcatraz, and that was a true symbol of hope for Indians.

The Trudels named the boy Wovoka, after the Paiute holy man who started the Ghost Dance movement in the decade before the tragedy at Wounded Knee in 1890.[37] The holy man Wovoka created a Ghost Dance prophesy that predicted the removal of the White man from the continent. In his vision, Wovoka saw Indian ancestors rise from the dead and the buffalo return to the prairie. In the Ghost Dance, Indians wore Ghost Shirts that made them invincible; bullets would simply bounce off. If Indians did the Ghost Dance with the proper belief, they would be able to regain their lost lands and get America back for the Indians.[38] The Indian sovereignty movement from the start had identified with Wounded Knee and the Ghost Dance, and these images were clearly being applied to the Alcatraz occupation.

Despite the seeming chaos at Alcatraz, by the summer of 1970, the Indian sovereignty movement was gaining a foothold on numerous fronts. While island occupiers caught the attention and partial sympathy of the nation, the National Council of Indian Opportunity (NCIO) was gaining influence in Washington through more traditional and peaceful means. About a month after the threat of another Wounded Knee at Alcatraz on Memorial Day, Nixon addressed the Congress on the subject of Indian affairs. His message represented a great victory for Deloria and the group at Alcatraz, and would prove to be much more significant for Indians than title to a 17-acre rock. The "Indian Problem" as Nixon saw it (and as Indians have since seen it) concerned both too little or too much dependence on the government. Nixon's views on Indian affairs bear an uncanny resemblance to those espoused by Indian leaders. Earlier in 1968, a presidential order had created the National Council of Indian Opportunity (NCIO) in response to Indian demands for participation in the development of Indian policy. The council members included Chairman Vice President Spiro T. Agnew, the attorney general, the director of the Office of Economic Opportunity, secretaries of Housing and Urban Development, Agriculture, Labor, Commerce, Health, the Interior, and Education and Welfare, as well as eight Indian members.[39] This powerful group played a significant role in forming Nixon's attitudes towards Indian affairs.

On January 26, 1970, the Indian members of the NCIO delivered a statement to the vice president and cabinet at the White House. The Indians began by saying it was the first time Indian leaders met as equals with the president's cabinet in Washington. They understood the uniqueness of their position and said, "We realize that every group in America would like to have you arrayed before them, commanding your attention."[40] They proceeded to discuss their great fear of cutting the trust relationship between Indians and the federal government. If they lost the trust relationship through termination they would be treated the same way as all other Americans. Indians felt termination would lead to the destruction of tribes, and if tribes were destroyed, Indian culture would also be lost. The Indians said the fear of termination was "strangling" every negotiation, meeting and encounter between tribes and the government.

Along with the fear of termination, NCIO leaders complained about the inadequacies of the Bureau of Indian Affairs (BIA). There were two main problems with the BIA. One was the sense that Indian's standard of living was far behind that of other Americans, and more BIA services were needed to allow Indians to catch up. The second, which the Indians admitted seemed to contradict the first, was that the BIA had a paternalistic attitude toward Indians, and Indians were overly dependent on it. Indians wanted to become less dependent on the

BIA, but keep the "special relationship" they have with the government. "In short," the Indian council members said, "the Indian people want more services, more self determination and relief from the hovering specter of termination."[41]

Nixon's speech to Congress in July of 1970 was conspicuous because NCIO leaders had dictated the specifics to the presidential cabinet in January. The president found himself caught between the Alcatraz protesters on the West Coast who had the attention of the world press, and the NCIO members who held up his campaign promise to the cabinet. Nixon was caught between "The Rock" and a hard place. In his July speech to Congress regarding Indian policy, Nixon declared that "the fear of one extreme policy, forced termination, has often worked to produce the opposite extreme: excessive dependence on the Federal government." Nixon advocated for Indian control of federal programs without "being cut off from Federal concern and Federal support." When Indians control federal programs, Nixon identified the process as "self-determination." He also makes it clear that this "historic relationship between the Federal government and the Indian communities cannot be abridged without the consent of the Indians."[42]

It is interesting to note that the government's approach to the demonstrators at Alcatraz was in marked contrast to that applied to mainstream civil protests going on simultaneously elsewhere in the U.S. Students demonstrating at the National Democratic Convention in Chicago in 1968 were brutally suppressed in a virtual police riot. Police often used tear gas and clubs to control antiwar protests. In the most infamous incident at Kent State University in 1970, the national guard fired into a group of unarmed students, killing four and wounding several. By contrast, Indian protests produced special White House task forces, significant financial concessions, and policy changes that ignored constitutional law and precedent.

Alcatraz was unquestionable proof that violence and threats were highly effective as a political strategy in the Indian movement, even if they weren't as effective for other protesting groups. They also discovered the soft underbelly of "political correctness" decades before the phrase was coined. This double standard allowed Indians to be held to a different standard of conduct than other Americans. Vine Deloria Jr. commented on this emerging trend in his essay for *The New York Times* magazine in March 1970. "Churches," he noted, "have given money to Indians who have been willing to copy black militant activist tactics, and the more violent and insulting the Indians can be, the more the churches seem to love it. They are wallowing in self-guilt and piety over the lot of the poor."[43] The government reacted to Indian activism with a similar guilt-ridden approach.

By the end of 1970, Indian radicalism was beginning to spread from disenfranchised Indian youth to the ranks of the more conservative NCIO. Bob Robertson, who had handled the Alcatraz negotiations and worked directly under Vice President Spiro Agnew, arranged a NCIO conference in Warrenton, Virginia on Monday, December 14, 1970. The conference attracted about 150 Indians from around the country following urban affairs hearings held earlier in places like Minneapolis, Cleveland, Chicago and San Francisco. Some of the participants were immediately disappointed that the meeting was being held in the Virginia countryside rather than nearby Washington. They had expected to meet with President Nixon or Vice President Agnew.

By early evening, when some of the attendees had gone to one of the bars located on the 3,000-acre complex, a dispute broke out between the Indians and a group from IBM. A short time later, Indians set up a drum and upset another group. The director of the center then shut down the bars, but an Indian official from the Office of Economic Opportunity was able to get the bars reopened. Later that night, some Indians vandalized the International House, one of the buildings where the Indian group was staying, and stole food and beverages from the kitchen.[44]

On Tuesday, the conference went on as usual, but in Warrenton, Indians were sighted drinking whiskey in public areas and later formed a human chain blocking traffic. Late that night more serious trouble occurred. Indians took over the entire complex, placed guards at every door, and held three staff members of the Airlie Conference Center hostage. The group was wildly drunk and vandalism was rampant. The director of the center called the Virginia State Police and Bob Robertson in Washington. The director got a rundown on the night's mayhem from his employees, one of whom was told "they (Indians) wanted to show the white man they could take over his property as he had taken over theirs."[45]   Thus went the first official conference between urban Indian leaders and the administration of Richard Nixon.

On Thursday, December 17, the NCIO issued a statement stressing the positive aspects of the Airlie Conference and admitted that a small group of people had gotten drunk and caused some property damage. Dennis Banks of the American Indian Movement (AIM) was reported to have said the conference signaled the start of real communication between urban Indians and the federal government.[46] One can assume Nixon got the message.

By the summer of 1971, the occupation of Alcatraz had lost all momentum. Only 10 or 15 people remained on the island, and when federal agents finally attempted to take back the island, it took less than an hour to place all remaining protesters under arrest with little resistance. Had these actions taken place 19 months earlier, the Indian protesters might have left just as easily. But by now the Indian movement understood the power of public opinion and Nixon's weakness in managing domestic affairs, and were ready to take full advantage.

One of the newest and most radical of Indian groups to gain influence and attention during this time was the American Indian Movement (AIM), created in Minneapolis, Minnesota in July of 1968 by about 250 Indians, mostly Chippewa, from various local Indian organizations.[47]   The leaders of AIM were three streetwise activists: Dennis Banks, Clyde Bellecourt and George Mitchell. Banks was from the Leech Lake Reservation in northern Minnesota. While serving time for several criminal convictions, Banks avidly studied the civil rights movement, antiwar protests and Indian treaties. Eventually, Banks landed a job with Honeywell Corporation. The company actively recruited minorities, and Banks helped the company hire more than 400 Indians. Honeywell gave money to Banks for organizing the community and granted a leave of absence when he began to work at AIM.

Clyde Bellecourt developed his activist philosophy while in prison in Stillwater, Minnesota. He had spent 12 years in prison and felt that he would never survive. After a brief hunger strike, a friend managed to get Bellecourt interested in Ojibwe culture and religion which turned his life around. Soon Bellecourt earned a high school diploma and an operator's license in the prison's heating plant. When Bellecourt was elected the first chairman of AIM he had a job with Northern States Power, the largest power company in Minnesota.

When it was first formed, AIM focused on local issues and the big problem of alleged harassment of Indians by the Minneapolis Police Department. With a grant from church organizations, a special AIM patrol was formed to counteract police brutality. This group monitored police dispatches and sent AIM observers in red vests to bars and street corners to record and photograph police tactics. After the patrol was established, the arrest rate for Indians dropped dramatically, and during one twenty-two week period, there were no arrests.[48]

Russell Means is perhaps the best known member of the American Indian Movement, but he did not get involved in the organization until October, 1969 in San Francisco. Means was in the city to attend a meeting of the National Urban Indian Organization (NUIO). Bellecourt and Banks showed up at the meeting, not to add their support, but to radicalize it. Unlike the other Indians at the meeting who were dressed in the mainstream fashion of the time, the two AIM leaders wore traditional Indian gear including moccasins, headbands, beaded belts and chokers. According to Russell Means' autobiography, Banks told the assembly, "You have one of two choices — either radically change your organization, or we'll destroy it. Tomorrow, we're going to come back and tell you how to change it." The next day Banks and Bellecourt argued that the NUIO didn't properly represent the Indian community and suggested they move the group to Minneapolis where AIM could be actively involved.

The NUIO did not respond favorably to this demand, and the AIM leaders walked out in disgust but gained a believer in Russell Means. The occupation of Alcatraz would begin in a month, and although Means, Banks, and Bellecourt did not take part in the protest due to responsibilities with their own organizations, they would be profoundly inspired by the audacity of the student group. Through the leadership of Means, Banks and Bellecourt, AIM would play an important role in several key events like that in Gordon, Nebraska that simmered civil unrest among Indians and later came to a boil in the takeover of the Bureau of Indian Affairs building in late 1972 and the stand-off at Wounded Knee in 1973 — events that would eventually lead to the landmark American Indian Policy Review Commission.

Means helped found the Cleveland American Indian Center in 1970. Soon afterwards, Means got a call from Banks who wanted his assistance at a National Council of Churches convention in nearby Detroit. The event marked Means' first collaboration with the AIM activists. AIM felt the churches were not giving enough of the funds solicited for Indians *to* Indian causes and demanded direct Indian involvement in church committees. Bellecourt and Banks were allowed to speak to the church convocation and charged the churchmen with not following the Ten Commandments. The AIM leaders said, "You say, 'Thou Shalt Not Steal' — unless you're stealing Indian land. You preach, 'Thou Shalt Not Lie' — unless it's an Indian treaty — and 'Thou Shalt Not Kill' - unless you kill an Indian."[49] When the AIM leaders finished, the Council of Churches members voted to accept AIM's list of demands. According to Means' autobiography, the churches gave Christian Indian groups millions of dollars over the next few years. Clyde Bellecourt loved to challenge the churches. At one church, Clyde is reported to have said, "The missionaries came with the Bible in one hand and the sword in the other. They had the book and we had the land. Now we've got the book and they've got our land."[50] When Means opened the Cleveland American Indian Center, there was no money to pay his salary as director, so he petitioned the Episcopal Diocese of Cleveland for a grant. The Diocese came up with $1,600 for Means, who later established the first AIM chapter outside of Minneapolis.

A 1970 AIM rally in New York brought Means together with Hank Adams. Over drinks they discussed strategies for the coming Indian revolution, spelling out specifics on placemats and napkins. Adams felt Indians needed to return to their historical roots to discover traditional methods of leadership, social interaction, and economic independence, rather than try to revamp the Bureau of Indian Affairs. Russell Means saw the necessity for a cataclysmic confrontation with the U.S. government — an all-or-nothing epic struggle leading to a major victory or defeat for the Indian nations. Because Indians were only a small part of the American experience, Means believed that Indians needed to make an unforgettable statement or their struggle would disappear from the common memory.

For Means, a Lakota Indian, the area around the Black Hills was of special significance. In a life or death struggle, he envisioned Indian lands would be liberated from non-Indian domination by occupying and securing an area of symbolic importance. Means hoped to force the government to either acknowledge demands based on old treaties or kill all the Indians involved. AIM did not have significant ties with reservation Indians yet, but Russell felt there were several sites on the Pine Ridge Reservation of South Dakota that were strategically acceptable for such a stand-off including Wounded Knee, the site of a tragic massacre in 1890, located half-way between Badlands National Monument and Gordon, Nebraska.[51]

Ironically, Gordon, Nebraska would serve as a test-pilot of sorts for the type of demonstration Means envisioned. In February 1972, Raymond Yellow Thunder, a 51-year-old Oglala Sioux, was found dead in his pickup truck on a used car lot in the small Nebraska town. According to police reports, he had been dead for about five days. The story of his torment was an all-too-common one for the border town of 2,000 located south of the Pine Ridge Reservation.[52] Indians referred to the general area as the "Mississippi of the North," in reference to racial prejudice reminiscent of the treatment of Blacks in the segregated South.[53] Because of the lack of services and stores on the reservation, Indians had to go to towns like Gordon for necessities, but they were often treated badly, cheated or insulted, in spite of the fact that residents of the town depended on Indian business for a good portion of their livelihood.[54]

Yellow Thunder had been seized by four Whites in front of a bar, beaten, stripped below the waist, and thrown in the trunk of a car. The next destination was the American Legion Post where his abductors forced the intoxicated Indian to dance. Then Yellow Thunder was shoved outside into the cold night. A few Whites allegedly went outside to help him, but claimed Yellow Thunder told them he was all right and sent them away. When he did not return home, his relatives looked for him for days. Finally two teenage boys discovered the body in the car lot.[55]

The coroner would not allow the family to view the body, raising speculation that Raymond had been tortured or mutilated in addition to the beating. The family frantically petitioned the Oglala tribe, attorneys, and the BIA for help investigating Yellow Thunder's death, but no one would help. One of Yellow Thunder's nephews, Severt Young Bear, had friends in AIM, so the family begged him to ask for AIM's help, especially that of Russell Means, an Oglala Indian whose family came from the same town as Yellow Thunder.[56] The AIM group arrived in March, along with many residents from Pine Ridge and the Winnebago Reservations.[57] Within a short time, 1,400 Indians had come to Gordon, representing over 80 tribes.[58] Here was the coalition of radical youth and tribal elders that Clyde Warrior had predicted in 1966, when he said some towns in American had "better look out" when the two groups got together.[59]

This Indian coalition, led by Means, Banks and Bellecourt, demonstrated in Gordon for days. Indians took over the city hall for two days and met with the chief of police, county attorney, mayor and a representative of the governor. They demanded that the charges against the accused Whites be changed from manslaughter to murder and the death penalty be sought.[60] Yellow Thunder's body was exhumed and a new autopsy was ordered, done in the presence of an attorney for the Indians. The second autopsy confirmed that Yellow Thunder died from a brain hemorrhage with no evidence of torture or mutilation.[61] However, the discovery did not lessen the Indian's anger.

Non-stop Indian protests brought daily activity in Gordon to a grinding halt. Indians boycotted stores and businesses, disrupted government routines, and the Oglala Tribe transferred $1 million in funds out of Gordon banks. To ease tensions, an Indian "people's grand jury" was formed. Local officials agreed to form a commission to study violations of human rights and to suspend police officers found guilty of brutality toward Indian prisoners. Officials from the state and federal governments began to investigate Yellow Thunder's death.[62]

The uniting of AIM and its urban radicals with Indians from reservations was a critical step in the Indian sovereignty movement because it allowed each group to educate the other. AIM activists learned about their cultural heritage while reservation people discovered the power of public opinion and social protest. Many of the Indians who belonged to organizations like AIM were out of touch with reservation life because often their families had lived for a generation or two in mainstream society. Likewise, many on the reservation still hated and feared AIM and its leaders. Indeed, Means, Banks and Bellecourt were often as critical of Indian reservation leaders as they were of the BIA or state and federal governments. AIM characterized Indians who worked too closely with the White establishment as "Apples," Indians who were red on the outside but white on the inside.[63] The heavy-handed tactics of AIM would never be completely acceptable to many Indian people or to mainstream society, but the demonstrations in Nebraska proved AIM had the power to cause change. For many people, that was enough. Power creates its own legitimacy, and AIM would be a force to be reckoned with.

In his autobiography, Russell Means talks about the methods by which AIM was able to exert its power. "AIM had its own axiom," Means writes. "When we chose to fight, we would pick the time and the battlefield."[64] This strategy would prove to be effective in the takeover of the BIA building in Washington D.C., just as Nixon won his second term of office. Nixon's negotiations in the takeover were predicated on the notion that it was not a good time for him to deal with Indian problems in his own back yard. Indian leaders also learned that to get attention and action, the movement had to sidestep government red tape and go directly to the top. According to Means, Dennis Banks discovered this tactic. "He (Banks)…lobbied the federal agencies and both houses of Congress on Indian legislation, and quickly learned that wading through the bureaucracy was for dummies. AIM's policy of starting at the top and moving down expedited our work. To this day, I believe that's the way to deal with the white world."[65]

The Trail Of Broken Treaties Caravan

In the spring of 1972, after the protests in Gordon, Nebraska, AIM activists stayed in rural South Dakota rather than return to metropolitan areas. They decided to expose racist policies in the government by holding a series of public meetings. They caravaned in groups between town meetings, collecting support and sympathy along the way. AIM called their inquiries the "Red Ribbon Grand Jury Hearings" and was able to get assistance from the community relations branch of the Department of Justice. Church groups responded to pleas for money to support the endeavor, as did many Indians. The Indian grand juries gathered information, complaints and news coverage at places like the Pine Ridge and Rosebud reservations. A number of reservations in South Dakota were visited including Standing Rock, Vine Deloria Jr.'s home area, and the Crow Creek and Yankton reservations. The caravan visited many reservations bordering the Missouri River as it cuts across the center of the state from Mobridge in the north (near Chief Sitting Bull's grave) to the Yankton Reservation on the Nebraska border.[66]

Many of the complaints received by the Red Ribbon Grand Jury Hearings dealt with reservation lands lost to White men and reservation trading posts that did not deal fairly with Indian customers. Other problems were sub-standard housing, poor service and impersonal treatment from BIA institutions. Tribal courts and BIA Indian police were also frequently mentioned, as beatings and improper procedures were common.[67] In addition, many traditionalist Indians expressed dissatisfaction with the corporate type of tribal government that was imposed upon reservations by the Indian Reorganization Act of 1934. Indians were not only dissatisfied with elected officials but with the process and structure by which they were ruled.[68] They preferred traditional Indian governments which did not use parliamentary procedures or balloting and election campaigns, but instead used a council of elders whose rule was suggestive in nature, though highly respected.

Means gained a lot of insight from these journeys and began to see that the biggest Indian problems were on the reservations, not in the cities, and he began to long for his people, their culture and their homelands. Means decided to resign his post in Cleveland and devote all his time to AIM as the national coordinator so he could adequately address the most urgent needs on the reservations.

The affidavits from the Indian grand juries were given to the Department of Justice, but by August the government had not

responded.   At the annual Rosebud Fair on the Rosebud Sioux
Reservation, Dennis Banks and Robert Burnett, a former Rosebud official, organized a meeting of Indian visitors from around the country.[69]
During the meeting Burnett, who was not an AIM activist, suggested a
march on Washington that would arrive during the presidential elections in November.   It would be the perfect time to educate the new
president, the American people and the government about Indian problems.   An additional impetus for the caravan had come with the death
of Richard Oakes on September 21, 1972, in a fight in Mendicino
County, California.   At the funeral, Hank Adams delivered a touching
eulogy and the subject of the national caravan was later mentioned as a
fitting tribute to the fallen leader.   Shortly thereafter, a meeting of 50
Indian leaders took place in Denver to finalize the plan.   After three
days of work in Denver, the final plan for the "Trail of Broken Treaties"
caravan was finished.[70]

The Trail of Broken Treaties caravan began at three points on
the West Coast and was due to converge in St. Paul, Minnesota on
October 23, 1972.[71]   Russell Means led a group that started in Seattle,
Washington and went through Idaho, Montana and South Dakota.
Dennis Banks brought a contingent from San Francisco and traveled
through Nevada, Utah, and Wyoming. The third group, led by George
Martin, started in Los Angeles and recruited activists in Arizona, New
Mexico and Oklahoma.[72]   Before they left Denver, the caravan leaders
were careful to emphasize the peaceful nature of the planned march and
demonstration in Washington.   Participants were expected to be on their
best behavior.

Robert Burnett, a former president of the NCAI, lectured the
group on Washington protocol.[73]   No drugs or alcohol, and violators
must be excluded from the caravan.   They were to honor the poor, help-
less and elderly, taking their cause to Washington.   He said, "The caravan must be our finest hour."   Because of his long experience in the
nation's capitol, Burnett was entrusted with making arrangements for
lodging and other necessities.[74]   However, his arrangements for the
group in Washington turned out to be virtually non-existent.   A good
deal of trouble ensued from this simple error.

Along the caravan trail, the Indians solicited operating funds from Indians and church groups. At the Saint Libra Catholic School near the Cheyenne Reservation in Montana, the group lead by Means was able to get a $1,000 donation.[75] Vernon Bellecourt, whose demanding fund raising style caused him to be physically removed from the Mormon Church in Salt Lake, was able to collect another $1,000 for his effort.[76] By the time they got to St. Paul, the group had raised several thousand dollars. Along the way, they also supported themselves by doing a little "AIM shopping." According to Means:

> I was always amazed that (people) wouldn't lift a phone to call the cops while our guys came out of their stores with new jeans, shirts, gloves, axes, candy, soft drinks, chips — even coin boxes from soda-pop coolers. Everything that wasn't nailed down went into someone's jacket or pants pocket. We did that with clear consciences: We were repossessing, in another form, that which had been taken from us. As Clyde often said…'We're the landlords of this country, and we're here to collect the rent.'[77]

When the caravan reached St. Paul, Minnesota in late October, its 300 participants stayed at the State Fairgrounds. At that point, Means temporarily took over as the head representative for AIM since Banks and other officials were busy elsewhere. In St. Paul the group worked on suggestions for a policy statement to be given to the government in Washington, hopefully to the president himself. These ideas about treaties, government, law and resources were given to Hank Adams who spent two days in a motel writing what became known as the "Twenty Points."[78] Though Adams was not an AIM member, he had a reputation as a treaty expert. While he had input and suggestions from the larger group, he did most of the drafting himself.[79]

The Twenty Points

The Twenty Points represented a radical Indian viewpoint aimed at returning tribes to treaty relations with the United States. Briefly, here are some of the most significant demands:

- Repeal the 1871 statute that officially ended treaty making with tribes.
- Establish a commission to write new treaties, and re-affirm all existing treaties.
- All Indians are to be governed by treaty relations.
- Require the U.S. Supreme Court to hear Indian appeals on treaty violations.
- Increase reservation area in the United States to 110 million acres. (In 1977, the reservation land area was about 50 million acres.[80])
- Revoke all non-Indian land ownership on reservations.
- Place reservation resources under control of Indians.
- Eliminate all state jurisdiction over Indians.
- Increase funding for housing, health services, education and economic development.
- Give control to Indians at a local level.[81]

The Twenty Points would be a major accomplishment of the Trail of Broken Treaties. In spite of the fact that the points were ultimately dismissed by the Nixon Administration as "unconstitutional in concept, misleading to the Indian people, and diversionary from the real problems that do need our combined energies," the Twenty Points caused a revolution in the way Indians think about their relationship to the United States.[82] They were demands that have been repeated by Indians ever since. They are completely one-sided and would greatly expand Indian reservations, giving Indians complete jurisdiction over the land. At the same time, Indians would receive funding for all social welfare without any federal government control. According to Vine Deloria Jr., the Twenty Points are "the best...reforms put forth in this century."[83] He also said acceptance of the Twenty Points by the government would give Indian treaties a deserved legal status "equal to the legal status afforded foreign treaties."[8]

Washington D.C. and the BIA Takeover

On November 1, 1972, the Trail of Broken Treaties caravan reached the streets of Washington, winding its serpentine way to its temporary home base at the seedy St. Stephen and the Incarnation Church, a decrepit ministry that catered to the poor and unwanted. The first AIM group to arrive hoped to set up a kitchen in the church basement, but instead of finding the food that Robert Burnett had been charged with providing, they discovered rats. Burnett's logistics people had provided assurances to the government and the caravan that food and lodging would be taken care of. Now, 700 people had nothing but a tiny rat infested church.[85]

The Trail of Broken Treaties caravan of 700 peaceful Indians was a less-than-impressive demonstration in a town that had recently seen anti-war demonstrations of a quarter-million. According to Robert Burnett, the planned activities included a symbolic Indian village complete with sweat lodges and teepees in West Potomac Park, religious rituals in Arlington National Cemetery and the Iwo Jima Memorial where Indian war heroes were honored, a program to discuss the Twenty Points, and a parade past the White House. Both presidential candidates, Richard Nixon and George McGovern, were invited to speak during the evening festivities at the Sylvan Theater.

The Bureau of Indian Affairs building had never been a planned destination for the Washington demonstration, but meeting with the president was a clear goal. Despite the advanced planning, however, coming to Washington to meet Nixon during the last days of the presidential campaign had several strategic flaws. For one, the president was out campaigning and was not in Washington. For another, the American public and the press were preoccupied with the election process and the Paris Peace Talks aimed at ending the war in Vietnam. While the president, who was almost certain to win re-election, might be wary of any trouble with the Indians, the public and press showed little interest in the small Indian presence in Washington. Had the protest remained peaceful, it probably would have had little or no impact.[86]

The breakdown in plans lcd to more frustrations among the weary caravan group. Not only were the accommodations a disaster, but the Park Service denied permission for the ceremonies at Arlington Cemetery and the Iwo Jima Memorial.[87] Early in the morning on November 2, the group leaders headed for the White House in a fruitless search for solutions. After a few hours, they decided to go to the Bureau of Indian Affairs building which fronted Constitution Avenue near the Lincoln Memorial. Soon caravan cars were parked on the side streets and hundreds of Indians entered the BIA building. It was a place to which they felt some connection. It was "their" building where many reservation friends worked, yet it was also a symbol of a hated bureaucracy that treated Indians like unwanted children.[88]

Past behavior at Alcatraz, Gordon, and the Warrenton Conference created suspicion about the AIM group that now filled the BIA auditorium, cafeteria and film library. Bob Robertson, former negotiator with the Alcatraz activists, had a strong feeling AIM would try some kind of takeover, perhaps of the Washington Monument.[89] As the caravan group relaxed in the BIA — by then over 1,000 strong — 200 riot police secretly waited for orders in the Interior Department auditorium next door.

Harrison Loesch and John Crow of the BIA spent most of the day negotiating with caravan leaders. Lodging was found for the protesters at Andrews Air Force Base, the Salvation Army, and a number of churches and synagogues. It was already too late in the day to relocate to these quarters, so Loesch, not trusting the group in the BIA overnight, suggested they move to the Labor Department auditorium a short distance away. By then, however, the Indian group was remembering the purpose of its cross-country trek and demanded to speak with a White House representative, preferably John Ehrlichman. Loesch contacted Ehrlichman, who sent Assistant Brad Patterson for an evening meeting with the Indians. It looked as if the problems had been solved and the week of peaceful demonstrations would take place.[90]

After confirming the meeting, Dennis Banks told reporters at a news conference that the Indians were satisfied with the situation. At the same time, however, a different scene was unfolding in the BIA lobby. Earlier in the afternoon, officials had made plans to evict the Indians at 5 p.m. when the building closed for the day. The order was later canceled, but not all of the police were aware of the change of plans.[91] At 5 p.m., a contingent of police entered the BIA and told the protesters to leave. After a moment of hesitation, Clyde Bellecourt yelled, "We're staying here!" and Russell Means added, "This is no longer the BIA building! This is now the American Indian Embassy."[92] At that point, a fight broke out as Indians spontaneously pushed the police into the street and barricaded the doors with chairs and filing cabinets. In a few minutes of confusion, the peaceful demonstration had become a takeover complete with hand-to-hand combat, blood and broken glass.

The evening meeting went on as planned as White House representatives Robertson and Patterson did the negotiating for the government. Already Means and Banks had emerged as leaders of the takeover. The evening meeting consisted of hours of threats and harsh words from various protesters. Patterson left a few times to consult with other administration officials. A decision had to be made whether to forcefully remove the activists or wait them out. Robertson and Loesch favored action while Patterson argued for restraint. Communication with Nixon quickly finalized the course of action. With only five days left before elections, bad publicity could not be risked. The Indian occupiers included dozens of children and elderly, making a bloody assault a public relations disaster. It was decided to obtain a court order for the eviction to distance the president from the entire situation. The negotiations for the day ended with Patterson promising to carefully study the Twenty Points.[93]

Two days of frustration in Washington was enough to overturn the plans for a peaceful dialogue with the president. No longer were the Twenty Points a suggestion, they were a demand. Once the building was taken, terroristic threats began to surface and the occupation became a test for the kind of confrontation Russell Means had envisioned two years earlier in New York. The Indians raised the possibility of a cataclysmic end, one protester was quoted, "You know Mr. Patterson, we are going to die tonight." They were willing to die rather than quit.[94] Quite probably it was just bravado, but the risk was real enough, and with each passing day the Indians would up the ante.

Governments, with all their levels of communication, are a recipe for mistakes to happen. In their attempts to defuse the situation, the Washington bureaucrats only infuriated the demonstrators. On Friday, the housing situation appeared to be solved when the government attempted to move the Indians from the BIA to the nearby Labor Department auditorium. The new facility would have food, beds and showers, the protesters were assured, but when they arrived the door was locked. An official refused to open it until all the Indians were out of the BIA, which the protesters interpreted as a trick to push them into the street, so everyone quickly returned to the BIA. A court order was soon in place to remove the demonstrators, and this prompted a frenzy of defiance. The AIM leadership consisted of men who were accustomed to a lifetime of abuse from society, the law, perhaps even themselves. With enough abuse the psyche is blinded, a deep-seeded rage begins to dull the edge of reason, and every setback is met with fury. War paint was applied to faces, and so many molotov cocktails were made the gasoline could be smelled in the street. The *Washington Post* reported fears of another Wounded Knee, and for a time the eviction was called off.[95]

A confrontation in Washington could not be prolonged a year and half as it had on a remote island like Alcatraz. The BIA was not an abandoned federal site; it was only blocks from the White House. On Sunday night, November 5, the government issued an ultimatum for the Indians to be out by 8 a.m. Monday. Other accommodations would be provided, and only limited access to the BIA would be allowed during regular hours. A few negotiators could meet with the secretary of the Interior. The negotiating team, led by Hank Adams, refused the government offer. The occupation continued on Monday, the day before the elections, and another court order was issued that called for eviction of the Indians by 6 p.m.[96]

During the afternoon, there was a virtual riot of vandalism in the BIA building, but the Indian authors do not agree on who caused it.

Vine Deloria Jr., author of *Behind the Trial of Broken Treaties* in 1974, claims the damage was mostly the work of government agents planted among the Indians. According to his version, some of the Indians returned to the building weeks later and noticed additional damage that wasn't there during the occupation.[97] *Like a Hurricane*, by Paul Smith and Robert Warrior, makes no mention of government agents. The authors say that the vandalism began from a combination of an inspirational movie about Indian political activism, news of the coming eviction, and rage over past BIA paternalism and corruption. Warrior and Smith claim Hank Adams was engaged in negotiations with the government during the destruction.[98] Both of these accounts differ from the story told by Russell Means in his autobiography, *Where White Men Fear to Tread*. Means, the only one of these authors who was actually there, says the vandalism was started by Hank Adams, who left for the government negotiations soon afterward. According to Means, at 4 p.m. on Friday (Warrior and Smith say Monday) the activists had a meeting in the commissioner's third floor office which had a huge desk and overstuffed leather chairs. Hank Adams was sitting behind the commissioner's desk, and he and his followers insisted the Indians trash the building rather than give up at 6 p.m.. They were opposed by most of the AIM leadership, including Clyde and Vernon Bellecourt and Dennis Banks who thought AIM would get the blame for any destruction. Adams did not belong to AIM. Means claims he wanted to be loyal to AIM, but leaned toward the Adams' method of non-verbal communication.

Adams solved the argument by proclaiming, "I've always wanted to do this," then pulled out a pocketknife and proceeded to skin one of the commissioner's fancy leather chairs. All of this is disputed history, but *somebody* trashed the building enough for it to be closed for six weeks.[99] These discrepancies are interesting because Indian leaders dismiss a great deal of what is written in "white" history books as "White lies." In fact, in the 1997 book, *Red Earth White Lies*, Vine Deloria Jr. suggests Indian oral histories are more accurate than the biased "facts" produced by modern scientists. It seems, however, that these Indian authors have as much trouble remembering the facts as anyone else.

What is not disputed is that the 6 p.m. negotiations produced an agreement between the government and the activists. The government agreed to create a task force to study Indian grievances, promised a response to each of the Twenty Points, and money for the protesters to get back home. Two U-Haul trucks were rented and the Indians loaded up their belongings plus art work, pottery, rugs and jewelry taken from BIA collections. A ton and a half of BIA documents were also stolen. Government officials handed the group $66,650 in cash and provided a police escort out of town. No one had been arrested.[100] If Nixon breathed a sigh of relief as the caravan left town, it was to be a short-lived rest from the escalating violence of the American Indian Movement.

The Twenty Points

As promised, the Nixon administration reviewed each of the Twenty Points, but they found that the demands were an attempt to erase one hundred years of American history. The response from the Nixon administration was quite a disappointment to the Indians. In *American Indian Treaties*, author Francis Prucha quotes the January 1973 response of government negotiator Frank Carlucci:

Over one hundred years ago the Congress decided that it was no longer appropriate for the United States to make treaties with Indian tribes. By 1924, all Indians were citizens of the United States and of the states in which they resided. The citizenship relationship with one's government and the treaty relationship are mutually exclusive; a government makes treaties with for-eign nations, not with its own citizens. If renunciation of citi-zenship is implied here, or secession, these are wholly back-ward steps, inappropriate for a nation which is a Union.[101]

Carlucci also pointed out that some of the demands amounted to special preferences for Indians which would be against American judicial principles, so calling for new treaties was an unconstitutional

concept.[102]   Ironically, Nixon's speech calling for Indian self-determination in 1970 had set the stage for Indian control of federal programs,
and Supreme Court rulings during the 1970s would open the way
toward giving Indian tribes the sovereign status demanded in the
Twenty Points. Though the demands of the Twenty Points were denied,
the courts today have, in fact, met these demands by re-interpreting
Indian treaties without getting Congress or the American people to
approve the process.

Wounded Knee

Chasing 1,000 Indians out of Washington D.C. with a pay-off of
$66,650 and a few promises to look at the Twenty Points was not
enough to quiet the tensions within the American Indian Movement.
Radical Indian leader Russell Means had been planning a violent all-
or-nothing confrontation with the federal government over treaty rights
since 1970, and the siege at Wounded Knee in 1973 gave him the
opportunity to carry out his plan.[103] The cumulative effect of a number
of events in the previous few years had made Wounded Knee the perfect location for the media event that would ensue. During the Alcatraz
occupation, Indians warned that federal attempts to end the occupation
would result "in another Wounded Knee."[104] When violence flared during the takeover of the BIA, the *Washington Post* ran a story headlined
"Another 'Wounded Knee' was feared Friday night."[105]

By the late 1960s and early 1970s, the United States was wallowing in the deepest quagmire of self-doubt and capitalist guilt since
the Great Depression of the 1930s. Foremost among American failures
was the war in Vietnam which was increasingly seen as an uncon-
scionable attempt by the U.S. to interfere with the internal affairs of a
backward third world country.

The massacre of 450 unarmed Vietnamese civilians at My Lai
in 1968 underscored the sordid nature of the war and gave the Indian
activists a perfect tie-in to their own disasters at the hands of the U.S.
Army. Deloria noted in a 1970 *The New York Times* magazine article
titled "This Country Was a Lot Better off When the Indians Were

Running It" that, "The most memorable event of my early childhood was visiting Wounded Knee where 200 Sioux, including women and children, were slaughtered in 1890 by troopers of the Seventh Cavalry in what is believed to have been a delayed act of vengeance for Custer's defeat. The people were simply lined up and shot down much as was allegedly done, according to newspaper reports, at Songmy."[106]   In 1970, the best selling book *Bury My Heart At Wounded Knee* was published, giving the 1890 massacre world-wide name recognition. Books explaining the massacre do not tell the story of another My Lai, however.

On December 28, 1890, the Sioux, under a leader named Big Foot, were overcome by four troops of cavalry sent to arrest the group for being involved with the Ghost Dance movement. The Ghost Dance was started by a Paiute Messiah named Wovoka who preached that the Indians' ancestors would soon rise from the dead, the buffalo would return to the prairie, and the land would be purged of the White man. As the legend developed, it was believed that Ghost Dancers who had the proper faith would be invincible and bullets simply would bounce off their Ghost Shirts. Fear of an Indian uprising prompted the army to ban Ghost Dance rituals and return all Indians to reservation land where they could be watched.

Big Foot's band was nearing Porcupine Creek as the soldiers approached and ran up a white flag of truce. The commanding officer decided to march the Indians to a cavalry camp at Wounded Knee Creek where the Indians would be disarmed before the trip to the Pine Ridge Reservation. The band contained about 120 men and 230 women and children. Because it was nearly dark when the Indians arrived at camp, the warriors were not disarmed until the next morning. The next day, while soldiers collected weapons from the Indians, medicine man Yellow Bird danced a few steps of the Ghost Dance and told the Indians their shirts would make them invincible to the soldier's bullets. At about this time, an Indian named Black Coyote (described by other Indians as a crazy man in reports given in 1892) fired his gun.[107]

The soldiers' reply was immediate and devastating. About 470 soldiers opened fire with carbines and four Hochkiss guns (primitive machine guns). The total number of Indians killed will never be known, but estimates range from about 170 to 300.[108] Among soldiers, 25 were killed and 39 wounded. Actual events at Wounded Knee do not fit Deloria's assertion that unarmed Indians "were simply lined up and shot down." Soldiers are trained to react violently when fired upon, and no officer could have stopped or ordered the instantaneous response to Black Coyote's rifle shot. After the initial fighting, the Indian retreat was followed up with brutal vengeance, however, and it is a disgrace that the fighting was not stopped quickly by the officers in charge. This was probably an act of revenge for the slaughter of Custer's 212 men at the Little Big Horn 14 years earlier when some of the same soldiers of the Seventh Cavalry faced some of the same Indian warriors.[109]

On February 27, 1973, Russell Means and a group of activist Indians prepared themselves for the modern version of Wounded Knee, complete with U.S. soldiers, Indian warriors, and plenty of women and children. The initial occupation force of about 350 Indians included 100 men and 250 women and children.[110] While Wounded Knee was the perfect place for a demonstration from a media point of view, local events on the Pine Ridge Reservation also contributed greatly to unrest that led to the occupation. A constant source of trouble at Pine Ridge was the tribal government which was notoriously corrupt. The tribal chairman at the time, Dick Wilson, was liked no more than most of his predecessors, and many on the reservation wanted him impeached. Only one tribal chairman had been re-elected in the previous 30 years, and even he had been impeached twice before. Many traditional tribal chiefs opposed Wilson, but he had an iron grip on the reservation, enforced by members of his feared "goon squad" who brutally sup-pressed any dissidents on the reservation. With AIM becoming a more powerful force in Indian politics, Wilson called for government help, and the Nixon administration responded in usual form by turning Pine Ridge into an armed camp. The government reinforced Wilson with more than 75 members of the elite Special Operations Group. The gov-ernment forces completed the spectacle by placing a .50 caliber machine gun atop the tribal office.

Unable to find a voice in tribal government, the chiefs threw in their lot with Russell Means, and the government was left with the satisfaction of having turned a local problem into one the whole world would watch for 71 days.[111] Upon taking over the church and trading post that were located at Wounded Knee, the protesters took the priest and store owners hostage. The military responded by bringing out armored personnel carriers, more machine guns, and a host of federal marshals. It was everything Means had dreamed of and more.

Because of the hostage "crisis," Senators George McGovern and James Abourezk soon showed up to see if the hostages were being treated well.[112] Abourezk insisted the news media be present for the hostage interviews and the AIM leadership agreed. According to Means, McGovern then asked Agnes Gildersleeve, one of the trading post owners, if she was a hostage. The 70-year-old shopkeeper replied:

Of course we're not hostages! These Indians are here and they have legitimate grievances. You people — it's your fault. If you people had done something about their problems, they wouldn't be here today. We're here not only to protect our property, but also because we want to help save the Indians, and we know you're ready to massacre them.[113]

Means later wrote, "We knew this was bullshit, of course, but we didn't care. Knowing the whole scene was going to be on national television, we looked at one another, grins all but swallowing our faces. The spirits haunting Wounded Knee must have worked hard for that moment."[114]

Although Wounded Knee is touted as a death-defying struggle against a constant barrage of government machine guns and small arms fire, there seemed to be an element of shadow boxing to much of the fighting. The major news networks set up communications vans at Wounded Knee, and Means claims that he ate dinner with a different news crew almost every night. Not wanting to wear out his welcome, Means would vary his diet with government C-rations smuggled in by Justice Department negotiators on other nights.[115] Some Indians later chided Means and Banks for their vanity, saying they continually posed for photographers during the takeover.[116]

On March 10, the government lifted the roadblocks and pulled back their forces in the hope of defusing the situation. People could come and go as they pleased. To the government's dismay, however, few left. The chiefs at Wounded Knee responded by declaring the area a sovereign nation for the Oglala, based on the Treaty of 1868, and demanded the right to negotiate with the government on a nation-to-nation basis. They also proposed that the IRA-style government on the reservation be abolished.[117] Russell Means saw the let-up in hostilities as a disaster in the making. In his autobiography, he states:

> We still hadn't forced the government to enter into real negoti-
> ations about our treaty. Without a confrontation to focus public
> attention on Wounded Knee, the government could ignore us.
> The war would be over, and we would lose. I decided to start a
> firefight so the marshals would put the roadblocks back up and
> we could continue the battle.[118]

Means claims he and a few of the protesters went out on patrol toward the government positions and were soon shot at. The protesters returned the fire, but soon ran out of ammunition and retreated. Other patrol groups joined their retreat, and one of the warriors, identified by Means as a Canadian named Black Horse, thought he shot an FBI agent and was upset. The other fighters began to curse him for putting all of their lives in danger, but Means remembers Dennis Banks saying, "Wait a minute, this man's a hero. We should be celebrating."[119]

The purpose of the fight for the Indians was to get the government to capitulate to their list of demands, which had been laid out for the government since the beginning of the confrontation. The list of demands called for Senate committees to review treaties, uncover abuses in the BIA and the Department of Interior, and investigate conditions on all Sioux reservations in South Dakota. Negotiations were called for with John Ehrlichman of the White House, as well as Senators William Fulbright, Edward Kennedy, and James Abourezk. The Indians gave the government two options: negotiate our demands, or "wipe out the old people, women, children and men by attacking us."[120]

By the end of the confrontation at Wounded Knee, two Indians would be dead and one federal Marshall was paralyzed from the waist down, all from gunshot wounds.[121] The occupation ended on May 8, 1973, after the government agreed to hold meetings on the Pine Ridge Reservation within a few weeks to discuss treaty issues. By early June, an Indian affairs subcommittee, led by Senator James Abourezk, was holding meetings on Pine Ridge to listen to grievances.[122] In July, the senator proposed a joint resolution to the Senate to create the American Indian Policy Review Commission.[123] For the Indian sovereignty movement, legitimacy had finally come. Public opinion was strongly on the side of the Indians, and the government would give them almost any concession.

A Harris Poll in the spring of 1973 showed that 98 percent of respondents had heard of the Wounded Knee takeover, 51 percent of whom sympathized with the Indians. Only 21 percent sided with the government and 28 percent were not sure.[124] Public opinion is everything.

Seven leaders of the Wounded Knee occupation were indicted for conspiracy. Russell Means and Dennis Banks were the first to be tried with charges including theft, burglary, arson, interference with federal officers and assault. Thirty-five lawyers from the National Association of Criminal Defense Lawyers committed themselves to helping the Indians, as well as many lawyers from the National Lawyers Guild.[125] The attorneys who actually defended Means and Banks were William Kunstler, Mark Lane, Larry Leventhal, Doug Hall and Ken Tilsen.[126]

The trial dragged on for almost eight and a half months. On Thursday, September 12, 1973, the jury went into deliberations. The next day one of the jurors became ill and had to be removed. There was then some wrangling between the defense and prosecution as to whether to proceed with 11 jurors. On Monday, September 16, presiding Judge Fred Nichol solved the dilemma by dismissing the remaining charges against Means and Banks, citing government misconduct. Many suspected that it was the judge who should have been dismissed for misconduct, however. A reporter for the St. Paul *Pioneer Press*, J. C. Wolfe, noted that Judge Nichol seemed to have little control over the courtroom and had let Russell Means do pretty much as he pleased in the courtroom. Nichol had allowed Means and Banks to act as co-councils in the trial. In effect, this meant they could act as if they were lawyers and cross-examine witnesses, but did not have to be examined on the stand as defendants.[127] In his autobiography, Means explains the court-room antics that took place daily.

> We continued to jump up and do and say things that no lawyer would. We knew we could get away with giving speeches while pretending to cross-examine. The government always objected, and the judge always told the jury to disregard what they heard — but you can't unring a bell. After the umpteenth time, Nichol told us he knew we were doing it just to influence the jury. By that time, we had accomplished our purpose.[128]

CHAPTER SIX

The Government Cave-In
The American Indian Review Commission

The American Indian Policy Review Commission of 1977 has had perhaps more impact on Indians than any other event in 200 years of U.S. history, yet it is an event that is virtually unknown to the American people. It is truly the "missing link" in the evolution of Indian policy and explains the status of tribes today. Without knowledge of the changes in policy that occurred as a result of this Senate commission, it is difficult to make informed judgments about Indian sovereignty. Few people understand the transformation of the Indian sovereignty movement created by the American Indian Policy Review Commission of 1977. Most people do not know the commission ever existed, yet it allowed Indians to virtually write their own federal policy and imprint these radical reforms on the Congress and the courts of the United States.

The original Senate committee, called the Senate Select Committee on Indian Affairs, was convened as a result of the publicity generated by the three major Indian protests: the occupation of Alcatraz Island in 1969, the takeover of the Bureau of Indian Affairs in November 1972, and the 71-day stand-off at Wounded Knee in February 1973. While it took almost four years of civil protest to get formal action by the federal government, the protests were leaving their mark from the very beginning, particularly with President Richard Nixon.

Nixon, in fact, expressed sympathy for the Indian movement even before the Indians organized their civil protest movement. In a campaign speech of September 28, 1968, Nixon promised, "Termination of tribal recognition will not be a policy objective, and in no case will it be imposed without Indian consent."[1] The National Council for Indian Opportunity (NCIO) was created in 1968 by a presidential order in response to Indian demands for participation in policy development. Then in 1970, the NCIO met with Vice President Spiro Agnew and cabinet members at the White House to discuss their dissatisfaction with the policy of termination and the Bureau of Indian Affairs. Indians believed their standard of living was far behind that of other Americans, and they expected the BIA to close the gap for them. On the flip side, which the Indians admitted seemed contradictory, was a feeling that the BIA was too paternalistic and made Indians overly dependent on federal handouts — a catch-22 if ever there was one. Though Indians wanted to be less dependent on the BIA, they also wanted to keep the "trust relationship" with the government.[2]

Nixon's sympathies were clear as he spoke to Congress in a July 1970 speech:

> This policy of forced termination is wrong, in my judgment, for a number of reasons. First, the premises on which it rests are wrong. Termination implies that the Federal government has taken on a trusteeship responsibility for Indian communities as an act of generosity toward a disadvantaged people and that it can therefore discontinue this responsibility on a unilateral basis whenever it sees fit. But the unique status of Indian tribes does not rest on any premise such as this. The special relationship between Indians and the Federal government is the result instead of solemn obligations which have been entered into by the United States Government. Down through the years, through written treaties and through formal and informal agreements, our government has made specific commitments to the Indian people. For their part, the Indians have often surrendered claims to vast tracts of land and have accepted life on government reservations. In exchange, the government has agreed to provide community services such as health, education, and public safety, services which would presumably allow

Indian communities to enjoy a standard of living comparable to other Americans.

This goal, of course, has never been achieved. But the special relationship between the tribes and the Federal Government which arises from these agreements continues to carry immense moral and legal force. To terminate this relationship would be no more appropriate than to terminate the citizenship rights of any other American.[3]

Nixon goes on to say that fear of termination has led to apprehension in the tribes, and this in turn has inhibited tribal progress. "Any step that might result in greater social, economic or political autonomy is regarded with suspicion by many Indians who fear that it will only bring them closer to the day when the Federal government will disavow its responsibility and cut them adrift," Nixon said. "In short, the fear of one extreme policy, forced termination, has often worked to produce the opposite extreme: excessive dependence on the Federal government."[4]

At this point, Nixon advocates for Indian control of federal programs without "being cut off from Federal concern and Federal support." Ironically, when Indians control federal programs, Nixon identifies this as Indian "self-determination." He also makes it clear that this "historic relationship between the Federal government and the Indian communities cannot be abridged without the consent of the Indians."[5]

Beyond Nixon's seemingly puppet-like repetition of Indian concerns, Nixon's speech is noteworthy for other reasons as well. Certainly, it displays a remarkable ignorance of the most basic fact of American Indian policy. Congress has plenary power over Indian tribes. In simple terms, this means Congress can *unilaterally* terminate any tribe from the federal trust relationship at any time. Congress has always had this power, and it gets the power from the Constitution, not from the president. Indians have always *wished* that Congress did not have plenary power over tribes, and President Nixon was expressing misplaced agreement with this wish as well.

The most interesting element in the speech is the idea that

termination of the trust relationship must rest not in the plenary power of Congress, but in the consent of the tribe. Nixon states that the government must provide services such as health, education, and public safety to tribes, but he fails to mention that under the trust relationship, tribal lands, homes and businesses are not taxed for these services. Under the president's plan, Indian tribes would continue to be free from obligatory taxes for services, so of course the tribes have chosen *not* to pay taxes (like the rest of us would if given the opportunity).

The tribes and Nixon both speak of the pressing need for self-determination. As defined in the speech, however, self-determination appears to be nothing more than autonomy and total freedom to spend federal money as Indians see fit. A more standard definition of self-determination is self-*sufficiency*, or depending on oneself for one's livelihood. Nixon's idea of self-determination, in contrast, would have the opposite effect. Indians would depend on the federal government for their livelihood, sans accountability for their actions or any return on this federal investment. To be sure, the framers of Indian treaties did not intend to create permanent welfare states for Indians.

Finally, Nixon equates loss of trust status for Indians to the loss of rights as U.S. citizens. In fact, the loss of trust status would finally put Indian rights on an *equal* playing field with average Americans. Nowadays, Indians enjoy constitutional rights — freedom of speech, religion, the equal treatment of the laws, — as well as a second tier of rights, not the least of which is tribal exemption from taxation.

The Legacy of Wounded Knee

The 71-day Wounded Knee takeover in 1973 happened at the worst possible time for Nixon, who was embroiled in the Watergate controversy at the time. On April 30, Nixon gave a televised national address to try to distance himself from his Watergate problems. Amid talk of the president's impeachment, Attorney General Richard Kleindienst and Nixon's two top aids, John Erlichman and H.R. Haldeman, resigned. White House Council John Dean was fired and replaced with Leonard Garment, who had represented the Nixon administration during negotiations with Hank Adams and other Indians during the takeovers of

Alcatraz and the BIA.[6]

On May 3, the Lakota chiefs asked the White House to establish a presidential treaty commission, repeating a demand stated at the beginning of the stand-off. They also asked Senator James Abourezk to head the commission. On May 5, Garment sent Hank Adams, acting as a personal envoy of the president, to try and settle the Wounded Knee stand-off. Garment promised Chief Fools Crow that the White House would hold a meeting at Pine Ridge Reservation the third week of May. On May 6, an agreement was reached to end the occupation on May 8, 1973. On May 17, Garment sent his aid, Brad Patterson, to meet with the chiefs about the old treaties. As a result, Nixon got what would be a rare respite from unfavorable Watergate press coverage — a picture of an old chief in a war bonnet leading Presidential Emissary Patterson by the hand across a field.[7] On July 16, 1973, Abourezk proposed Joint Resolution Number 133 to the House and Senate.[8] On January 3, 1975, the resolution became law and created the American Indian Policy Review Commission.[9]

Senator James Abourezk, a Democrat from South Dakota, was appointed as the chairman of the Senate commission. For Russell Means and AIM, there could not have been a better choice. Means had been friends with Abourezk since the summer of 1965.[10] At that time, Abourezk owned a bar and restaurant in the town of Rockerville, South Dakota, located in the Black Hills south of Rapid City and not far from Mount Rushmore and the Wyoming border. Rockerville catered to the tourist trade, using cowboy and Indian shows as tourist attractions. Means moved to the area in 1965 because his father told him there was good money in Indian dancing in that part of western South Dakota. Abourezk put two canvas Indian teepees outside the restaurant and Indians were hired to do Indian dances and drumming to attract tourists. Russell Means and his younger brother Ted danced on Monday, Tuesday and Wednesday to attract business on the slowest days of the week.

Means did not like doing Indian dances for the tourists. In his autobiography, he said, "Dancing for the tourists, I came to know exactly how prostitutes feel when they sell their bodies."[11] Regardless, Means got to know Abourezk and Bill Janklow, a law school classmate of Abourezk's. Janklow worked as a bartender at Abourezk's restaurant in 1965 and would later become governor of South Dakota in the 1970s. In the 1960s, Janklow also worked as a legal aid attorney at the Rosebud Sioux Reservation where he made many good Indian friends. According to Means' autobiography, "Years later, when Bill was elected governor of South Dakota, they all got jobs."[12] Means describes both politicians as very friendly and talkative when he was working as a dancer.[13]

Abourezk was first elected to the U.S. House of Representatives and later to the Senate. In 1970, Russell and Ted Means again worked for Abourezk, this time in a political capacity during Abourezk's election campaign for a seat in the House of Representatives. Abourezk rented the brothers a car and paid them $200 a week cash to go to Indian reservations and campaign for him.[14] Abourezk himself was well acquainted with reservation life. He grew up on the Rosebud Sioux Reservation in South Dakota on the Nebraska border. Russell Means also was well acquainted with Senator Abourezk's son, Charles who wore his blond hair in braids, was married to an Indian woman, and was a dedicated member of the American Indian Movement.[15] It's not hard to understand why Senator James Abourezk was the perfect choice, as far as the American Indian Movement was concerned, to head the Senate Select Committee on Indian Affairs. Having grown up in South Dakota on the Rosebud Indian Reservation, he could hardly be characterized as an impartial observer of the events at Wounded Knee in 1973, nor an impartial member and chairman of the committee.

As a Senator from South Dakota, Abourezk had a duty to represent the American people, the people of South Dakota, the interests of the state, and the interests of the Indians during the Senate Select Committee hearings. The question we should ask about his chairmanship of that committee, however, is whether he impartially represented the interests of all Americans — *including* Indians — or whether he represented *only* Indians. There is ample evidence to suggest he was largely biased toward the Indian point of view. By examining more than 3,000 pages of government documents that make up the record of the committee hearings and recommendations, it is possible to see how Senator Abourezk performed his duties for the American people with a biased perspective.

The American Indian Policy Review Commission, which I will refer to as the "Indian Commission" for brevity, also featured Lloyd Meeds as vice chairman. Meeds was a Democrat from the state of Washington. By the time the Indian Commission had finished its work, Meeds and Abourezk would disagree completely on the conclusions and recommendations made. Meeds' objections to the Indian Commission's final report were so strong, in fact, that he hired two lawyers in January 1977 to assist him in preparing a dissent to the Indian Commission. This dissent is 40 pages long and covers all of the major legal points of law considered by the Indian Commission.

Meeds begins by lambasting the objectivity of this supposedly non-partisan commission:

With the creation of this Commission it was hoped that Congress would have before it an objective statement of past and current American Indian Law and policy so that it could exercise its powers wisely in legislating a coherent and lasting policy toward American Indians.

Unfortunately, the majority report of this Commission is the product of one-sided advocacy in favor of American Indian tribes. The interests of the United States, the States, and non-Indian citizens, if considered at all, were largely ignored. This was perhaps inevitable because the enabling legislation... required that 5 out of the 11 Commissioners be American Indians, and that each of the investigating task forces be composed of 3 persons, a majority of whom were required to be of Indian descent....As a result, of the 33 persons appointed to lead the task forces, 31 were Indian.

With due regard to those who worked on the task forces, the reports were often based on what the members wished the law to be. Their findings were often poorly documented. Recommendations ignored contemporary reality. As an example, the report of Task Force No. 1 would require the return to Indian possession and jurisdiction large parts of California, Oregon, Nebraska, North Dakota, South Dakota, and Oklahoma.   Despite contemporary litigation, most Americans are justified in believing that 400 years have been sufficient to quiet title to the continent.[16]

Here is a fundamental problem that is encountered whenever the subject of Indian treaties is raised in the Indian community. There is a belief that somehow, by some magic or political slight of hand, the clock can be turned back hundreds of years, and a significantly large piece of American real estate can be simply "given back" to tribes, free of all non-Indian influence. This is the radical viewpoint that motivated the protesters at the famous Indian protests of the 70s. The face that the Indians put on at Indian Commission meetings is a different one from that seen at Alcatraz, the BIA, and what activists began to call "the Knee." Gone were the rusty rifles, raised fists, and molotov cocktails, replaced by task forces, briefcases, expense accounts, and most importantly, a newfound legitimacy. But underneath the bureaucratic jargon, the dream was still the same, namely to take back the land and turn back time.

Early in his critique of the review, Meeds points out that the Commission failed to address controversial and unresolved issues concerning modern Indian law. He essentially called the document one-sided propaganda for a special interest group. He writes:

Instead, it assumed as first principles, the resolution of all contemporary legal and policy issues in favor of the Indian tribes. Hence, the report is advocacy and cannot be relied upon as a statement of existing law nor as a statement of what future policy should be. The report's utility, then is limited to informing the Congress of the special interests of some American Indian tribes and their non-Indian advocates. Congress will either have to authorize another Commission to ascertain the views of non-Indians, the States, and the United States or perform that function on its own.[17]

The problem for Meeds and the rest of America, however, was that as a final report the commission was not honor-bound to address these basic gaps in its policy analysis. Meeds, for his part, did his best to point out some of the problems after the fact. He felt the most basic error in the report was its interpretation of tribal sovereignty. The Indian Commission saw Indian sovereignty as a form of *territorial* government rather than as a form of self-governance for Indians. Meeds accurately notes that federal and state governments are the sole sovereign in the territory of the United States of America, and that the federal government, as an exercise of its sovereign power, merely permits tribes to govern themselves and their *internal* affairs, but not the affairs of others. Meeds continued:

> In our Federal system, as ordained and established by the United States Constitution, there are but two sovereign entities: the United States and the States. This is obvious not only from an examination of the Constitution, its structure, and its amendments, but also from the express language of the 10th amendment which provides:
>
> The powers not delegated to the United States by the Constitution, nor prohibited by it to the States, are reserved to the States respectively, or to the people. And, under the 14th amendment, all citizens of the United States who are residents of a particular State are also citizens of that State.
>
> The Commission report...would have us believe that there is a third source of sovereign and governmental power in the United States. It argues that American Indian tribes have the characteristics of sovereignty over the lands they occupy analogous to the kind of sovereignty possessed by the United States and the States. The report describes Indian tribes as governmental units in the territorial sense. This fundamental error infects the balance of the report in a way which is contrary to American Federalism and unacceptable to the United States, the States, and non-Indian people.[18]

The Indian Commission repeatedly makes baseless claims for increasing Indian authority where the Constitution neither provides nor intended. A section called "Indian Country" clearly shows that tribes desired a territorial form of government and wanted to impose jurisdiction on non-Indians who reside within reservation boundaries. Not only is jurisdiction claimed within reservations, but even on land allotments outside reservations. The Commission notes:

> The Indian country statute has three separate parts. First, Indian country is defined as all lands within the limits of any Federal Indian reservation, 'not withstanding the issuance of any patent.' Land within reservation boundaries which has been opened to settlement by non-Indians is Indian country unless Congress intended to diminish the reservation. Thus, Indian country includes all land within the reservation boundaries, including 'checkerboard' land — that is, those areas within Indian reservations where non-Indian land is interspersed with Indian land. Second, Indian country includes all dependent Indian communities within the borders of the United States. Third, Indian country includes all Indian trust allotments, even though they may not be within the boundaries of a reservation.[19]

But Meeds rejects this argument whole-cloth, arguing that Indian tribes are not sovereign nations. He makes it clear that while tribes were given the power to be "self-governing entities" they were not allowed to exercise jurisdiction over the land.

> The blunt fact of the matter is that American Indian tribes are not a third set of governments in the American federal system. They are not sovereigns. The Congress of the United States has permitted them to be self-governing entities but not entities which would govern others. American Indian tribal self-government has meant that the Congress permits Indian tribes to make their own laws and be ruled by them. The erroneous view adopted by the Commission's report is that American Indian tribal self-government is territorial in nature. On the contrary,

American Indian tribal self-government is purposive. The Congress has permitted Indian tribes to govern themselves for the purpose of maintaining tribal integrity and identity. But this does not mean that the Congress has permitted them to exercise general governmental powers over the lands they occupy. This is the critical distinction which the Commission report fails to make. The Commission has failed to deal with the ultimate legal issue, which is the very subject of its charter.[20]

Another issue with sovereignty is whether Indians can be prosecuted for offenses done on reservations. Many believe the answer is no, but Meeds rightfully corrects this erroneous assumption.

The United States Supreme Court has over and again upheld the power of the State to impose its law on non-Indians within the reservation. If American Indian tribes had the kind of sovereignty which this Commission urges, and if Indian tribal self-government were territorial rather than purposive, the States could not have jurisdiction over non-Indians within the reservation.[21]

A recent court case in Minnesota demonstrates that the federal government can impose laws on Indians living within the boundaries of reservations. In June 1996, Darryl "Chip" Wadena, chairman of the White Earth Reservation in Minnesota was convicted on 15 counts of theft, conspiracy, bribery and money laundering.[22] Wadena allegedly stole more than $428,000 by rigging construction bids for the tribe's Shooting Star Casino. Another alleged scheme involved the creation of a tribal fishing commission that paid Wadena and others salaries of $65,000 to $75,000, although the tribal biologist and Conservation Department did not know anything about the jobs.[23] Wadena appealed his conviction in October of 1997. His lawyer asserted that the federal government had no jurisdiction on the reservation because of Indian sovereignty. He compared Wadena's conviction to a coup d'etat of a foreign nation and said the prosecution violated the Indian right of self-government. The federal attorneys disagreed, however, stating that the members of the White Earth Tribe were also U.S. citizens, and they would not be adequately protected by tribal government.[24]

In this case, the government relied on the equal protection guaranteed by the Constitution to justify prosecuting Wadena. Since Indians are citizens and live within the boundaries of states, they are clearly subject to the jurisdiction of the United States. By contrast, being subjected to Indian courts and jurisdiction is not equal treatment. Each tribe would have a different set of laws which would revive the concept of "separate but equal." This was discarded 50 years ago as an unacceptable form of racism. Meeds explains how the legal status of Indians has changed over time:

> Tribal government, no doubt, had one purpose when Indians were neither citizens of the United States nor of the State in which they lived...But all non-citizen Indians were made citizens of the United States by the Act of June 2, 1924...And, under the 14th amendment to the United States Constitution, citizens of the United States are citizens of the State wherein they reside. American Indians, therefore, are citizens of the State in which they reside and the United States. They cannot now claim that their tribal entity gives to them a source of governmental power in an extra-constitutional sense.[25]

The U.S. government gave Indians citizenship in 1924 to correct the inequities of segregation. Prior the 1924 Indian Citizenship Act, Indians needed some form of separate government because they were segregated from other Americans. With the Citizenship Act, the legal separation ended. But instead of acknowledging this reality, the Indian Commission feigned ignorance and continued to act as if Indians were not citizens of the U.S. As a result, the commission assumes that a policy of extreme *laissez faire* is not only possible and practical, but logical. Little consideration is given to the ramifications of Indian quasi-sovereignty, and disturbingly little attention is given to the rights of non-Indians, particularly those owning land within reservations where the commission takes a "let them eat cake" attitude. Meeds questions such an approach:

The commission has not explained why, for policy reasons, it would be a good thing for Indian tribes to exercise general governmental powers over the lands they occupy. The Commission has just assumed that because Indian tribes would like to exercise governmental powers over their territory, it would be wise to let them. There is no adequate discussion in the Commission report of the detriments of such a course of action, much less any weighing of the advantages and disadvantages. The report fails to take into consideration that Indian tribes are no longer isolated communities. Indian reservations now abut major metropolitan areas in this country. The Commission report makes much of the fact that reservation Indians want to be left alone and be free of State interference (even though they are citizens of the State, vote in State elections, and help create State laws that are inapplicable to them), yet fails to understand that by arguing for the exercise by Indian tribes of general governmental powers, Indian tribes cannot be left alone. For example, the Commission's recommendations would leave us with the following results. Reservation Indians would be citizens of the State but be wholly free of State law and State taxing schemes. In short, reservation Indians would have all the benefits of citizenship and none of its burdens. On the other hand, non-Indian citizens of the State would have no say in the creation of Indian law and policy on the reservation, even if they were residents of the reservation, and yet be subject to tribal jurisdiction. In short, non-Indians would have all of the burdens of citizenship but none of the benefits. This is a strange scheme to behold.[26]

It is more than a little näive to assume that such a contradictory jurisdictional scheme would solve the "Indian Problem" in the United States. It could only make things worse. But Indians claim that their sovereignty is inherent, so it cannot be limited by the states. Meeds attacks the idea of inherent tribal sovereignty as mythical and unfounded in any legal sense.

The assertion of inherent tribal sovereignty proves too much. It would mean that whenever there is a group of American Indians living together on land which is allocated to them by the Federal Government, they would have the power to exercise general governmental powers. The source of those powers would then be some magical combination of their Indianness and their ownership of the land. Governmental powers do not have as their source such magic. Governmental powers in these United States have as their source the State and Federal Constitutions.[27]

Meeds also sees a problem with the allocation of federal services to Indians as a special class of people. He points out that Indians insist on having a social welfare system created specially for their benefit and use. As such, Indian law and policy went from dealing with Indians on Indian lands to servicing Indians wherever they are located and regardless of assimilation. When this happens, Meeds says that the objectives have shifted from the preservation of tribal cultural identity and separation to the treatment of Indians, qua Indians, as a special and preferred class of people. The shift cannot be tied rationally to Congress' purpose of permitting reservation Indians to make their own laws and be ruled by them."[28]

Taxation is another question that becomes hopelessly muddled in the present checkerboard of ownership that comprises most Indian reservations. As an example, the White Earth Reservation in Minnesota comprises about 887,000 acres. About 90 percent of this reservation land is owned by non-Indians, yet the Indian Commission asserts that the Indians should be able to collect taxes from everyone within the reservation boundaries.[29] How could the Commission justify taxing non-Indians while denying them participation in the government? This would give rise to serious constitutional questions. Meeds cautions:

It would be irrational for Congress to tolerate a system wherein the costs of Indian tribal separatism are not borne by all the taxpayers of the United States, but rather are to be borne inordinately by those non-Indian taxpayers who, by accident, conduct activities or have property on reservations. While Congress may insulate Indians from state law and may subsidize their efforts at government and social welfare, I seriously doubt that Congress could levy a tax on persons or property situated on Indian reservations and then remit those tax funds to the Indian tribes. The same result is achieved by allowing Indian tribes to tax nonmembers on their lands. It is a denial of due process of law for Congress to tolerate a scheme in which the financial burden of supporting Indians and Indian government falls disproportionately on non-Indians or on non-Indian property on Indian reservations.[30]

At issue is whether Indians want autonomy to harken back to the romantic notions of traditional Indian hunting and gathering, or whether they simply want and expect federal intervention to help them become prosperous in an economy that has passed by the Indian culture. By most signs, Indians want to protect traditions that make tribes culturally unique, but in many other respects, Indians want to live in the "western" economic world when it benefits them. Unfortunately, on many reservations, they are poorly prepared to compete in the global economy today and expect the federal government to essentially pay off the economic gap, and then to stop bothering them, thank you.

In their rebuttal to Meeds' dissent, five of the Indian commissioners for the Indian Commission outlined just such an argument:

It is our judgment that the goal of Indian self-sufficiency is indeed a matter of over-riding importance. Every single Indian tribe in this Nation aspires to this goal and we have recommended that, as a policy of the highest priority, the Federal Government should make a concerted effort to assist Indian tribes in their efforts to achieve economic self-sufficiency. There are two elements essential to the ability of all Indian tribes to progress toward economic development and eventual self-sufficiency; self-government i.e., sovereignty and the trust relationship. Without governmental authority to enact laws regulating natural resource and industrial development or to license and possibly tax commercial activities within reservations, or without the judicial authority to enforce and interpret tribal laws, it is simply not possible for Indian tribes to achieve economic independence.[31]

Even with all the special concessions, education and services that the federal government has given to the Indians, they are the most economically isolated ethnic group in America. In 50 years, there has been little economic improvement on many reservations in spite of the infusion of billions of dollars in federal aid. Most reservation societies continue to be economically and socially dysfunctional. Economic success has come to some tribes because of casino development, but this success is based on the monopoly status of the enterprise rather than any legitimate ability to create enterprise in real-world competition. Economic self-sufficiency will be achieved when Indians can interact and compete with other Americans at the same level. But the isolated existence of many reservation residents makes it difficult for them to gain access to the benefits of the larger culture such as education and jobs. For example, today on the Pine Ridge Reservation in South Dakota, the unemployment rate is 80 percent. The national rate is about 4 percent, the lowest in 25 years. The suicide rate on Indian reservations today is nearly 7 times the national average and the alcoholism rate on some reservations is above 50 percent.[32]

The Commission's demand for Indian sovereignty also raises questions of how Indian courts will regard both Indian and non-Indian civil rights. Courts operate in two areas: civil and criminal jurisdiction. If Indians can subject non-Indians to the enforcement powers of tribal courts, in effect, Indians would be governing non-Indians. Meeds argues this serves both parties poorly. Indians have the same access to state and federal courts as all other American citizens. Not only is their access equal to that of all other Americans, but they can participate in the lawmaking process like everyone else. In contrast, non-Indians are subject to tribal court jurisdictions, but without any accompanying rights to participate in the lawmaking process or the selection of judges within the tribal court system. Meeds accurately points out that this violates the most basic American principles of democracy, particularly the value of government deriving its power from the consent of those governed.

Government by Indian tribes over non-Indians, if allowed to take place, would be a clear exception to that principle. A heavy burden of justification should fall on those who would subject some of our citizens to the coercive powers of others without any opportunity or right to join in the deliberations and decisions which determine how that power is exercised."[33]

The Indian Commission, however, was not focused on the ideals of democracy but on getting Indian treaties renegotiated and to give as many concessions as possible to themselves. Indeed, despite the abuse that Indians suffered under past treaties, it is a bit ironic that the report wished the relationship between the government and Indians to be renegotiated by treaty. According to the Indian Commission's report, "Perhaps someday in the future, the Indian people may return to the bargaining table to renegotiate and reshape those solemn agreements (treaties). But it must be done as equals, and not as one party coming, on its knees, pleading as inferiors."[34] This idea originated from the "Twenty Points" which was drawn up by Hank Adams while staying at the Minnesota State Fairgrounds in 1972, during the Trail of Broken Treaties caravan. It was presented to the White House during the takeover of the Bureau of Indian Affairs, but rejected by the Nixon administration on the grounds that Indians became citizens in 1924 and a nation cannot make treaties with its own citizens. In spite of this rejection, the Indian Commission raised the demand again, this time in a congressional report written to suggest future Indian policy. The Indian Commission looked backward instead of forward, hoping to reinstitute the Indian treaty-making process that was ended by congressional action in 1871.[35]

When it does look forward, the Indian Commission sees an America where Indians govern non-Indians and Indians alike in Indian Country. As Meeds notes, "The Commission finds that the growth and development of tribal government into fully functioning governments necessarily encompasses the exercise of tribal jurisdiction over non-Indian people and property within reservation boundaries."[36] In 1977, that meant perhaps 100 million acres of U.S. territory would have been under ethnic jurisdiction. Sovereign tribes would then have had the power to create courts with civil and criminal jurisdiction, regulate land use, tax property and economic activity, and control natural resources.[37]

Congressman Meeds provided ample evidence of the conflicts such Indian jurisdiction would cause non-Indian residents of reservations. The Indian Commission dismisses his argument by saying non-Indians don't belong on the reservation in the first place. It states:

> There are also complaints that people should not be subjected to the authority of government in which they are not allowed to participate — a complaint with a solid patriotic ring but one which does not reach the core of the problem of government in Indian country; it overlooks the history of Federal policy which opened the Indian lands for non-Indian settlement against the wishes of the Indian community and in violation of treaty agreements.[38]

Yet, what the Indian members of the commission failed to admit is that in many states, land had been given to Indians who could keep the land title free after 25 years of occupation or sell the land to whomever they wished. They were private owners of reservation lands. After the 25 years of homesteading, many Indian land owners sold their land to non-Indians. Some reservations today have as much as 90 percent of the land owned by non-Indian people.

The Indian Commission was forced to deal with this "checkerboard" reality of modern-day reservations. They chose to confer special and elite status to Indians as a race and to recommend buy-back programs in order to regain Indian country and create a purer, more segregated society. They wrote, "Tribal members are United States citizens, yet they are citizens of their tribes also, giving them rights and privileges distinct from any other racial or cultural group in the Nation."[39] One of these rights, asserted over and over in the Commission report, is the right of Indians to live separately from all other races and cultures. The Indian Commission suggested consolidation programs that would accelerate land acquisition using tribal funds and federal loans.[40] The Standing Rock Sioux Tribe was one tribe looking to do just that:

> We believe that since there seems to be a steady and growing

group who want to move from the reservation and since it is our objective to gain back as much of the land that was taken from us without our consent, that it is morally, as well as economically reasonable, that the Indian Administration develop a program whereby the Tribe can regain trust title of those alienated lands as they become available for sale.[41]

In essence, this argues that American taxpayers should provide funds for Indians to buy out non-Indian property owners on reservations, and then allow Indians to promptly close the governance door behind them. Apart from the obvious potential for abusive practices in gaining back non-Indian owned land, is it wise for the federal government to make loans to tribes for the purpose of creating a culturally pure land mass? When tribes believe that they have a "morally reasonable" mandate to regain "alienated lands" from non-Indian owners, is there reason to wonder if tribal governments will treat such landowners fairly? Draconian tax codes and unreasonable property regulations could be used by unscrupulous tribal governments to encourage non-Indian landowners to sell their land. Is there reason to believe this could happen on reservations with an avowed grudge against non-Indian land owners? American government is structured with checks and balances to prevent one group, especially a particular racial or cultural group, from gaining unilateral control of the government, but tribal governments have no such checks.

A parallel can be drawn to White separatist groups who wish to be ethnically pure and segregated from "undesirables." Today, America has several of these groups who wish to create a White homeland in America. Their policy statements sound remarkably like those of the Indian tribes. The National Alliance, formed in 1974, speaks of the need for what it calls "White Living Space." The group says, "we must have a racially clean area of the earth for the further development of our people. We must have White schools, White residential neighborhoods and recreation areas, White workplaces, White farms and countryside. We must have no non-whites in our living space, and we must have open space around us for expansion." In a section called "An Aryan Society," the National Alliance says, "We do not need to homogenize

the White world: there will be room for Germanic societies, Celtic societies, Baltic societies, and so on, each with its own roots, traditions, and
language. ...It means neighborhoods, schools, work groups, and universities in which there is a feeling of family and comradeship, of a
shared heritage and a shared destiny."[42] This is not exactly a public service announcement for America's melting pot, yet Indians make many
similar claims, and policy makers and other sympathizers seem only
too eager to help them achieve their mission of elitist segregation.

The American Indian Research and Policy Institute of St. Paul,
Minnesota, is a nonprofit organization* dedicated to promoting accurate knowledge of the legal and political status of Indians. In a 1996
report published by the institute, Marge Anderson, chief executive of
the Mille Lacs Band of Chippewa, defined Indian sovereignty in this
way:

> First and most important are people. There must be a distinct,
> unique group of people. These people must have a distinct lan-
> guage, a distinct moral and religious structure, and a distinct
> cultural base. They must have a specific geographic area that
> they control and regulate. Within that area, they must possess
> governmental powers, including the power to tax and the power
> to change their government as they see fit. These governmen-
> tal powers must be acknowledged by the people who are subject
> to them.[43]

The Indian Commission placed great importance on the need
for a living space for each culturally distinct tribe. "The desire for land
is not a romantic notion. It springs from a serious analysis by Indians
of their needs for cultural survival and economic improvement of their
people."[44] According to the group, the integrity of their land base is
essential for the preservation and enhancement of all other resources —
water rights, fishing, hunting, trapping, timber and mineral reserves —
because Indian livelihood is derived from the land. Indians often assert
that their cultural values include a long-term respect for the land; they
say they must preserve land and resources "for the next seven generations to come." They believe that American capitalist society will

---

* Funding sources for the Policy Institute include Little Six, Inc., a wholly owned enterprise of the Shakopee
Mdewakanton Dakota Community, the Northwest Area Foundation, the General Mills Foundation, The Minneapolis
Foundation, The Saint Paul Companies, the Otto Bremer Foundation, the Emma B. Howe Foundation, The St. Paul
Foundation, and the Bigelow Foundation. [45]

destroy the environment unless Indians have jurisdiction over land use. Ultimately, however, we all share the natural environment, depend upon it for our survival, and must preserve it for our children. Dividing America into hundreds of separate racial or cultural "nations" whose interaction is defined by treaty relationships will only make it more difficult for us to live together and create solutions that are mutually beneficial.

Today, our interests are interrelated. Not only do more than half of all American Indians live off reservations, but on most reservations, assimilation has already taken place. Most Indians live in close proximity to non-Indians, and most Indians already have non-Indian ancestors. Their cultural experience today has far more in common with the rest of America than it does with 19th century Indian cultures.

Is there a way for Indians to protect their cultural values and live within the American system? Abourezk and Meeds do not agree on how this can be accomplished. Abourezk says that following Meeds' recommendations would severely curtail the general governmental powers of the tribes.

> By turning its back on the goal of economic independence, the dissent would entrench the governmental paternalism which Indian people have worked so hard to eradicate. The ultimate consequence would be the virtual assimilation of Native Americans into the dominant culture, destroying the last vestiges of a distinctively proud and independent way of life.[46]

It is interesting to note that Abourezk in particular, and Indians in general, feel that assimilation of Indians into American culture would be destructive to the Indian way of life. For other Americans, assimilation is the ultimate goal rather than the ultimate horror. America tolerates a wide range of religious and cultural beliefs, even ones which are completely at odds with mainstream values. Jews, Catholics and Muslims practice their faiths without the violence and repression they encounter in many other parts of the world. A wide range of political beliefs exist side by side; we tolerate Republicans and Democrats, Communists and the American Nazi Party. By giving everyone equal access to government and freedom of speech, we can tolerate what many other nations brutally repress. Through assimilation we have created a whole which is greater than the sum of its parts and which allows everyone a chance to succeed. It is segregation rather than integration that impoverishes minority cultures.

Even the Indian Commission seems to question whether isolation on reservation life is positive or negative. In a section of the review called "A Policy for the Future," the Commission decries the isolation on reservations.

What are the explanations for the circumstances in which the Indian finds himself today? First and foremost are the consistently damaging Federal policies of the past - policies which sought through the first three-quarters of the 19th century to remove the Indian people from the midst of the European settlers by isolating them on reservations; and policies which after accomplishing isolation were then directed toward breaking down their social and governmental structures and throwing their land, water, timber and mineral resources open to exploitation by non-Indians. These policies were repudiated by Congress with the passage of the Indian Reorganization Act of 1934, but by this time severe damage had been done.[47]

Here the Commission repudiates three-quarters of a century of isolation as oppressive, but fails to explain how this oppressive structure has since been transformed into something useful and endearing. Let me suggest that it is not isolation that is so appealing, but Indian sovereignty which seeks to replace White supremacy with Red supremacy. We will not solve the Indian problem by recycling intolerance. We should learn from our mistakes, not repeat them in another form. In continuing to demand ethnic sovereignty, Indians ignore the civil rights legislation that became law just as the Indian sovereignty movement was beginning its violent protests. Meeds seemed to have a more balanced solution to maintain the ethnic identity of Indians and yet protect the rights of all American citizens. He writes:

The United States is prepared to accommodate Indian interests, and to provide a substantial degree of self-determination. But there is a point beyond which it cannot go — our federal framework will not be compromised, nor will the rights of non-Indians be ignored. Where tribal aspirations collide with constitutional values, the tribe's interests must yield. Nor can the rights of the non-Indian majority be compromised to support tribal aspirations. Doing justice by Indians does not require doing injustices to non-Indians.[48]

After the Indian Commission report was released in 1977, many Indians were dissatisfied that it did not go far enough, just as many non-Indians thought it went too far. About a year later, in April 1978, Vine Deloria Jr. debated Senator Meeds at San Diego State University. A point of disagreement between the two was Meeds' assertion that "you can't rewrite 400 years of history." Deloria felt Meeds' "400 years of history" represented a biased viewpoint that was full of inaccuracies. Deloria believed that a long-term educational process of maybe 100 years was needed to re-educate non-Indians about these inaccuracies.[49] To Deloria, the Indian Commission was just another failure in a long list of government commissions that accomplished little or perhaps even provided another obstacle for Indians to overcome.[50] Hank Adams also was disappointed with the Indian Commission. He had progressed from "fish in" protester in the 1960s, to government negotiator during the 70s, to chairman of Task Force #1 for the Indian Commission.[51] He had high hopes for what the Commission could accomplish, but after the report was presented, it is said that he "was ashamed for being associated with the Commission."[52]

What famous Indian activists like Deloria and Adams failed to understand in 1978, however, was how much credibility the Indian Commission gave to the Indian sovereignty movement. As Abourezk had said, "(W)e have advertised this as the only time in the history of this country that the Indian people themselves have really written their own policy."[53] Commissioners writing policy reports in Washington offices could accomplish what the AIM protesters could never achieve with rifles and molotov cocktails, and that is legitimacy. The

Commission did not accomplish what Russell Means had hoped for —
the return of the Black Hills to the Sioux — but it did a lot to clear the
way for the 100-year re-education plan that Vine Deloria Jr. envisioned.

It is the slow, steady progress of Indian sovereignty that is a
threat to the constitutional rights of Americans. The raised fist of
enraged radicals has no real long-term effect. The Indian Commission
was a watershed for Indian public relations. Public opinion is the most
powerful influence in American politics, and the credibility of the
Indian Commission marked the acceptance of Indian radicalism into
the American mainstream. Hank Adams and Vine Deloria Jr. had progressed from being obscure Indian activists to men who could successfully debate with congressmen and negotiate with the president. They
were idealized by the press and courted by the biggest names in
Hollywood such as Marlon Brando and Jane Fonda. Indians had
arrived, and they hardly knew what they had accomplished.

CHAPTER SEVEN

The Indian Sovereignty Movement

During the last 30 years, Indians have had a goal of establishing themselves as a third source of general government in the United States, to go along with state and federal governments that we traditionally recognize. Whether people realize it or not, they have largely succeeded despite the fact that it violates the U.S. Constitution. What's more, most non-Indians don't realize the ramifications of recognizing a sovereign power within the existing state and federal legal framework, although some non-Indian citizens and policy makers are finding out the hard way.

Prior to events in the early 1970s, Indians were considered to have limited powers of government over their own affairs, known in legalese as having *purposive* government whereby tribal governments have the power to govern (only) Indians. Over the last 40 years, however, Indians have successfully managed to shift this governance structure to one that is *territorial* in nature, whereby Indians have full governing powers over a defined tract of land and all Indians and non-Indians who live, work or play within its confines.

The 1950s and 60s created a foundation for a grassroots movement among Indians for this cause. The American Indian Policy Review Commission of 1977 was an official acknowledgment of the movement, giving it legitimacy with the establishment and generating sympathy from a misinformed American public (Senator Meeds' efforts not withstanding). The last two decades have seen significant efforts to implement this shift in the governance of Indian affairs.

At an Indian sovereignty symposium in Oklahoma on June 4, 1996, Supreme Court Justice Sandra Day O'Connor outlined her views on the current sovereign status of tribes.

> Today, in the United States, we have three types of sovereign entities — the Federal government, the States, and the Indian Tribes. Each of the three governments has its own judicial system, and each play an important role in the administration of justice in this country. The part played by tribal courts is expanding.[1]

O'Connor's designation of tribes as a third source of sovereign territorial power in the United States is nothing short of remarkable. To allow an ethnic tribe to rule a geographic area that includes many non-tribal people differs from all other forms of American government. The American governance structure is expressly designed to prevent the concentration of power by any ethnic, religious, political or socioeconomic group, and ensures that all groups have equal access to governmental power. In federal and state government, we do not allow one group singular access to government. To do so would violate every principle upon which our democracy is founded. In the case of Indian tribes, the government has decided to ignore this principle and allow government to be based on ethnic heritage, a philosophical shift which represents great harm for the country in the long run.

Most Americans have no idea that this change in government policy has occurred. There have been few dramatic events. Instead, the shift has occurred in small steps over the course of decades and largely beneath the public's view and interest. More importantly, few people comprehend the rights they have been stripped of in the process. A trip to an Indian casino can be the legal equivalent of a journey to a foreign country with different police, laws, and court procedures, despite the fact that Indian reservations and trust lands are American soil, and all Indians are American citizens. Without publicly announced borders, like that of Mexico and Canada, most people do not realize when they are crossing into Indian-controlled land. Non-Indian American citizens, however, lose many of their rights when they enter lands or do business subject to Indian sovereignty. This reality may not be apparent until you find yourself in a legal dispute with an Indian tribe. Then, the meaning of "Indian country" might become painfully apparent.

For example, on October 7, 1994, Sylvia Cohen entered Mystic Lake Casino in Prior Lake, Minnesota.[2] When she attempted to sit on a chair in front of a slot machine, the chair collapsed, and the 82-year-old patron broke her hip. She has undergone two operations in the last three years, and might never walk normally again.[3] Cohen attempted to sue Little Six, Inc., the tribal corporation that manages the casino for the Mdewakanton Sioux (Dakota) Reservation in Shakopee, Minnesota. The casino said it was protected by sovereign immunity, and Minnesota courts, therefore, had no jurisdiction over the matter. That left Sylvia Cohen with no recourse except tribal court which provides for a jury trial by her "peers," many of whom are likely tribal members who receive a check from the casino every month. Tribal judges get their appointments from the tribal council which may own the casino and pay the judge from the profits.

Consider the case of a Minnesota resident named Jill Gavle. Gavle also filed a lawsuit against Little Six, Inc. She claimed the former chief executive officer, Leonard Prescott, forced her into a sexual relationship as a condition of keeping her job. In 1993, Gavle became pregnant and was fired. Both the county court and state court of appeals ruled that the tribal business had sovereign immunity, even if the sexual assaults and harassment occurred in Little Six's corporate offices which are not on the Indian reservation. In 1995, three Appeals Court judges unanimously threw out Jill Gavle's suit and she was told to pursue her case in tribal court.[4] The headline from a local newspaper at the time proclaimed, "Tribes often can't be touched in court." The article went on to say that two lawyers who worked for the Shakopee Dakota Tribe for three years couldn't recall a single non-Indian winning a case. The newspaper also quoted a lawyer who had a case dismissed in tribal court as saying, "Basically, it's justice bought and paid for."[5]   The Shakopee Mdewakanton Dakota Tribe can afford as much casino justice as it desires because every member of the tribe who is 18 or older currently receives about $600,000 a year from the casino, or about $50,000 per month per person.[6] Gavle is appealing her case to the United States Supreme Court.[7]

In both the Cohen and Gavle cases, the tribe claimed sovereign immunity as a defense. Throughout the nation, similar claims are arising in connection with Indian tribes. As a result, great pressure has been put on Congress to address the problem. A Senate committee on Indian affairs met in September of 1996 to review problems associated with tribal sovereign immunity. According to Senator Slade Gorton of Washington, the concept of sovereign immunity arises from English law where the traditional immunity of the English king is expressed in the phrase, "The king can do no wrong."[8] This meant the king was immune from any legal prosecution because of his special status. Sovereign immunity as expressed in its original form, however, has been severely restricted in the United States in the last century. According to Gorton, sovereign immunity retains its original scope and extent only in connection with Indian tribes in the United States.[9]

Ron Allen, president of the National Congress of American Indians, outlined the need for sovereign immunity among tribes at a Senate hearing in 1996.

> The notion that tribal immunity ought to be waived contradicts and works against the well-settled federal principle of encouraging business and economic development on Indian lands. Since the dawning of the Era of Self-Determination with President Nixon in 1970, a number of federal initiatives have attempted to foster development in Indian Country.[10]

Marge Anderson of the Mille Lacs Band of Chippewa in Minnesota charged that sovereign immunity was an inherent right of tribes.

> It is my view that sovereign immunity is one of the most fundamental aspects of the sovereign status of any governmental

entity. Sovereign immunity precludes tribal governments, like state governments and the federal government, from being subjected to frivolous, time-consuming lawsuits. Sovereign immunity protects tribal assets from the perils of the many entities who seek to attack and impoverish tribal governments.[11]

Echoing Ron Allen, Anderson then traces the current ethnic sovereignty of tribes, euphemistically called the "Era of Self Determination," to Nixon. Perhaps a more accurate term would be the Era of Ethnic Sovereign Segregation. As a result of this change in the status of Indian tribes, the injury claims of Jill Gavle and Sylvia Cohen could be reduced to the status of "frivolous, time-consuming lawsuits" by a tribal band that pays $50,000 in casino profits to each adult member per month.

The Mashantucket Pequot Tribe of Connecticut is another extremely wealthy tribe that uses sovereign immunity as would the kings of England. Their reservation is in eastern Connecticut, not far from Long Island Sound and the Rhode Island border. Until 1983, the tribe was not recognized by the federal government. In 1637, the Pequots were defeated by the Massachusetts Bay Colony and gradually began to disperse and intermarry with the Connecticut population of Whites and Blacks. By the 1850s, the reservation had been reduced to a few acres. In 1900, there were about two dozen tribal members in a single family still associated with the reservation, and by 1930 only two Indian women still lived on the reservation. The resurrection of the tribe began in 1975 when Richard "Skip" Hayward became chairman of the tribe. Hayward tracked down relatives from as far as Michigan and Florida and began a 10-year legal battle to get the tribe federally recognized. In gaining recognition, the tribe was awarded $900,000 for lost lands.[12]

Generations of inter-racial marriages had thinned the tribe's pure heritage considerably. Nonetheless, tribal members have arbitrarily designated their late 19th century ancestors as "full blood for the purpose of enrollment."[13] Today, the extended tribal family numbers about 500. The reservation's culture revolves around one of the largest casinos in the world. Near the casino are three small towns, Ledyard,

North Stonington, and Preston, with a combined population of about 25,000. These non-Indians now find themselves totally dominated by the casino culture of the Pequots, who have parlayed a few acres 60 years ago into a reservation now comprising 2,210 acres, with an additional 4,500 acres under tribal control in the surrounding area. The tribe has become the dominant economic force and by far the largest landowner in the region, which has dramatically changed the social, economic and environmental character of the area, according to the mayors of the three towns near the casino.[14] Estimates of the annual revenue for the casino are now over $1.3 billion, with profits in excess of $300 million. Besides gaming, the tribe has interests in resorts, pharmaceuticals and shipbuilding, and the tribe intends to buy more land to engage in more business ventures with future casino profits.

The casino is open 365 days a year and on a typical summer weekend attracts about 60,000 gamblers. The area of the casino is 7.6 acres, with 4,000 slot machines (if placed in a row they would stretch about a mile and a half), a 24-hour poker room and a bingo hall as large as a football field seating 3,100 players. Tribal finances can only be estimated, since the tribe is exempt from federal and state taxes. When the tribe initially petitioned for a casino, Connecticut Governor Lowell Weicker seriously objected. His objections were appeased by a tribal promise to contribute a fixed percentage of profits to state government. Recently, the tribal contribution to the state was about $130 million. In July of 1996, the take from slot machines alone exceeded $60 million.[15]

For its members, the tribe provides housing, full medical insurance, a wide range of public services, and scholarships that provide for education to the Ph.D. level. The tribe also guarantees all of its members a job. An annual Indian dance powwow is held with prizes totaling $500,000 for the competition.[16] The casino also is one of the largest employers in the state, with 9,000 employees in mostly low-skill, low-wage jobs. Only a few of the employees are from the tribe. The gambling revenues of the Pequot Tribe represent about 15 percent of all money taken in by tribal casinos in the United States.[17] Because we allow gambling monopolies based on ethnic heritage, 500 American citizens in Connecticut collect almost one-sixth of all Indian gaming revenues.

Given the excellent state of economic affairs on the Mashantucket Pequot Reservation, how does this "sovereign nation" interact with other Americans? The tribe hired its own attorneys and judges to form its tribal legal system. Tribal courts have jurisdiction over all accidents, injuries and civil disputes on the reservation except inside the casino, where state police jurisdiction is granted to prevent infiltration of organized crime. There are no juries in the Pequot tribal court system, giving judges unprecedented power. According to tribal law, labor unions are not allowed, and labor disputes cannot be sent to state or federal courts. Author Fergus Bordewich correctly points out that such an arrangement makes the tribe "simultaneously employer, judge, and jury."[18]

The towns face a number of problems created by the Pequot Tribe, its reservation and the casino. The tribe lacks a comprehensive environmental plan for development as required by the Environmental Protection Agency. The tribe also is able to buy and convert land to trust status, including lands not designated as reservation land, thereby exempting such lands from paying local property taxes that municipalities depend on to provide local services. What's more, the tribe has claimed that certain city zoning restrictions cannot be enforced on the reservation. Finally, sovereign immunity is used not only to shield the tribe and its members from liability, but is used to protect those firms which contract services for the tribe. When a person was injured on a casino commuter bus, the tribe claimed sovereign immunity, a defense that could also have been raised by the tribe's non-Indian owned insurance company.

In testimony to the U.S. Senate, the mayor of a town near the Pequot Reservation asked, "What good is such insurance to injured parties if the tribe's sovereign immunity will be used, even by third parties, to bar such claims?"[19] Tribal immunity from taxation has also been used by non-Indian corporations. In one instance, a high-tech company claimed tax exempt status on property it leased to the Pequot Tribe because the equipment was located on Indian lands. When the non-Indian owned corporation was taken to court, it used the claim of sovereign immunity as a defense.[20]

The use of sovereign immunity as a defense has also been used for incidents occurring off the reservation. In 1994, an employee of the tribe's Foxwoods Casino was injured in the casino parking lot, which is not on reservation land. The tribe was able to defeat the woman's claim using sovereign immunity as the defense. The court ruled that "the tribe's immunity from suit extends to commercial activities occurring off the reservation."[21] Such protections make the Pequot Tribe virtually exempt from all social, economic and other community responsibilities.

One of the Foxwood-area mayors told the Senate, "We fail to see how stopping a Tribe from conducting a legal wrong or compensating an injured party 'undermines Indian self-government and self-sufficiency.' To the contrary, we believe a fundamental attribute of sovereignty is for the government entity involved to live up to its obligations and defend its actions on the merits, not hide from them."[22]

Stories like that of the Mashantucket Pequot are not isolated to affluent areas on the eastern seaboard, but happen wherever ethnic sovereignty is practiced. On June 8, 1997, I attended a conference of the Citizens Equal Rights Alliance (CERA) in Washington D.C. One of the conference speakers was Verna Lawrence, a Native American who is a commissioner for the city of Sault Ste. Marie, Michigan. Lawrence discussed conflicts occurring between the city and the local Chippewa tribe. At the conference, she presented a position paper from Mayor Bill Lynn concerning a controversy over tribal land in the city that Indians wanted to convert to trust land status. If Indians were successful, the city would lose jurisdiction for police, zoning, and building code enforcement on the land in question, and forfeit all future property taxes generated by commercial or residential property.

In 1974, the Sault Ste. Marie Tribe of Chippewa Indians petitioned the Secretary of the Interior to place 76.5 acres of land within the city in trust land status. In 1985, the tribe opened a casino on the land. It negotiated fee-for-service agreements with the city, but the agreements are non-binding and the tribe can back out of them at any time. The success of its casino allowed the tribe to buy more land in 1996, nearly tripling its property holdings within the city to 210 acres, worth more than $20 million. The tribe is now trying to get trust status for nearly 500 acres more, which the Department of the Interior can grant without the consent of the city. The additional lands would mean more than a square mile of city land would be in trust and free from zoning or building codes. Service payments on the new trust land is currently voluntary, so a change in leadership in the tribe might result in a decision not to pay for city services such as police, fire, sewer and water.

The Sault Ste. Marie Chippewa are currently in the process of acquiring property 350 miles away in Detroit, Michigan and converting it to trust status for additional casino ventures.[23] They aren't the only tribe with large amounts of land in trust status. The Apache Indians may have the record for trust lands in the United States, holding approximately 20 million acres in 3 states, an area larger than the state of West Virginia.[24] While this might seem innocuous to some, it demonstrates a dangerous trend, namely that tribes could conceivably purchase land in any area of the United States and create a tax and zoning-free mecca for business ventures. Such schemes go far beyond the goal of preserving the traditional culture of Indian tribes. Sovereignty, in this case, is being used to capture economic and competitive advantages for Indian businesses. Allowing tribes to pay for services on a voluntary basis puts the tribe in an unfair bargaining position with the city, which has to provide services for trust lands whether they are paid for or not.

Waivers of sovereign immunity are sometimes used by tribes as a bargaining tactic to get concessions from towns, investors or the government. When the Mashantucket Pequot Tribe wanted to secure financing for its casino from outside investors, it waived its sovereign immunity. To transfer off-reservation land into trust status, the tribe agreed to a limited waiver of immunity in order to get approval from the Department of the Interior. According to Senate testimony by three government officials from the Ledyard (Connecticut) area, the Mashantucket Tribe only agrees to waivers of immunity when its self-interest is strong enough. "The tribe's dominant political and economic position," they wrote, "give it very little motivation to compromise on such issues, and as a result non-Indian entities negotiating with the tribe are frequently presented with a take it or leave it position on the sovereign immunity issue."[25]

In 1995, the Shakopee Mdewakanton Sioux petitioned the

Bureau of Indian Affairs to place 590 acres of land into trust in Scott County, Minnesota. Tribal Chairman Stanley Crooks submitted a letter to the Shakopee newspaper to assure people that the tribe would pay its share of public costs associated with development.[26] However, when Scott County asked the tribe to pay the $2.3 million dollar yearly costs for public services associated with the tribe's existing Mystic Lake Casino, the tribe refused. Negotiations broke down in January of 1997. The county commissioners finally settled for a payment of $200,000 per year in June of 1997, after concluding they had little leverage to make a better deal.[27]

Even when tribes agree to waive sovereign immunity, there is no guarantee they will honor that commitment. In February 1997, a decision was handed down by the Minnesota Court of Appeals on a dispute between Granite Valley Hotel and Jackpot Junction Bingo and Casino located in Morton, Minnesota. Jackpot Junction is owned by the Lower Sioux Indian Community. The town of Morton is less than two miles from the Birch Coulee battlefield of the 1862 Sioux Uprising, and about thirty-five miles northeast of Walnut Grove where Plum Creek flows past the site of Laura Ingalls Wilder's little house on the prairie. This is an area of small towns and mid-sized farms, too far from any large metropolitan area to support more than a modest casino and hotel. A representative of the tribe signed a contract between the casino and Granite Valley Hotel for the mutual benefit of the local tribe and the non-Indian owners of the hotel. The hotel would attract patrons to the casino, increasing profits, and the hotel would in turn have a guarantee of enough customers to survive as a business. The casino agreed that "if the agreed-upon occupancy percentage was not satisfied, Jackpot Junction was obligated to pay Granite Valley an amount equal to the charter rates for the balance of the unsold rooms." Granite Valley required "safeguards in the form of contract provisions waiving sovereign immunity and consenting to jurisdiction of Minnesota courts."[28]   After several years of successful cooperation with the Granite Falls Hotel, the tribe decided to revoke the original contract with the Granite Valley Hotel and build their own hotel. Their defense? Sovereign immunity. In this case, "sovereign immunity" could be defined as cold-blooded greed. Arbitrary abuse like that of Jackpot

Junction makes non-Indian enterprises wary of doing business with Indian tribes because of the legal uncertainties associated with sovereign immunity.

At the Senate hearings on sovereign immunity, an attorney who has participated in about 35 cases involving tribal law had this to say about sovereign immunity: "When tribes act more like gangs than governments, there must be a remedy. An unexpected secondary effect is that persons and companies which could do business adding to reservation economic development choose not to do so."[29]

Friendly Courts

As stated previously, federal and state governments in the United States are designed to prevent any ethnic, religious, political or socioeconomic group from gaining coercive power over others. The Bill of Rights and U.S. Constitution apply equally to every state. All state court systems must meet federal standards. We also have separation of powers between the executive, judicial and legislative branches of government.

Indian tribes seemingly have a very different goal in mind, one that is arguably less noble. Instead of striving for fairness and justice, tribal courts are pervaded by ethnic bias that enhances the power of a tribe over non-Indians and forwards their mission of segregation to preserve Indian identity and culture.

Judge R. A. Randall of the Minnesota Court of Appeals made a careful analysis of the Indian judicial system in the Jackpot Junction/Granite Valley Hotel decision.

Evidence is accumulating that the fairly recent creation of tribal courts in Minnesota may be part of a calculated plan by tribal governments and their advisors to create a totally controlled in-house court system to shield themselves from lawsuits and accountability in state district court where the mandates of state and federal constitutions apply.

Randall notes that the Lower Sioux Indian Community created its court system the same year it built its own motel.

> Appellant's (Sioux) decision to breach the contract was the product of pure opportunism and not the product of any 'cultural decision' to have its own motel. At the same time its own hotel was constructed, appellant instituted its own tribal court that would be a friendly forum for appellant, which is perhaps more than a coincidence.[30]

Randall points out that the Sioux constitution and judicial code have no checks and balances, allowing the Reservation Business Council (the equivalent of a city council) to maintain "absolute control over the qualifications, appointments, salaries, and hiring and firing of those who serve as tribal judges."[31] Even though this person possesses authority over Minnesota Indians and non-Indians alike, a judge for the tribe can be a non-lawyer and exempt from state laws overseeing judicial appointments, qualifications and code of ethics used for other state judges. In fact, Randall notes, it would be possible for all three Lower Sioux judges to have a criminal record and no state-recognized legal training. In Minnesota, there are 11 recognized tribes, each of which claims to be sovereign and thus able to develop its own legal system, rules and constitution. "So far," Judge Randall asserts, "we have not seen fit to require tribal governments to abide by the United States Constitution, its Bill of Rights or individual state constitutions. This is both morally and legally inexcusable, as it is a race-based distinction — not helping a race, but killing a race."[32]

Protections and rights we take for granted in the U.S. court system are often lacking in tribal courts. In one example, tribal judges were given the right to overturn jury decisions without providing any explanation. Ordinance 407.115 of the Red Lake Indian Reservation in Minnesota states, "The judge in a criminal case may render a verdict contrary to that reached by the jury." With the ability to arbitrarily overturn a guilty or not guilty verdict, the ordinance reduces the jury process to irrelevancy.

Here we see how the fuzzy, quasi-sovereign status of Indians actually fails to protect even the civil rights of Indians living on the reservation. Tribal court ordinances giving judges free reign over final verdicts are a violation of the 4th and 6th Amendments of the U.S. Constitution, and also are illegal under the Indian Civil Rights Act of 1968. All of these laws guarantee "due process of law," including the right to a trial by a jury of peers, with the assumption that the jury holds ultimate power over final decisions.

In a case on the Red Lake Reservation in January of 1996, Chief Magistrate Wanda Lyons overturned a jury verdict of not guilty against Ronald Smith, a Native American who had been charged with possession of marijuana. Citing Ordinance 407.115 of Red Lake tribal law, Lyons sentenced Smith to a 150-day sentence in the reservation jail. Judge Randall, who has practiced law for 30 years, says this about the Smith ruling:

> It is the worst case of abuse of judicial process, and abuse of a state citizen, that I have ever seen...I have no knowledge that even in any part of the deep South between the Emancipation Proclamation in 1863 and Brown v. the Board of Education that any sitting judge, trial or appellate, claimed the right in a criminal case to take a verdict of not guilty away from the jury, convict the defendant, and sentence him to prison.[33]

Randall's analysis stands in marked contrast to the address given by Supreme Court Justice Sandra Day O'Connor at the Indian Sovereignty Symposium in Tulsa, Oklahoma, on June 4, 1996. Her speech is titled "Lessons from the Third Sovereign, Indian Tribal Courts." Consider this section:

> To fulfill their role as an essential branch of tribal government, the tribal courts must provide a forum that commands the respect of both the tribal community and the non-tribal courts, governments, and litigants. To do so, these courts need to be perceived as both fair and principled. And at the same time the courts seek to satisfy these conditions, they strive to embody tribal values — values that, at times, suggest the use of differ-

ent methods than those used in the Anglo-American, adversarial, common-law tradition.[34]

O'Connor goes so far as to say that our own U.S. court system could learn something from such "flexibility" in tribal justice.

The development of different methods of solving disputes in tribal legal systems provides the tribal courts with a way both to incorporate traditional values and to hold up an example to the nation about the possibilities of alternative dispute resolution. New methods have much to offer to the tribal communities, and much to teach the other court systems operating in the United States. For about the last fifteen years, in recognition of the plain fact that the adversarial process is often not the best means to a fair outcome, both the State and Federal systems have turned with increasing interest to the possibilities offered by mediation, arbitration, and other forms of alternate dispute resolution. In many situations, alternative methods offer quicker, more personal, and more efficient ways of arriving at an answer to the parties' difficulties.[35]

Indeed, alternative forms of dispute resolution used by tribes can be, as Justice O'Connor claims, quicker and more efficient. Doing away with juries and the due process of law saves time and money, although it might "conveniently" railroad justice for innocent people along the way or fall prey to corruption, undermining the basic civil rights of Indians and non-Indians. Claims of sovereign immunity can also go a long way in reducing the number of "frivolous" and "time consuming" lawsuits tribes have to contend with, regardless of whether such cases actually have legal merit. Under tribal law, "legal merit" is conveniently and sometimes arbitrary determined by the tribe, instead of by those whose rights have been violated.

All of this is teaching the American people and the American courts much about the benefits of ethnic sovereignty. The most important fact we should learn is that race-based courts are not only a legal and moral disaster for people who aren't members of a tribe, but even for those who are. As Judge Randall points out, tribal governments who ignore basic American rights are not helping a race, but killing a race. In the unlikely event that an Indian casino stool collapses under Justice O'Connor, I think she would come to the same conclusion. Until then, we can only assume it's difficult to see all the way to Indian Country from the lofty perch of a Supreme Court bench.

The "alternative dispute resolution" about which Justice O'Connor speaks is used by some Minnesota tribes in family law disputes. Rather than allowing a person to bring a self-selected attorney to court, these tribes require you to use a "court appointed advocate" who is selected by the tribe. These advocates are under the complete control of the tribe which sets standards of qualification. The advocate is paid by the tribe and can be fired at will. In a recent case in Minnesota, a non-Indian woman filed for divorce from an enrolled member of a tribe. The woman sued for divorce in state court and her spouse did the same in tribal court. The tribe obtained jurisdiction and forced the woman to go to court with an Indian court-appointed advocate rather than the attorney of her choice. The tribal court granted joint custody and visitation rights, but as Judge Randall notes, "She and others similarly situated have faced severe obstacles getting visitation and in the collection of child support from the on reservation obligors."[36]

Few people in the United States realize the extent to which basic American rights have been erased on many Indian reservations. In his Jackpot Junction opinion, Judge Randall lists the legal deficiencies that apply to many Minnesota reservations.

There is no guarantee that the Minnesota Constitution, the United States Constitution and its precious Bill of Rights will control. There are no guarantees that Civil Rights Acts, federal or state legislation against age discrimination, gender discrimination, etc. will be honored. There are no guarantees of the Veteran's Preference Act, no civil service classification to protect tribal government employees, no guarantees of OSHA, no guarantees of the American with Disabilities Act (1990), no guarantees of the right to unionize, no right to Minnesota's teacher tenure laws, no right to the benefit of federal and state "whistleblower" statutes, no guarantees against blatant nepotism, no guarantees of a fair and orderly process concerning access to reservation housing, and no freedom of the press and no freedom of speech. In other words, all the basic human rights we take for granted, that allow us to live in dignity with our neighbors, are not guaranteed on Indian reservations under the present version of sovereignty....The recent flow of Minnesota cases, trial and appellate, have nothing to do with cultural preservation. They have to do only with money and a tribal government's continued insistence on the right to be unaccountable to anyone, Indian or non-Indian, in any state court, unless they choose to go to state court. Otherwise they try to force parties into their own hired tribal courts.[37]

The "lethal flaw" that Judge Randall finds in tribal courts is the lack of independence between tribal judges and the executive and legislative officials on reservations. The people who run reservations — reservation boards, community committees, and reservation business committees — have complete power to appoint, hire or fire judges. Tribal court judges are appointed for a fixed term on paper, but there are no constitutional obstacles preventing the arbitrary dismissal of tribal judges in mid-term. As a result, conflicts of interest abound in the tribal justice system.

In a recent Minnesota case, a tribal judge found irregularities in a tribal election and allowed the political candidates who lost to get a hearing and begin an investigation for election fraud. The elected tribal officials, according to Randall, appealed the ruling to an Indian appellate court, and that court agreed with the tribal judge. At that point, the reservation business committee simply fired the tribal judge.[38]

But all differences of structure and procedure aside, tribal courts are based on a fundamental premise expressly avoided by the U.S. court system — the need for race-based justice. In an opinion on the Sylvia Cohen injury case, Judge Randall warns of the dangers of setting up race-based courts. He correctly points out that many areas of the country have high concentrations of African-Americans, Hispanics, and Asian Americans (e.g., the Chinatowns of San Francisco and New York), yet the idea of a separate system of courts based on race or ethnicity for such areas seems ludicrous.

> Why do we not have 'African-American courts,' 'Hispanic courts,' 'Chinese courts,' or 'Korean courts?' Why do we not have special court systems in those areas where outsiders, that is, nonresidents, do not have automatic access to that state's district court system for redress of wrongs, but must first submit their claim to a local or ethnic court? I suggest that if we tried to establish 'racially based courts,' the constitutional issue of the denial of due process issue, the race-related and race-baiting issues, and the ill-will and divisiveness that would follow would serve to overcome us as a country.

> We try to go out of our way in Minnesota, and hopefully other states in the federal court system do as well, to ensure equal access and fair treatment to all people, whether plaintiffs or defendants, of any race, color, creed or ethnic origin. Why here, are we tolerating segregating out the American Indians by race and allowing them to maintain a parallel court system and further, subjecting non-Indians to it? To me, this is red apartheid.

Most disturbing and bewildering — even fascinating in a darker sense — is our utter failure to apply the historical lessons of Black segregation and Jim Crow laws to our dealings with Indians. The origin of Jim Crow laws in the South dates from 1887, when Tennessee and Florida passed laws segregating railroad coaches into cars for Blacks and Whites. Texas passed similar laws in 1889 and Louisiana in 1890. These laws were tested before the Supreme Court in 1896 in *Plessy v. Ferguson*, which established the principle that segregation was legal as long as the accommodations for each race were equal. According to the court, this did not constitute a violation of the 14th Amendment which guarantees equal protection under the law.[39] This decision led to other forms of discrimination, including separate schools, and "colored" sections in restaurants, bathrooms and busses. It also reinforced the idea that towns could have districts for particular races where other groups were not welcome.

Jim Crow segregation was the law of the land until 1954, when *Brown v. the Board of Education* reversed the "separate but equal" doctrine of *Plessy v. Ferguson*. The Brown case dealt specifically with segregation in schools, and the court unanimously ruled separate schools for African-Americans *were* a violation of the 14th Amendment. In spite of the ruling, the Alabama Senate passed a "nullification" resolution in defiance of the court in 1956, and the Virginia legislature asserted its right to "interpose its sovereignty" against the desegregation ruling. In March of 1956, one hundred Congressmen issued a "Southern Manifesto" vowing to use every lawful means to bring back segregation. In 1958, the Court clarified the matter in *Cooper v. Aaron*, and declared that when a state managed a school system, no form of segregation could be allowed.[40]

In the United States, we experienced legalized slavery from 1776 to 1865 until the 13th Amendment finally abolished it. In 1868, the 14th Amendment was ratified, guaranteeing citizenship for all persons born or naturalized in the United States and granting them equal protection under the law. In violation of this amendment, however, citizenship was not given to all Indians until 1924, and African-Americans were segregated until the *Brown* decision in 1954. Despite these lessons, the Supreme Court continues to support the re-segregation of American Indians. It took America almost 90 years after its birth to abolish slavery, and almost a century more to finally provide African-Americans with rights truly equal with mainstream White America. For Indians, however, the U.S. has supported segregation for well over 200 years. Yet, we continue to wonder why, of all minorities, Indians have the worst problems, especially on segregated reservations.

Red Supremacy and Tribal Homelands

Two fundamental goals define the Indian sovereignty movement, one legal in nature, the other territorial and geographical in nature. The first goal is to create exclusive governmental power just for Indian tribes, equal in authority to that of federal and state government. A second goal is to reclaim Indian lands "lost" or "taken" by early settlers and subsequent U.S. governments. Particularly prominent today is the push to return all land within reservations to tribal ownership. At the present time, most reservations contain what is called "checkerboard" land, or land owned by non-Indians interspersed with that controlled by tribes. On many reservations, more than half of the landowners are non-Indians. Nationally, about 500,000 non-Indian Americans own land on reservations.[41]

Indians would like to regain ownership of all land in reservations so they might create a geographically specific, Indian-only enclave — tribal homelands, if you will. What's more, Indians also want to increase the size of reservations to encompass lands that Indians controlled in the 18th and 19th centuries. Ron Allen, president of the National Congress of American Indians, told the U.S. Senate:

The fact that we have checkerboard reservations is not the fault of the Indian people. It is the fault of the Federal policies, the gyrations of the Federal policies in their attempt to take over Indian land, Indian resources, to dominate the Indian people, from the very beginning....We currently only own, still, 4 percent of the land in this nation. Is the issue that they (Indians) really want more than 4 percent, or should we be moving toward providing the tribes the opportunity to reacquire the fee patent lands (non-Indian owned) within the reservation boundaries to help resolve some of those problems....So we are here to help, we're here to make sure that the picture is clear, it's crisp and you understand the truth. The notion that our sovereignty, our governments are an anachronism is the reverse really of what the situation is. The anachronism is to go back to any notions of termination or assimilation. The true solution here is to strengthen the tribal governments so we can co-exist in a very meaningful way, to the benefit of everybody, including our people.[42]

Allen makes it clear Indians do not want to assimilate with other Americans, but rather "co-exist" without fear of termination. In his testimony before the Senate committee, Allen held up the Lummi Tribe near Bellingham, Washington as one of the tribes reflecting "the theme of the NCIA convention…that we're standing our ground. We're not going to back off."[43]

The Lummi Tribe found out they could "stand their ground" in 1974, when Judge George Boldt handed down a fishing decision which gave Lummi Indians rights to half of the fish resources, basing the court decision on anachronistic treaties. Once these treaties are held to be superior to the U.S. Constitution, the concept of sovereignty soon leads to trouble. Since the 1974 fishing decision, the Lummi Tribe has come into serious conflict with non-Indian landowners living on the reservation. They have gone from a desire to "co-exist" to a *demand* for Indian-only living areas. The Lummi Indian Business Council submitted a lengthy statement to the Senate committee on Indian sovereignty explaining the position of the tribe. The Lummi Tribe does not want to "co-exist," they want to be isolated and free from any "co-existing" with Whites on their land. Regarding reservation lands they said:

> The Lummi Nation recognizes that increased numbers of non-members on the reservation have led to jurisdictional conflicts over water and land use. In addition, like most Indian governments, we make no secret of our intent to purchase reservation fee lands taken or sold in violation of our treaty, *in order to fulfill the treaty intent of a tribal homeland.* The tribe has purchased hundreds of acres of reservation land in the past 20 years, and in every case we have paid fair market value or above. Our land acquisition program is openly discussed as a long-term solution to the need for reservation land for homes for our people (emphasis added).[44]

The racist nature of Indian treaties is openly defined in the

Lummi testimony. The language of many treaties dramatically reveals the intent to form racially segregated tribal homelands. The treaty below was given to the Senate committee as proof that racially pure lands were promised under past treaty agreements:

TREATY WITH THE SAUK AND FOXES, 1804

Article 1. The United States receive the united Sac and Fox tribes into their friendship and protection, and the said tribes agree to consider themselves under the protection of the United States, and of no other power whatsoever.

Article 4. The United States will never interrupt the said tribes in the possession of the lands which they rightfully claim, but will on the contrary protect them in the quiet enjoyment of the same against their own citizens and against all other white persons who may intrude upon them. And the said tribes do hereby engage that they will never sell their lands or any part thereof to any sovereign power, but the United States, not to the citizens or subjects of any other sovereign power, nor to the citizens of the United States.

Article 6. If any citizen of the United States or other white person should form a settlement upon lands which are the property of the Sac and Fox tribes, upon complaint being made thereof to the superintendent or other person having charge of the affairs of Indians, such intruder shall forthwith be removed.[45]

While to some this may seem like a reasonable goal for Indians, accomplishing that goal has resulted in pressures on non-Indians to sell their land by denying them water on their land and regulating and taxing them without representation in government. Let me remind the reader that when the Dawes Act (described in detail in chapter four) allocated reservation land to individual Indians, Indians often sold their land to non-Indians after homesteading it for 25 years, thus creating "checkerboard' landscape on the reservations. This land has since been bought and sold for generations without restrictions. Sales were legal and land was not stolen. But the current owners nonetheless find themselves in a tremendous bind.

Tribes have openly and repeatedly stated their desire to remove non-Indians from reservation lands, and to claim the right to govern, tax, and regulate non-Indians on reservations without giving them any voice in the government. For example, the Confederated Tribes of the Warm Springs Reservation in Oregon issued a proclamation in 1992 stating, "We declare the existence of this inherent sovereign authority — the absolute right to govern, to determine our destiny, and to control all persons, land, water, resources, and activities, free from all outside interference — throughout our homeland and over all our rights, property, and people, wherever located."[46]

Indians are forthright in their assertion that treaties give them license to form racially pure homelands. Lummi Tribal Chairman Henry Cagey gave a radio interview on Bellingham (Washington) radio station KGMI, on August 11, 1995, with talk show host Jeff Kent. Here is a transcript from that program:

Cagey - *What I've got to worry about, Jeff, we got over 4,000 members down here on Lummi.*

Kent - Are they all living on the reservation?

Cagey - *They would like to. They would like to eventually, and like I said, we are going to be there for generations. And I've got three girls myself and they eventually are gonna want to have their own families and their own homes. Hopefully, on the reservation.*

Kent - Well, and I've seen some papers recently that indicate that that is a concern, of course, of the Lummi Nation, that there is actually physical room for Lummi people to be able to live and expand and develop and so forth. Is it possible that the properties out on Sandy Point (non-Indian owned) are something that the Lummi Nation would like to get back? Certainly the documents I've seen indicate that. And that they'd like to secure that land back in order to present it to the future generations of Lummi people.

Cagey - *That's right.*

Kent - And is there any truth then to the fear then that this water dispute, the utility disputes, etc. etc., are merely a mechanism to try and pressure non-tribal members to either sell that property or to lose that property?

Cagey - *That's something that might be a last resort here to do. If we're pushed to a corner here, we're going to have to do something real drastic here, and we may launch a land claims settlement.*[47]

For the 600 non-Indians who live on the Lummi Reservation, the meaning of Indian control and jurisdiction over reservation resources is as clear as water. These people live in a development called Sandy Point. Their water supply was threatened when the tribe drilled a well 40 feet deeper and less than 100 feet away from the Sandy Point supply well. According to Whatcom County Council member Marlene Dawson, the tribe did not have a state permit to drill so close to the other well and had land 1,000 feet away that could have been used to erect a well and avoid interference.[48] The illegal well was used to supply water for a fish hatchery. Although reports state that the fish hatchery should require less than 80 gallons per minute, the Indian well had a pump capable of producing 300 gallons per minute (432,000 gallons per day) and was run for as much as 22 hours a day.[49] A television report on KVOS-TV reported that by the spring of 1995, excessive pumping had caused the residential water supply to run dangerously low, and Sandy Point residents were told their well was running dry. The nearby city of Ferndale expressed willingness to supply city water if the tribe would allow it, but the tribe refused.   Tribal Chairman Henry Cagey said, "It's not okay with us, as far as we're concerned right now, any water coming to the reservation belongs to the tribe and we've maintained we're the sole purveyor on that reservation. Any water that does come in belongs to the tribe."[50]

In 1990, non-Indian property owner Paul Jones tried to build homes on reservation property he bought in 1983. The Lummi Indian Business Council denied him the right to develop lots that would use reservation groundwater.[51] Availability of alternate water sources is not a problem on the Lummi Reservation — at least not for Indians. In 1990, the Lummi Tribe contracted with the city of Bellingham to provide up to one million gallons per day of city water to the reservation. As of 1995, the tribe was using only 127,000 gallons per day of city water (less than 13 percent of the contract's capacity), leaving a significant amount unused despite documented needs by non-Indians.[52] Early evidence of this no-growth hostility toward non-Indians can be found in a document on water resources from a 1981 Lummi Indian Business Council document which states, "Another goal is to minimize growth of non-Indian land ownership and residence on the reservation. In theory, utility extensions can be used as a method of growth control."[53]

Albert Sperry found this out the hard way after buying land on the Lummi Reservation in 1988. A tribal representative told Sperry he could have water when he retired in 1992. In 1992, Vern Johnson, the tribal member in charge of the reservation water district, said there was a "little problem" with the water and it would take another year. In 1993, Sperry received a letter from Henry Cagey that said it would take another year to complete a "water survey" to find out how much water they could give out. According to written Senate testimony, Cagey sent a letter to Sperry in May of 1994 quoting Lummi Council Resolution # 90-108, "that the Lummi Indian Reservation has no surplus water for additional non-Indian development, and that all water present on the Lummi Indian Reservation is subject to the sole regulatory authority of the Lummi Indian Reservation."[54]

Sperry could not get water even though Lummi Indians had about 875,000 gallons of excess daily water capacity through its contract with the city of Bellingham. In his last communication with Cagey, Sperry said, "He told me that the only way I'd *ever* get water out there would be to give the land back to the Indians and lease it, or sell it to an Indian and lease it."[55]

Non-Indian residents of Sandy Point also have to deal with taxation without representation. The Lummi Tribe puts a tax on non-Indian utility bills from public utilities located off the reservation. The utility lines are not on reservation land, but on county roads and easements that are not under tribal jurisdiction.[56] Yet, the tribe adds a tax to every non-Indian's utility bill. What's more, the tax goes to pay for "needed and desired services to the Lummi tribal members and the reservation community."[57]

A letter from Cagey to the Senate Committee on Sovereign Immunity shows the extent to which Indian leaders try to make sovereignty an after-the-fact reality. He proposes that non-Indian residents of the reservation have a relationship with Indian residents which is similar to the relationship between residents of two foreign countries.

Tribal members, fee land owners, neighbors, and any interested party have the ability and right to present their case and seek protection of property rights through the tribal appeal system. The fact that only enrolled Lummi Tribal members are eligible to vote in Tribal elections has no bearing on this issue on land use jurisdiction. Canadian citizens who own property in Whatcom County (Washington) are not eligible to vote in County elections just as U.S. citizens are not eligible to vote in Canadian elections, even if they own land and live in British Columbia. The fact that all residents of the Reservation have the right and ability to influence land use decisions through established legal process sufficiently protects their legitimate property rights.[58]

Those who see great virtue in Indian declarations of sovereignty would do well to carefully consider the implications of Cagey's analogy. As one of the most respected Indian leaders in America today, Cagey's Senate testimony has great credibility. As is clear from the testimony, Indian leaders increasingly see themselves as the rulers of foreign countries, subject not to the U.S. Constitution, but still eligible for the monetary benefits of U.S. citizenship — what is often referred to as "foreign aid" or "rent" by Indian leaders.[59]

Jessie Taken Alive, the tribal chairman of the Standing Rock Sioux Tribe in South Dakota, believes that non-Indians can be assured of fair treatment where Indians have full jurisdiction. "It is simply not the case that non-Indians need to be provided with access to state or federal courts to address claims that arise on the reservation. The Tribal Court treats Indians and non-Indians alike in an evenhanded and fair manner."[60] Not everyone agrees, however.

A common service provided in South Dakota is custom wheat harvesting where combine operators contract to harvest crops. In dealing with a tribal farm corporation, one harvester negotiated a bid of about $15,000. When the job was done and the harvester went for payment, the tribe told him, "Here's $5,000. Take it or leave it. You can't sue us."[61]

In April of 1992, Lisa Hanson contracted with the Yankton Sioux Tribe to provide transportation services for the Fort Randall Casino. She was to be paid $15 per person for a round trip. When her contract was terminated in January of 1993, the tribe owed her $41,566. When she brought suit in state court, the tribe claimed sovereign immunity. Craig Katt had a similar experience. He contracted with the same tribe to book live entertainment for the casino at a 10 percent commission. After booking acts which cost the casino $504,250, he was denied his fee of $50,425. Katt's claim was dismissed in January of 1994 when the tribe claimed sovereign immunity.[62]

While some tribal court judges have ruled to actively enforce civil rights laws on reservations, tribes in South Dakota have often removed these judges from office, according to Lawrence Long, assistant deputy attorney general of South Dakota, who testified at Senate hearings. At the Rosebud Sioux Reservation, Tribal Judge Trudell Guerue placed a temporary restraining order on a tribal election the day before the polls were to open, but he was fired on election day so the election could proceed in spite of the judicial action. Judges for the Sisseton Wahpeton Sioux Tribal Court issued several decisions enforcing the Indian Civil Rights Act against actions of tribal officials in the late 1980s. The tribe subsequently dissolved the tribal court and reorganized it in a way that disqualified the judges. In 1983, Tribal Judge Matthews strongly enforced the Indian Civil Rights Act against the Oglala Sioux Tribe, but he is no longer a judge on that reservation. According to Long, "Tribal judges and tribal courts exist only at the pleasure of the tribal council. Attempts by tribal judiciary, absent assistance of the federal courts or Congress, to enforce the Indian Civil Rights Act and similar claims are simply unrealistic."[63]

Daryl Smith, a non-Indian, is a rancher who owns land near Mobridge, South Dakota, on the Standing Rock Sioux Reservation. Smith pays tribal taxes that Indians themselves are exempt from. Not surprisingly, Smith feels he has little recourse in dealing with civil rights abuses:

What if the position of Indians and non-Indians were exactly reversed on reservations. Suppose tribes were governed exclusively by Whites. Imagine that they excluded non-Whites from participation in their government while they taxed, licensed and regulated them, often discriminately. Suppose these same Whites could participate in local government, while being excluded from many of the taxes and ordinances of that same government. If this were the case, how long would you tolerate the situation? Sometimes basic, subtle, symbolic words can teach us much. You have invited me to represent testimony about how tribal sovereignty impacts non-Indians. In presenting my testimony I have used that same term — non-Indians. It speaks volumes about our position on reservations. How would others like to be classified as non-Whites? The use of the term non-Indians accurately describes me as a non-somebody, as a non-person, and that is how I am treated on the reservation. As a 'non-Indian' I thank you for finally allowing my voice to, at least, be heard.[64]

Throughout Indian country, tribes are asserting their rights to tax and regulate land and people, and to defy the ability of any other governmental power to interfere. Lana Marcussen, an attorney who lives in New Mexico, deals with many cases in federal district courts involving Indians and non-Indians who feel they have not been treated fairly in tribal courts. One of her clients is a Navajo man named Dennis Williams. He inherited land from his mother and the transfer was approved by the Navajo Probate Court. Two years later, however, the Navajo Court of Appeals notified him that the case had been reopened and the land might belong to his cousin. Williams objected, to no avail, stating that the court didn't have the right to reopen the case, but the court ruled on the matter without giving him notice and without his presence in court.

Williams began to research the matter and discovered documents pertaining to his land case in the Navajo Supreme Court building. It turned out someone had tampered with his case document by switching numbers from an open appeals case to his case (which had been closed for two years). Assuming this information would solve the problem, Williams went to the Navajo District Court and asked them to correct the switched numbers. Instead, the court refused and made him go through the entire appeals process, all the way to the Navajo Supreme Court. The court did not dispute the fact that the numbers had been switched, but Williams still did not get his land back. To add insult to injury, Williams' cousin then initiated a damage claim against Williams. Williams refused to pay the claim because he believed he had been totally deprived of his rights, and was promptly thrown in jail for contempt of court. The Williams land case began in 1984, and 12 years later it ended up in the federal district court in Arizona which had agreed to review the case as ruled by the Navajo court.[65]

A relevant question, however, is whether the Navajo Tribe would honor a federal court ruling. According to Marcussen, tribes have refused to follow federal court orders. In 1996, the Mescalero Apache Tribe refused to obey a federal district court order to close their casino. When tribes no longer accept the jurisdiction of the federal government, the rights of Indians and non-Indians are jeopardized. Tribes have taken this sovereignty argument to the point where they believe that disputes between tribes and the federal government should be resolved by international courts.[66]

The recognition of Indian tribes as nations with international status has long been a goal of many Indian groups in the United States. The Iroquois Confederacy, also known as the Six Nations, sent a delegate to the League of Nations in the 1920s to request international recognition of Indian sovereignty. The Iroquois were the only Indians to formally object to U.S. citizenship because they thought it would limit their sovereignty.[67] In the summer of 1974, the Standing Rock Reservation hosted the First International Treaty Conference, attended by about 5,000 people from the U.S. and Canada. Representatives from 97 tribes attended the conference held in Mobridge, South Dakota.[68] In September of 1977, the United Nations held a conference on Indian treatment in the Western Hemisphere at its Geneva headquarters. The conference was attended by approximately 35 members from the UN General Assembly. The main topics discussed were land and treaties, with emphasis on North America.[69]

In reality, however, such questions were settled long ago in the United States. In the early part of the 1800s, Chief Justice John Marshall ruled on the question of federal jurisdiction over tribes. In the landmark case of *Cherokee Nation v. the State of Georgia* in 1831, Marshall wrote:

Though the Indians are acknowledged to have an unquestionable, and, heretofore unquestioned right to the lands they occupy until that right shall be extinguished by a voluntary cession to our government, yet it may well be doubted whether those tribes which reside within the acknowledged boundaries of the United States can, with strict accuracy, be denominated foreign nations. They may, more correctly be denominated domestic dependent nations. They occupy a territory to which we assert a title independent of their will, which must take effect in point of possession when their right of possession ceases. Meanwhile they are in a state of pupilage. Their relation to the United States resembles that of a ward to his guardian.

They look to our government for protection; rely upon its kindness and its power; appeal to it for relief to their wants; and address the President as their great father. They and their country are considered by foreign nations, as well as by ourselves, as being so completely under the sovereignty and dominion of the United States, that any attempt to acquire their lands, or to form a political connection with them, would be considered by all as an invasion of our territory, and an act of hostility.[70]

Apparently, this does not settle the matter for Indians. Indian activist Russell Means speaks for many Indians regarding sovereignty. "I have sworn on the sacred pipe that in my lifetime, I will see a free and independent Indian nation, responsible for its own economic destiny, beholden to no government, and recognized by the world community."[71]

CHAPTER EIGHT

Education and Propaganda

America today is filled with special interests and propaganda used to push individual agendas. Many of us belong to special interest groups of one kind or another, whether it be the Sierra Club, the National Rifle Association, the Democratic or Republican Party, or the local 4H Club. While some do it more legitimately than others, all special interest groups look to promote their own self-interests, sometimes at the expense of those who do not belong to their particular group.

Today, Indians represent a nation-wide special interest group, one that has gone from being abused and bullied to one that is now the abuser. Acknowledging that Indians were treated poorly in early American days, over the last 50 years, Indians have gained internal cohesiveness and public sympathy for a movement geared toward payback and then some. While reservation conditions remain desolate today in too many cases, this likely has as much to do with Indian mismanagement of their own affairs as it does with classic government do-nothingness. Ironically, Indians have successfully argued that more *and* less involvement from the U.S. government is necessary to repay them for past harm.

Indian tribes have done a remarkable job of convincing the American people that they deserve rights never promised them, and that Indians need not abide by the U.S. Constitution. Indians have publicly demanded secession from formal governance of the United States while simultaneously demanding continued financial aid from that same country. If this arrangement sounds like having your cake and

eating it too, you're not alone. But be careful in questioning the validity of such a special interest movement, lest you desire the name racist
or Indian hater.

Since becoming involved in treaties and other policy-related
Indian issues, I have often been labeled a racist. Indians often charge
that anyone posing a challenge to Indian rights — not as the U.S.
Constitution defines their rights, but *as Indians would define them* —
is simply an Indian hater. Talk of equal rights and the Constitution,
they say, is a smoke screen for a hidden racist agenda. Since treaties
are an unimpeachable example of international law, so the logic goes,
those who oppose treaties are not good Americans but racists with an
Indian ax to grind. This venom is directed toward those merely asking
for an open discussion of a basic American premise: equal rights.
Not special interest rights. Not race-based rights. *Equal rights.*
Constitutional rights.

In fact, if there is a racist tag to be attached anywhere, the
rhetoric of a number of leading Indian authors suggests the public is
being duped by a movement striving for sympathy but wanting nothing
whatsoever to do with the American people themselves. There is a
mountain of evidence demonstrating a racist Indian agenda, the handi-
work of leading Indian thinkers published neatly and purposefully for
all to see. There is so much racist rhetoric in Indian writing, it is amaz-
ing that Indians are so successful at escaping the racist label and are
instead able to apply it to others.

One need look no further than nationally recognized and respected Indian author and professor Vine Deloria Jr. He has written
many books on Indian activism and legal cases and is a professor of
history and law at the University of Colorado in Boulder. In 1974, he
wrote the book *Behind the Trail of Broken Treaties: An Indian
Declaration of Independence.* This book starts with a review of the history of the Indian relationship with the U.S. government, and recounts
the stories of Indian activism in the 1960s, events leading up to the
occupation of the Bureau of Indian Affairs building in 1972, and the
takeover at Wounded Knee in 1973. Most of the book is devoted to
making legal and moral arguments about the rights of Indians based on
their treaties with the United States. Early on, Deloria states in no

uncertain terms the inferiority in which Indians view non-Indians, particularly Whites.

> A substantial number of reservation Indians see the white man as little more than a passing episode in a tribal history which spans millennia. The white man may be the most destructive influence which the tribe has encountered, but he is still not regarded as a permanent fixture on the continent.[1]

Such rhetoric reminded me of something George Lincoln Rockwell said to me in my college days in the 1960s. This is not the Rockwell of *Saturday Evening Post* fame. George L. Rockwell was the leader of the American Nazi Party. My college in River Falls, Wisconsin had allowed him to speak at the student union — for what reason I'm not sure. I guess they wanted to show us what a real racist sounded like. I was a long-haired, 19-year-old "hippie" type. A few friends and I sat in the front row of the auditorium and asked Rockwell a few questions to see if we could smoke him out. I recall to this day his attempts to embarrass us by calling us "girls" or "ladies" when he answered our questions. I asked him what his attitudes toward Negroes were, and he said he had nothing against Negroes at all, "ma'am," but his party said they should live separately from Whites. This meant, he said, sending them back to Africa, "That's where they came from, that's where they belong."

Now fast-forward to Vine Deloria Jr. Could this be what he meant when he said Indians didn't regard White people as a "permanent" fixture on the continent? Did he mean Indians thought Whites belonged in Europe, in the same sense that Rockwell maintained Negroes belonged in Africa? Deloria further explained the early Indian activists' point of view:

> Imagining, therefore, that the coming Indian movement was an offshoot of the developments of the sixties, the New Left welcomed Indian Activists at its rallies, included Indians in the roll call of the oppressed, and sought Indian endorsement for schemes of fundamental reform. The Indian activists learned

the language of social protest, mastered the complicated hand-shakes used by the revolutionary elect, and began to raise funds for their activities. But the funding sources which were pouring money into the new fad of 'self-determination' for minority groups were often astounded to learn that the Indians were not planning to share the continent with their oppressed brothers once the revolution was over. Hell, no. The Indians were planning on taking the continent back and kicking out all the black, Chicano, Anglo, and Asian brothers who had made the whole thing possible.

The idea was so preposterous to the good liberals and their guilt-laden supporters that it was considered a good movement joke. There was even hearty applause when an Indian mentioned the plan, and it invoked solemn confessions of sin from those revolutionaries who sought to acknowledge and heal the psychic scars carried by each of the oppressed groups. Few people were able to look backward to the four-hundred-year struggle for freedom that the Indians had waged and recognize that if the United States and its inhabitants had regarded the Indians as another domestic minority group, the Indians did not see themselves as such. They were inundated by foreigners, perhaps, but for the majority of Indians their struggle was one of historical significance, not a temporary domestic discontent. Many Indians remained fully intent on raising their claims of national independence on the world scene.[2]

Was this just a joke for the "good liberals"? It seemed Deloria wasn't telling it as a joke, but as an attitude, unbelievable perhaps, but true nonetheless. The major thrust of Deloria's book *Behind the Trail of Broken Treaties* is the legal status of tribes and whether they should get compensation for unresolved disputes, including the return of land. But what would happen on these Indian lands after Indians got control? Would they become racial enclaves suitable for only one "color" of people? Deloria's first book, a smash hit published in 1969 entitled *Custer Died for Your Sins*, provides some insight to this question. In a chapter entitled "Red and Black," Deloria talks about problems and solutions for Blacks as well as Indians.

> Above all, Indian people have the possibility of total withdrawal from American society because of their special legal status. They can, when necessary, return to a recognized homeland where time is static and the world becomes a psychic unity again. To survive, blacks must have a homeland where they can withdraw, drop the facade of integration, and be themselves. Whites are inevitably torn because they have no roots, they do not understand the past, and they have mortgaged their future. Unless they can renew their psychic selves and achieve a sense of historical participation as a people they will be unable to survive.[3]

Deloria also shares some wisdom that might raise a few eyebrows among the politically correct crowd who believe minority groups have an all-for-one, one-for-all solidarity.

> People fool themselves when they visualize a great coalition of the minority groups to pressure Congress for additional programs and rights. Indians will not work within an ideological basis which is foreign to them. Any cooperative movement must come to terms with tribalism in the Indian context before it will gain Indian support. The future, therefore, as between the red, white and black, will depend on whether white and black begin to understand Indian nationalism....Hopefully the black militancy will return to nationalistic philosophies which relate to the ongoing conception of the tribe as a nation extending in time and occupying space.[4]

Deloria's unabashed push for tribalism relies on the creation of an Indian homeland where Indians can withdraw from American society, yet still enjoy the financial rewards of guardianship under the United States, returning repeatedly to American coffers, like the proverbial phoenix, to collect the "rent" which they believe is due them.

This neat juxtaposition is possible through the special legal status of Indians, allowing them to reap the benefits of American citizenship without assuming the responsibilities.

After finding these examples of racism in the books of Deloria, I began to look for similar attitudes in the writings of other Indian leaders and found them fairly easy to come by. A recent example of Indian separatist rhetoric is the book *Where White Men Fear to Tread* by Russell Means, an active, public leader of the Indian movement for more than two decades (see Chapter 5 on Indian activism in the 1970s). A good deal of Means' book deals with his actions as a revolutionary leader in the American Indian Movement during the takeover of the Bureau of Indian Affairs building in Washington D.C. in 1972 and the Wounded Knee stand-off in 1973.

When AIM Indians took over the BIA building in Washington, they were successful in intimidating even Richard Nixon who had just won re-election in a landslide. During the week-long occupation, Nixon called in additional police officers for security purposes, some of whom were Black. According to Means:

> Cops blocked off the streets on all four sides of the building. Along with several other men and women, I went out in front of the building and walked back and forth on the sidewalk, taunting the black cops and calling them 'house niggers.' 'Why are you going to kill for the white man?' I shouted. 'We're ready for you inside. Do you know what Indians do to buffalo soldiers? Do you know the tortures? Who's going to be the first nigger through the door?'[5]

Many Indian authors write with pent-up hatred toward Whites and toward American society in general and all its colors. In his autobiography, Means relates:

> I could feel the rage boiling from my every pore. I seethed and brooded and plotted for weeks — a mass of conflicting emotions. I began to compile an 'enemies list,' a la Nixon. I sorted through a roster of selected sellouts — presidents and chair-

men of tribal governments who had collaborated in the BIA's dirty work. I added others to the list — tribal judges and BIA police. I planned to kill a few rednecks at random, too, just the way they have butchered South Dakota Indians for generations. Most of the whites I wanted dead were U.S. congressmen, senators, federal and state appellate judges — the most visible opponents of the institutionalized racism that underlies government. I even developed scenarios for each killing. I believe I could succeed in carrying out many assassinations, but I also knew the law of averages was against me. Eventually, I would be caught. I planned to die in a gunfight, a martyr to my people. I told no one of my plan, not even Gloria. I added names to my list until I felt I probably couldn't kill many more before I was stopped. I was, of course, quite insane.[6]

Make no mistake, Means was and is one of the most respected and revered Indian leaders in America. His book is a bestseller all across the country and won high from Senator James Abourezk, former chairman of the American Indian Policy Review Commission, who writes, "Russell Means has written a moving, entertaining, and ultimately inspiring book that shows why and how he became a symbol of his peoples aspirations."[7]

Russell Means is considered to be one of the greatest and most charismatic speakers of all American Indian leaders. At the end of the book is printed what the book calls his most famous speech, "For America to Live, Europe Must Die," given in July 1980 at the South Dakota Black Hills International Survival Gathering. In it, Means says:

I don't really care whether my words reach whites or not...I'm more concerned with American Indian People, students and others, who have begun to be absorbed into the white world through universities and other institutions. But even then it's a marginal sort of concern. It's very possible to grow into a red face with a white mind; and if that's a person's individual choice, so be it, but I have no use for them. This is part of the process of cultural genocide being waged by Europeans against

American Indian peoples today.[8]

He leaves no doubt that Indian leaders like himself believe any mixing or assimilating into the White world, including university education, will destroy Indians. Means goes on to state that White Eurocentric ideas also must die.

In terms of the despiritualization of the universe, the mental process works so that it becomes virtuous to destroy the planet. Terms like *progress* and *development* are used as cover words here, the way *victory* and *freedom* are used to justify butchery in the dehumanization process. For example, a real-estate speculator may refer to 'developing' a parcel of ground by opening a gravel quarry; *development* here means total, permanent destruction, with the earth itself removed. But European logic has *gained* a few tons of gravel with which more land can be 'developed' through the construction of road beds. Ultimately the whole universe is open — in the European view — to this sort of insanity.[9]

As Means' speech goes on, he gets confused as to the distinction between hating what is "European" and what is "White."

The natural order will win out, and the offenders will die out, the way deer die when they offend the harmony by overpopulating a given region. It's only a matter of time until what Europeans call 'a major catastrophe of global proportions' will occur. It is the role of American Indian peoples, the role of all natural things, to survive. A part of our survival is to resist. We resist not to overthrow a government or to take political power, but because it is natural to resist extermination, to survive. We don't want power over white institutions; we want white institutions to disappear. *That's* revolution.[10]

Means goes on to tell us he's not a racist. "What I'm putting out here is not a racial proposition but a cultural proposition."[11] Is the revolutionary destruction of White institutions not a racist idea? Let's put another ethnic group in the phrase and see how it sounds. Suppose Hitler had said, "We don't want power over Jewish institutions, we want Jewish institutions to disappear. The natural order will win out, and the offenders will die out, the way deer die when they offend the harmony by overpopulating a given region. By the way, I'm not a racist, I'm just defending my culture."

Means also makes a disclaimer about his calling the Black cops in Washington "niggers." "I was just trying to play with their heads, but I got no response," he states.[12] OK then Russell, it's not a racist remark if you're an Indian and you just want to "play with their heads."

Toward the end of his speech at the International Survival Gathering, Means pulls no punches in his assessment of American values and their ancestral European roots.

> A culture which regularly confuses revolution with continuation, which confuses science and religion, which confuses revolt with resistance, has nothing helpful to teach you and nothing to offer you as a way of life. Europeans have long since lost all touch with reality, if ever they were in touch with it.[13]

In other portions of his book, Means himself seems almost unaware of the contradictory nature of Indian demands. At one point he asks, "How does one attain freedom? How can we fight city hall? The BIA? The Federal government? *How can we succeed in reestablishing our individual rights as guaranteed by the Constitution.*"[14] One short page later, Means expounds, "I have sworn on the sacred pipe that in my lifetime I will see a *free and independent Indian nation, responsible for its own economic destiny, beholden to no government*, and recognized by the world community" (emphasis added by author in both citations).[15]

I have only listed a fraction of the crime, violence and general lawlessness that is in the autobiography of Russell Means. It is interesting how Means puts a high moral purpose to much of what he did, in spite of dealing heroine, plotting to kill people, destroying property and stealing. He believes Indians should throw off White institutions like universities in the name of preserving Indian culture, and create separate nations to protect Indians rights under the U.S. Constitution. It is all a strange kind of logic, constantly contradicting itself.

Indian Revisionist History

Like all good cultural crusades, Indians have used propaganda to instill guilt and to increase support among non-Indians in their push for sovereignty. In particular, Indian authors have revisited history in an attempt to rewrite it in terms that are more favorable to their plight. In most cases, this has meant amplifying past abuses, discounting any Indian abuses, discrediting non-Indian accomplishments, and challenging the truthfulness of documented events through nothing more than Indian oral recollections.

Such revisionist history might normally be viewed as the ramblings of fringe elements, but the Indian crusade for sovereignty has reached such proportions that much of this revisionist history is actually being taught today from elementary schools to university classrooms. Their history of European abuses focuses much attention on Columbus and Cortez to the point where children today often believe that Columbus and Cortez were the worst demons in the world's history. While it is unquestionable that Columbus and Cortez did awful things to Indians, the distortion of history does not serve anyone justly. Means' interpretations of early American history are also very one-sided at best and bizarre at worst. In order to distort history to reflect well on all Indians and poorly on early explorers, Means claims that Aztecs did not practice human sacrifice, but instead were performing open-heart surgery 500 years before the procedure was done in modern hospitals.

> To persuade the church that they were subhuman, Columbus accused the Indians of such unnatural acts as cannibalism — a lie. Later Cortez accused the Aztecs of human sacrifice — another lie, but my own recent conversations and experiences with Aztec medicine men convinced me that their ancestors, aided by a masterful understanding of plants which temporarily

slow the bodies functions to near-paralysis, performed open heart surgery. This has been partly confirmed by recent archae-ological and pharmacological research. In order to conceal this truth and sell the lie of human sacrifice, the Franciscans who accompanied Cortez burned every Aztec book.[16]

While it's true that most Aztec books were burned by the church, the reason was not to create a myth about human sacrifice among the Aztecs. The church burned the books to stamp out the reli-gion of the Aztecs and replace it with Christianity. This was a terrible tragedy. But there are records of the Aztec slaughter of up to 20,000 victims per year that the Franciscans couldn't burn. In Central America, there are Aztec monuments of stone on which the Aztecs carved the record of their monstrous deeds. So the record stands, writ-ten by Aztec hands, and literally chiseled in stone.[17]

The book *Bury My Heart at Wounded Knee*, by Dee Brown, is one of the best-selling Indian history books of all time. It purports to tell the true story of historic Indian struggles in the United States. Brown's book, however, often relies on oral histories of Indian elders passed down through generations as its source of the truth. Not sur-prisingly, the book's stories and historical recollections sometimes fail to agree with versions in American history books. For instance, a Sioux woman is quoted by Brown as saying with regard to Wounded Knee, "the (white) soldiers must be mean to shoot women and children, the Indian soldiers would not do that to white children."[18] But history books are filled with irrefutable stories of the slaughter of women and children by Indians, even when Indians were fighting each other.[19] One example is the 1862 Minnesota Sioux Uprising when about 562 Whites were killed, many of whom were women and children.[20]

Continuing my research on Native Americans, I discovered the book *Indian Givers, How the Indians of the Americas Transformed the World*, by Jack Weatherford, chairman of the Anthropology Department at Macalaster College in St. Paul, Minnesota. He has written seven books and appeared on the "Today Show," "The Larry King Show," "ABC Nightly News with Peter Jennings," and in Kevin Costner's *Five Hundred Nations*.[21] *Indian Givers* is very popular in many classrooms, especially those dealing with cultural diversity issues and teaching about "real" Indians' contributions to civilization. The central theme of the book is that many of the marvelous advances in technology, science and human rights we normally attribute to European innovation really originated in the culture and knowledge of the Indians. A careful reading of the book, however, shows that a strange kind of logic is used to show how these innovations originated and what their ultimate value to society is.

On the one hand, the book talks about Indian contributions to the Industrial Revolution, science, agriculture, medicine, the development of the United States Constitution and the rise of democracy. The book implies that world progress would have been very retarded, perhaps by thousands of years, if not for the contributions of American Indians. But at the same time, the book condemns modern technology and European exploitation of Indians.

For example, Weatherford devotes significant space arguing that the Industrial Revolution started in the Americas through Spanish-owned silver mines, along with cotton and sugar plantations which produced the early factory system that formed the basic structure of the Industrial Revolution. Rather than stemming from the European craft system, as most historians believe, Weatherford gives the credit to Indians because he believes the European factory "modeled itself on the American plantation."[22]

Weatherford goes so far as to predict the retardation of the European world had it not been for the factory-like inducement brought on by American plantations.

> Had Europe and America not come together through Columbus or some other connection, the industrial revolution would never have happened in the way that we know it. The peasants of Europe, Asia, and Africa would have continued tilling their fields while the craftsmen produced small quantities of needed goods in their workshops. *Life would probably have continued as it had for thousands of years* (emphasis added).[23]

In making this assertion, Weatherford ignores the tremendous innovative and scientific trends occurring in Europe starting with the Renaissance. A major source for this surge in knowledge comes from the rediscovery by Europe of the knowledge of the ancient Greeks and Romans which was stored in the libraries of Egypt and the Near East. During the crusades, these libraries were plundered, bringing to Europe the books of many ancient civilizations plus the scientific and mathematical innovations of the Arabs (Arabic numerals), Persians and other empires in Asia Minor.[24] By the 1700s and early 1800s, Europeans had the knowledge and the will to embrace industry on a large scale. The discovery of the Americas undoubtedly accelerated the arrival of the Industrial Revolution, but hardly by "thousands of years" as Weatherford suggests.

At the same time, I don't understand how the Spanish plantations and mines were in any way an Indian innovation. Yes, Indians were needed in order to make plantations work, and Indians were an exploited resource, but this was hardly an Indian innovation in and of itself. Rome was built in just such a fashion 1500 years before these new world "innovations," and in Egypt they occurred 4,500 years ago. Moreover, using slaves by the thousands on Spanish plantations and in Spanish mines was an idea initiated by the Spaniards, not the Indians.

Besides the mines and plantations, Weatherford proposes that Indians were responsible for two other major innovations involved in the Industrial Revolution: the potato and cotton. Potatoes were first grown by American Indians, and American Indian cotton was superior to that grown in Asia. According to Weatherford, many towns in Europe had mills for grinding grain into flour. When the potato was introduced, many of these mills were idled since less flour was needed for feeding people. Thus, Weatherford concludes:

> The potato freed the mills but gave them nothing new to process....The situation changed with the massive influx of cotton from America. Suddenly, the peasants and weavers had more fiber than they could weave. They lacked the labor to process so much fiber. Europe desperately needed more energy than it had in human and animal power, and the most readily available source for creating new energy lay in the water-

wheels already in place throughout the continent. Thus were born the first textile factories.[25]

Weatherford is not content to merely give Indians patents on the production methods for textiles, he credits Indians and their dyes with the development of the European textile industry as well. "Without a consistent source of cheap yet high-quality dyes, the textile industry would scarcely have developed. The American Indians, however, had also developed a complex technology for producing superior dyes, and the Europeans immediately adopted it."[26] The implication here is multi-fold: without Indian dyes the textile industry would not have developed; without textiles and Spanish-plantation cotton — cultivated by Indian slaves — the weaving machine would not have been developed; without potatoes, there would not have been excess capacity at grain mills; without excess capacity, grain mills would not have re-tooled production from milling to weaving; and finally, without the weaving machines to produce textiles, there would be no Industrial Revolution.

If this seems to stretch the theory of cause and effect a bit thin, perhaps it is because the Industrial Revolution was the cumulative effect of thousands of separate innovations spread over millennia. To attribute the Industrial Revolution to two plants cultivated by Indians requires not only a vivid imagination but a determined effort to ignore historical developments and contributions from other cultures. To be sure, Indians were the creators of wonderful dyes and the cultivators of staple plants and crops used today to help feed the world. But every culture has such feathers of invention and ingenuity in their caps. Instead, *Indian Givers* appears to have been written with the sole intent to show how any activity associated *with* Indians was a creation *by* Indians that transformed the world, irrespective of how tenuous that connection might be or how many other groups might be involved. It is an obvious attempt to manipulate the facts to fit the hypothesis.

To credit Indian innovations as the root source of the Industrial Revolution is to ignore thousands of years of Western and Asian history. The major factors that lead to the Industrial Revolution are well known and well documented. Such things as steel, advancements in communications and transportation systems, and the mechanization of mass crop farming were all integral parts of the Industrial Revolution, and none have their roots in Native American history.

Ironically, after heroic efforts to place an Indian foundation under the Industrial Revolution, Weatherford then goes on to tell us how evil it all is, going so far as to blame the Spanish for the invention of a drug culture to deaden the humdrum boredom of factory work. He states:

> When the Spaniards found that the Indians would work longer and harder if mildly drugged (Indians in Bolivia had a tradition of chewing coca leaves, the source of cocaine), they made a major discovery of extensive consequences for workers around the world — that factory workers want drugs to help them withstand the drudgery and monotony of their work. Just as the money factory of Potosi served as prototype for factories of all kinds, the use of coca by the workers in Potosi served as a prototype of the use of drugs of all types as a way to alleviate the painful and unnatural conditions of work. The industrial revolution could just as easily be called the alcohol and drug revolution.[27]

Weatherford delights in showing us how we take the "gifts" of Indian cultures and turn them into monstrosities. If Europeans could produce nothing good from potatoes and cotton (merely the evil Industrial Revolution), neither should it be expected that they could do anything productive with corn or tobacco. Weatherford argues that Europeans could do nothing but find or invent detrimental uses for either crop. "Corn grew so luxuriantly in American fields that the settlers harvested much more than either humans or animals could consume. They turned it into corn liquor."[28] This development soon spread to Europe, Weatherford states, which "created a wholly new disease, alcoholism, which has spread steadily over the past few centuries. This rise closely parallels the development of industrialism; alcohol provided a psychic break from the monotonous and long work associated with industrial production."[29]

This creates a rather novel message for students reading *Indian Givers*: get a job in modern industry and you'll probably become an alcoholic or a drug addict. By this logic, perhaps we could solve the drug and alcohol problem in America by simply closing down all the factories. One wonders what Weatherford's defense might be concerning the Cheyenne River Souix Tribe. Here the unemployment rate is between 60 and 70 percent and the alcoholism rate is above 50 percent, which doesn't seem to agree with Weatherford's industrial-work-makes-alcoholics hypothesis.* Tobacco is another plant for which Indian Givers issues a double standard. When Indians use it, it has a religious and cultural benefit. When Whites use tobacco, it is merely part of the commercial drug trade. Weatherford leans on the guilt of a politically correct public to overstate his case, arguing that Westerners had no culturally prescribed place for tobacco as it did among the Indians. Instead, writes Weatherford:

> The first colony of the United States was settled by profiteering colonists, convicts, and indentured servants who arrived in Virginia to cultivate tobacco leaves for sale to Europeans, who ground it and snorted it up their noses in the form of snuff. Tobacco was the first of the New World drugs to be widely accepted in the Old World, and the European zest for it played a major role in opening North America to colonization. Contemporary civic mythology of the United States overlooks this role of America as drug supplier to the world.[30]

It is commonly assumed today that Indians always use plants wisely and are stewards of the land, while immigrant Americans are merely universal profiteers and convicts who can do nothing better with tobacco than create a drug trade in Europe. What is unfortunate about this method of reinventing history is that it does a great disservice to everyone, including the Indians. Reshaping historical facts to fit a particular viewpoint is not history at all, it is propaganda. Early Greek historians such as Thucydides (460-400 BC) were some of the first people to write authentic history because they tried to record facts objectively rather than modifying them to fit local prejudices. For centuries, his-

---

* Fergus Bordewich, *Killing the White Man's Indian,* pp. 250, 251. "A poor economy leads to alcoholism, and alcoholism leads to a poor economy." Quoting Greg Bourland.

torians have tried to live up to this ideal, though often they fall short. Indians and Indian sympathizers such as Weatherford complain that Western historians have consistently written history that promotes a White, Eurocentric world view. There is much truth to this assertion, but to rewrite history from an indigenous, anti-technology, anti-European world view is equally inaccurate and merely gives us more propaganda to sift through.

Weatherford is by no means alone in rewriting or reinterpreting history. After spending several years researching books on American Indians, I was amazed to find that most books about Indians written in the last 30 years have a strong bias toward revising history in favor of an indigenous world view. There was a tendency to portray American history as the lies of White men and to reject it in favor of the oral histories of Indians which were passed down verbally from generation to generation. Many of the ideas in these books seem to be filled with hatred and contempt for all things American and more specifically, all things White. There seems to be an undercurrent of racism in much of what was written, although sometimes the racism is obvious and blatant, as I have shown. The ideas presented are often illogical and ludicrous, even insane. I have yet to understand how these writings have not been found fraudulent by the reading public. These are popular books available in most bookstores. I wondered if these books represented mainstream Indian thought in America, or whether I was studying the lunatic fringe.

I decided it was time to go to a nationally recognized university and take a course in Native American Studies. I had spent almost six years in college, but most of that was 25 years ago. I knew universities to be places where different points of view were discussed. I had studied a good deal of psychology, sociology, history and philosophy and had been exposed to a number of world views. I had never taken a Native American Studies class, but I assumed these classes would cover multiple points of view, and I would be able to learn which viewpoints represented mainstream Indian thought.

The University of Minnesota had the best Native American program in my area, and there were a number of good classes to choose from. I picked "Topics in American Indian Studies: Native

Environmentalism at the Cusp of 2000," sub-titled, "Historic Survey, Present Struggles, Future Visions." This class seemed perfect because it covered most of the big issues connected with Indian treaties: the land, the environment, national and international law and the preservation of Indian culture. It promised to study past history, examine present-day situations and analyze the future direction of the Indian culture. It was a popular class filled with both undergraduate and graduate students.

The teacher was Winona LaDuke, a nationally recognized Native American with excellent credentials. LaDuke, a Harvard graduate and a frequent congressional lobbyist in Washington, has been very active as a tribal advocate throughout the United States for nearly two decades. In 1994, LaDuke was named by *Time* magazine as one of the 50 most promising leaders under 40 years of age in the United States. She has received numerous awards including the International Reebok Human Rights Award (worth $20,000). LaDuke is co-chair of the Indigenous Women's Network, an international organization, and she created the White Earth Land Recovery Project at her reservation in northern Minnesota. In 1996, Ralph Nader selected LaDuke as his vice presidential running mate. She is widely published, having written a novel about Indian history and experiences, called *Last Standing Woman*, and contributed selections to many other books. LaDuke, I remember thinking, was well qualified to teach about a wide range of Indian issues as they related to the national and international scene and could certainly represent the Indian viewpoint.[31]

LaDuke assigned material from the book *Struggle for the Land*, by Native American author Ward Churchill, in five out of ten classroom discussions. Churchill is the co-director of the American Indian Movement of Colorado, the vice chairperson of the American Indian Anti-Defamation Council, and an associate professor of American Indian Studies and Communications at the University of Colorado at Boulder. He is also associate director of the Center for Studies of Ethnicity and Race in America, and the author of many political books on Indians including Marxism and Native Americans, Fantasies of the Master Race, and Indians Are Us? Culture and Genocide in Native North America.[32]

Like Winona LaDuke, Ward Churchill has an impressive list of credentials, and appears well-versed and battle-tested in issues of racism. His books focus on the issue of Indian genocide and how Americans past and present wish to destroy Native Americans as a people and a culture. At the beginning of his book, *Struggle for the Land* is a foreword written by Winona LaDuke entitled "Succeeding Into Native North America: a Secessionist View." This foreword contains a map of North America over which are drawn huge areas to which Indians believe they have a legal land claim. LaDuke called these areas the "unceded territories." The dictionary defines unceded as "territory to which one has not given up rights." She writes, "Very little land in North America should rightly fall outside native jurisdiction, administered under indigenous rather than immigrant values."[33]

I was curious exactly what LaDuke meant by this, because according to the map, my entire state of Minnesota was "unceded territory." The map gave roughly the top half of the state to the Chippewa, with the rest of the state being given over to Sioux jurisdiction. LaDuke had talked extensively about this map during the first 3-hour class period. A week later, after I had read much of the book, I asked her to define jurisdiction as she had written it for the book. She answered, "That depends on the context." Since her foreword was supposed to provide the context for readers, it seemed to me that she was being evasive. This did not surprise me, however, because the ideas in the foreword were outrageous, to put it mildly, and I didn't think she would want to talk about them.

Hoping for some clarification, I read aloud her own definition of jurisdiction in class. It reads:

By extension, this [jurisdiction] would mean that much land which is currently taxed, regulated, strip-mined, militarized, drowned by hydroelectric generators or over-irrigation, and nuked by the U.S. and Canadian governments would no longer be under their control or jurisdiction. Surely, this is a prospect which all progressive and socially conscious people can embrace.[34]

Is that what you mean? I asked LaDuke in class, thinking that although I considered myself to be progressive and socially conscious, I could not embrace the idea that the state of Minnesota and much of the rest of the country should be under the control and jurisdiction of various Indian tribes.

LaDuke's body language was that of a kid caught with her hand in the cookie jar. "Well," she sighed, spreading her arms fully to each side in a gesture of resignation, "in a best case scenario, yes."

Then, I responded, suppose there is some White farmer in Malaca, Minnesota who did something with his land that the Chippewa Tribal Council wouldn't allow. What would his recourse be, and would there be any White people on the tribal council?

Now I thought LaDuke would explain what she really meant, but she would not. "These are good questions," LaDuke said, "and it shows you're really reading the material, but this is a question that we cover in another class, I think it is class nine, when we talk about the Buffalo Commons Project. So you can ask me about it then." This did not make any sense to me, because we had already covered the jurisdiction map in the previous class. I wasn't racing ahead of the material, I was digging into the material we had already covered.

This wasn't what I expected to happen at a class at a prestigious school like the University of Minnesota. During the first class period, LaDuke told us pointedly not to be afraid of asking questions and disagreeing with her. I wasn't. I asked her a reasonable question during the second class and she was putting me off. The following week she did it again. I kept my hand up during the question and discussion period which usually lasted a half-hour. She called on everyone but me. Then she said, "Well, the time is up, so you can go. David, I know you still have a question and I'll talk to you in private after class." It seemed to me that LaDuke's ideas, which perhaps could be skimmed over in a book, were not something that stood up well to a lot of questions.

In the end, I found class material and LaDuke to be cut from the same cloth as other Indian authors I had read. This "higher education" class was nothing but a front to push Indian propaganda and advance the Indian movement. To wit, most students faithfully read class materials, but few questioned the theories and beliefs being posited by

LaDuke or the reading material, including the following excerpt from her forward toward Churchill's book:

> The native struggle in North America today can only be properly understood as a pursuit of the recovery of land rights which are guaranteed through treaties. What Indians ask — what we really expect — from those who claim to be our friends and allies is respect and support for treaty rights. What does this mean? Well, it starts with advocating that Indians regain use of and jurisdiction over what the treaties define as being our lands. It means direct support of Indian efforts to recover these lands, but not governmental attempts to 'compensate' us with money for lands we never agreed to relinquish.... Native North America is struggling to break free of the colonialist, industrialist, militarist nation-state domination in which it is now engulfed. It is fighting to 'secede' from the U.S. and Canada. But, because of the broader implications of this, we refer to the results we seek not as 'secession,' but as 'success.'[35]

A careful reading of *Struggle for the Land* demonstrates some of the plans for the Indian control over different parts of America. It was shocking. I had come to the University of Minnesota to find out if the racist and ethnocentric viewpoints I was seeing in Indian books were an idea the Indian mainstream accepted, or if this was the ranting of the special-interest fringe. Almost all of the class books for other Native American Studies classes seemed to have the same bias that I was seeing in LaDuke's assigned readings. I made a careful study of the books for each class and found that most seemed to be full of the same type of propaganda, rather than offering a broad range of view points.

Unfortunately, I discovered that this university was not serving as a sorting ground for different viewpoints. It was not trying to find the most effective way to solve the problems of Indians in America. These classes were developed with an agenda in mind: to separate Indians as much as possible from the rest of America. The books I was seeing at the bookstores were not from the lunatic fringe; this was the whole cloth, the warp and the weft — the foundation — and the university classes were not serving the function of adding moderation, reason, and careful questioning to the arguments. The universities were the *source* of the radicalism, and the voice of reason was nowhere to be heard.

A reader of *Struggle for the Land* barely has time to get comfortable before Churchill is comparing the United States to Nazi Germany. Churchill, like a lot of other writers who create Indian sovereignty propaganda, spends a good deal of time talking about the history of the United States as if this country used concentration camps and biological and chemical warfare to exterminate the Indians in the 18th and 19th centuries. In the introduction, Churchill states:

> ...the present situation is simply the outgrowth of a juridical doctrine which has been evolving in the U.S. since before the very earliest moments of the republic. This ideology of expansionism — popularly known as 'Manifest Destiny' — has ongoing direct impacts upon the indigenous peoples of North America. The ideology also supported philosophical developments elsewhere. A salient example is Adolf Hitler's concept of lebenstraumpolitik ('politics of living space'). The ideology stipulated that Germans were innately entitled by virtue of an imagined racial and cultural superiority, to land belonging to others. This rendered Germany morally free in its own mind to take such lands through the aggressive use of military force.[36]

Many pages are devoted to describing Indian-American relations in horrifying terms that are tailored to create blinding feelings of White guilt in the reader, and to soften them up for when Churchill describes Indian intentions for their new territory. As Churchill approaches the delicate subject of the dismantling of the United States and forming a large Indian nation in the center, he begins to speak of secession as a highly moral and just solution for 500 years of Indian holocaust. He states:

This goal of creating government to government relations is

pursued with utmost seriousness because, in the end, it is through recognition of ourselves as fully sovereign entities within the international arena that indigenous people in the Americas perceive the sole possibility of a just and permanent resolution of the difficulties we now confront.[37]

Churchill compares the scourge of Nazism to the fundamental "Nation State" concept of the United States. Says Churchill, "The U.S. — at least as it has come to be known, and in the sense that it knows itself — must be driven from North America. In its stead resides the possibility, likely the only possibility, of a truly just and liberatory future for all humanity."[38] For sovereignty propagandists, the leap of logic from arguing about stale land claims to becoming the saviors of humanity is easily accomplished. The starting point for the sovereignty movement is old treaties that no longer reflect the realities of contemporary law and social reality. This matters little to Churchill, for his next trick is simply to dispense with nit-picking about the legality of old treaties.

The United States cannot pretend to even a shred of legitimacy in its occupancy and control of upwards of 30 percent of its 'home' territory…Leaving aside questions concerning the validity of various treaties, the beginning point for any indigents endeavor in the United States centers, logically enough, in efforts to restore direct Indian control over the huge portion of the continental U.S. which was never ceded by native nations.[39]

Should any of this talk cause us to worry about Indian demands for ethnic sovereignty? Some believe there is little to worry about regarding Indian unrest because the federal government would not allow any Indian tribe to secede from the United States. Perhaps, but remember the federal government has done its share of policy backflips in the past given enough public pressure from special-interest groups. In the 1950s, Indian tribes were being terminated, reservations shut down and Indians assimilated into American society. Then two decades later, the federal government changed its mind. Suddenly, tribes with no sovereignty and who were being unilaterally terminated in the 1950s were reconstituted and given a small amount of autonomy to govern their own affairs. Since then, the sovereign status of tribes has grown slowly and inexorably, and now there is serious talk of Indian tribes having powers superior to those of states.

In the brief span of about 20 years, federal and state governments have made a complete about-face in Indian policy, changes that the average American is scarcely aware of. We assume the government watches out for the best interests of all Americans, but often we're not sure who is in control. Over time, what is *possible* can change in astonishing ways. Churchill gives us a good example of unexpected changes in the makeup of nations and a hint of how he feels the U.S. can be brought down.

Anyone who doubts that it's possible to bring about the dismemberment of a super power state using internal forces in this day and age, ought to sit down and have a long talk with a guy named Mikhail Gorbechev. It would be better yet if you could chew the fat with Leonid Breznev, a man we can be sure would have replied in all sincerity — only a decade ago — that this was the most outlandish idea he'd ever heard. Well, look on a map today, and see if you can find the Union of Soviet Socialist Republics. It ain't there, my friends....These megastates are not immutable. They can be taken apart. They can be destroyed. But first we have to decide that we can do it, and that we *will* do it.[40]

Churchill has a name for his Indian Utopia; he calls it the North American Union of Indigenous Nations which would entail a land "give-back" plan equivalent to about one-third of the 48 continental states. Despite this seemingly huge land gift, Churchill believes it can be returned to the Indians without disrupting anyone's present way of life. First, he assures us that federal and state governments already hold title to 45 to 47 percent of the land in the United States, and that big corporations also hold a huge share. Having said this, he leaps to his conclusion by confidently declaring, "It is, and always has been, quite possible to accomplish the return of every square inch of unceded Indian Country in the United States without tossing a single non-Indian homeowner off the land on which they live."[41] Churchill then reassures us that we have nothing to fear.

> The Great Fear is within any settler state, that if indigenous land rights are ever openly acknowledged, and native people recover some significant portion of their land, the immigrants will correspondingly be dispossessed of what they've come to consider "theirs"; most notably individually held homes, small farms and ranches, and the like.[42]

He goes on to say that the "Great Fear" is just propaganda put out by groups such as the John Birch Society and the Klu Klux Klan. Handing over land jurisdiction to Indians, however, means a lot of non-Indians would be living in areas where the U.S. Constitution doesn't apply. Churchill assures us that this is not a big problem, at least not "once non-Indian America acknowledges that Indians have an absolute moral and legal right to the quantity of territory which was never ceded."[43] He then gives an example of his plan in action, a plan he considers non-intrusive and very workable.

Churchill cites a Rutger's University study done around 1980 that examined land-use patterns and local economies in the Great Plains region. The study found that 110 counties have been fiscally insolvent since originally incorporated under federal and state jurisdiction. These counties encompass one-fourth of all counties within the western portions of the states of North and South Dakota, Nebraska, Kansas, Oklahoma and Texas, along with eastern Montana, Wyoming, Colorado and New Mexico. This is an area of about 140,000 square miles, but sparsely populated by about 400,000 non-Indians.[44] Churchill is able to dispense of "only" 400,000 non-Indians rather easily within this secessionist scheme. He proposes that the government simply cut its on-going losses in these insolvent counties, buy out individual land holdings, and convert them into wildlife sanctuaries which Churchill refers to as the "Buffalo Commons."

In case any of this is beginning to give the reader cause for con-

cern, Churchill applies a bit of guilt lubrication to make the idea easier
to swallow.

> The whole area would, in effect, be turned back to the bison
> which were very nearly exterminated by Phil Sheridan's buffa-
> lo hunters back in the nineteenth century as a means of starving
> the 'recalcitrant' Indians into surrendering. The result...would
> be both environmentally and economically beneficial to the
> nation as a whole.[45]

Having so easily dispensed with the property rights of nearly a
half million people, Churchill unfolds the next level of his plan. To
complement the insolvent counties, Churchill suggests that the U.S.
give back "economically marginal" counties as well. While we're at it,
Churchill believes Indians should gain control of nearby areas like the
national grasslands in Wyoming, the national forest and parks in the
Black Hills and "extraneous" military reservations like Ellsworth Air
Force Base. "What you end up with is a huge territory lying east of
Denver, west of Lawrence, Kansas, and extending from the Canadian
border to southern Texas, all of it 'outside the loop' of U.S. business as
usual."[46] According to Churchill, the bulk of this land is unceded territory owned by the Lakota, Pawnee, Arikara, Hidatsa, Mandan, Crow,
Shoshone, Assiniboine, Cheyenne, Arapaho, Kiowa, Kiowa Apache,
Comanche, Jicarilla and Mescalero Apache. "There would be little cost
to the United States and virtually no arbitrary dispossession/dislocation
of non-Indians, if the entire Commons were restored to these people." [47]
He infers that such land is, in fact, already "owned" by Indians,
and the Buffalo Commons Project would merely be giving Indians back
what they already own. But in reality, most of this land is owned legally by individual Americans, corporations, and the federal and state government. Propagandists are skilled at hiding such fabrications in the
text to strengthen their arguments. Churchill rationalizes that there
would be "little cost" to the United States, assuming that the U.S.
wouldn't mind giving up its greatest national parks, not to mention the
lion's share of the coal, uranium, natural gas, copper, and other mineral, timber and water resources. Other matters — like dividing the West

Coast from the eastern part of the United States — would be a minor inconvenience. Whether such an undertaking is right or wrong, moral or not, the fact of the matter is it would be politically unworkable, even laughable.

There are some questions that must be answered, however. Why is this propaganda being taught in the classrooms of a major university? When the class period discussing the Buffalo Commons Project came around, I was anxious to find out how LaDuke felt about such a massive and radical "give-back" project. I waited for her to define Indian jurisdiction and describe how White people would be protected on Indian lands, but she did not talk about it. As students, we had all been assigned Churchill's writings from which I am quoting, yet none of my classmates raised questions about Indian jurisdiction of the ceded territories. These were not just undergraduates, but graduate students also, the people who would be going out into the schools of America to teach school children about Indian's rights and the Buffalo Commons Project. I didn't ask my questions about Indian jurisdiction because I wanted to see if anyone else was concerned enough to ask. No one was.

In the chapter we had been assigned to read, Churchill said plenty about what the new Indian Country would be like. But first, he had to make it a little bigger than it already was.

All right, as critics will undoubtedly be quick to point out, a sizable portion of the Buffalo Commons area I've sketched out — perhaps a million acres — lies outside the boundaries of unceded territory. That's the basis for the sorts of multilateral negotiations between the U.S. and indigenous nations I mentioned earlier. This land will need to be 'charged off' in some fashion against unceded land elsewhere, and in such a way as to bring other native peoples into the mix…the principle could extend as well to all native peoples willing to exchange land claims somewhere else for actual acreage in this locale.…From there, the Buffalo Commons cum Indian Territory could be extended westwards into areas which adjoin or are at least immediately proximate to the commons area itself.…Hence, it is reasonable — in my view at least — to expand the Commons territory to include most of Utah and Nevada, northern Montana and Idaho, quite a lot of western Washington and Oregon, most of New Mexico, and the lions share of Arizona....At this point we've arrived at an area comprising roughly one third of the continental U.S., a territory which — regardless of the internal political and geographic subdivisions effected by the array of native peoples within it — could be defined as a sort of 'North American Union of Indigenous Nations.'[48]

It is interesting to see how a propagandist like Churchill can begin a book by comparing Indian policy of the United States with the lebenstraumpolitik concept (politics of space) of Adolf Hitler and then end up proposing the same type of race-based space. He says Hitler's ideology was based on the idea that Germans were entitled to land belonging to others based on the German's innate racial and cultural superiority. He then implies that this ideology reflects how the federal government came to rationalize the taking of much of what is now America. Somewhere along the line, however, Churchill fails to recognize that the Buffalo Commons Project itself is a mirrored reflection of lebenstraumpolitik because of its desire to reclaim space for a separate race and culture — in this case, Indians. His arguments are circular, and by the time he gets back to the starting point, he has adopted what in the beginning he had rejected.

Churchill tries to soothe fears of non-Indians about losing their homes and ranches to Indian nations, playing such fears off as nothing but right-wing racist propaganda. Once he gets to the meat of his argument, however, it's obvious he believes the world is overpopulated and that industrialism is a great evil. According to Churchill, these two evils must be addressed, and he is very specific about how they will be tamed. Not surprisingly, they have something to do with non-Indians living on land that will be hypothetically ceded back to Indians.

Regarding overpopulation, Churchill claims he won't use forced abortion methods but will ask for voluntary abortion and sterilization. That alone won't bring down the population enough, according to Churchill, who would like to return to pre-settlement populations. "How many people have they got living in the valley down there-at Phoenix, a place which might be reasonably expected to support 500? Look at L.A., 20 million people where there ought to be maybe a few thousand."[49] His detailed plan for reducing the population to this acceptable level includes cutting off utilities like water to the areas that are overpopulated.

> In the scenario I've described, the entire Colorado watershed will be in Indian Country, under Indian control. So will the source of the Columbia. And diversion of the Yukon would have to go right through Indian Country. Now, here's the deal. No more use of water to fill swimming pools and sprinkle golf courses in Phoenix and L.A. No more watering Kentucky blue-grass lawns out on the yucca flats. No more drive thru car washes in Tucumcari. No more 'Big Surf' amusement parks in the middle of the desert. Drinking water and such for the whole population, yes, Indians should deliver that. But water for this other insanity? No way. I guarantee it'll start a pretty substan-tial out-flow. Most of these folks never wanted to live in the desert anyway. That's why they keep trying to make it look like Florida.[50]

He claims this "out-flow" will reduce the population to a rea-sonable size. Churchill also plans to do away with all unnecessary industrialization by doing away with power plants and other industrial evils.

> Virtually all the electrical power for the southwestern urban sprawls comes from the Four Corners area. This is smack dab in the middle of Indian Country, along with all the uranium with which a 'friendly atom' alternative might be attempted, and most of the low sulfur coal. Goodbye, to the neon glitter of Las Vegas and San Diego. Adios to air conditioners in every room. Sorry about your hundred mile expanses of formerly streetlit expressway. Basic needs will be met, and that's it....What I'm

saying probably sounds extraordinary cruel to a lot of people, particularly those imbued with the belief that they have a 'God-given right' to play a round of golf on the well-watered green beneath the imported palm trees outside the air-conditioned casino at the base of the Superstition Mountains. Tough. Those days can be ended without hesitation or apology. A much more legitimate concern rests on the fact that a lot of people who've drifted into the southwest have no place to go to. The areas they came from are crammed. In many cases, that's why they left. To them I say there's no need to panic; no one will abruptly pull the plug on you, or leave you to die of thirst. Nothing like that. But quantities of both water and power will be set at minimum levels. In order to have a surplus, you'll have to bring your number down to a certain level over a certain period. At that point, the levels will again be reduced, necessitating another population reduction. Things can be phased in over an extend-ed period, several generations, if need be.[51]

Well, there it is, the "great fear" completely debunked. Now that Churchill has explained it, non-Indians clearly have nothing to fear. Indian jurisdiction will not interfere with non-Indians, unless of course they want to live a life that is comfortable. I see we have nothing to fear but Indian sovereignty under Churchill's plan.

CHAPTER NINE

Re-Defining the Indian Problem

We have the power and the right to end the present system of red apartheid in this country, of wardship and dependency, all cloaked in the myth of sovereignty. But, do we have the will?

Judge R.A. Randall, Minnesota Court of Appeals
February 16, 1996

The white man says that the 1890 massacre was the end of the wars with the Indian, that it was the end of the Indian, the end of the Ghost Dance. Yet here we are at war, we're still Indians, and we're Ghost Dancing again.

Russell Means, Oglala, Lakota-Sioux, in 1973,
From *Ghost Dancing the Law*, by John Sayer, 1997

Taking in sum all of the treaties, all of the federal laws and policies enacted, and hundreds of years of rhetoric from both U.S. governments and Indians, the problem as it relates to American Indians has changed very little over the last 200 years. The central questions are fairly straight forward, but have never been fully answered or their answers fully agreed upon: do Indian tribes have inherent sovereign rights in the United States? Are Indian reservations sovereign nations in a territorial sense, where Indians will be permanently (and intentionally) segregated from the rest of the United States? Should Indians be governed by a separate set of rules and given additional rights over those received by other Americans?

The current state of Indian affairs is a compromised, hopelessly muddled version of "quasi-sovereignty" that satisfies neither side. This quasi-sovereignty has proved ineffective, even harmful, for the policy goals of both Indians and non-Indians, and each side is trying desperately to change the rules by which Indians are governed.

Today, Indians enjoy the benefits of dual citizenship. They are given the same rights as all other Americans, along with an additional set of rights and privileges granted them as members of Indian tribes. Indians insist that this special status arises out of old treaties, plus what they call original sovereignty. Hopefully, this book has convinced the reader that in fact the legal concept of Indian sovereignty was purposefully eliminated by treaties, the U.S. Constitution and subsequent U.S. laws. Treaties had two objectives, one of which was to establish the federal government as the sole and absolute sovereign over Indian tribes, and the other was to prepare Indians to become productive citizens of the United States. After Congress ended treaty making in 1871, it declared that "no Indian nation or tribe within the territory of the United States shall be acknowledged or recognized as an independent nation, tribe, or power with whom the United States may contract by treaty." Then in 1924, all Indians were made citizens of the United States, which provided a legal basis for ending the treaty relationship between the tribes and the United States for good.

How we've gotten to this point of quasi-sovereignty can only be blamed on government mismanagement, poor policy making and persistent tribal manipulation of a misinformed but sympathetic American public. Particularly harmful was the Indian Reorganization Act (IRA) of 1934, which gave tribes the right to draft their own tribal constitutions and for the first time set in law a separate set of Indian rights. Although Indians themselves despise the formal structure imposed on tribes and reservations by the IRA, IRA-based tribal governments have gradually assumed more territorially based powers and jurisdiction over the civil rights of Indians and non-Indians living on reservations or on Indian-owned land.

The sovereignty issue can be boiled down rather easily into two schools of thought. One view is encapsulated by Senator Lloyd Meeds in the American Indian Policy Review Commission report of 1977. Meeds believed that the U.S. Constitution — the very framework that incorporated the U.S. as a nation — provides for only two sovereign entities, namely federal and state governments. In contrast, Indian leaders like Marge Anderson, chief executive of the Minnesota Mille Lacs Band of Chippewa believes there are three sovereign entities in America: federal and state governments *and* Indian tribes. Regarding Indian sovereignty, Anderson had this to say at a meeting of the American Indian Research and Policy Institute, "Indian's sovereignty predates both federal and state governments. That means Indian governments have inherent sovereignty which is not derived from any other government, but rather from the people themselves."[1] She adds that sovereignty "is a hard concept for people to grasp. Part of the reason for this is that there is no clear definition of sovereignty."

While the sovereign status of Indians in the United States is indeed complex, the legal issue of sovereignty is a fairly unambiguous affair. Black's Law Dictionary states that sovereignty is:

> The international independence of a state, combined with the power of regulating its internal affairs without foreign dictation; the power to do everything in a state without accountability, to make laws, to execute and apply them, to impose and collect taxes and levy contributions, to make war and peace, to form treaties of alliance or of commerce with foreign nations, and the like.

By this definition, Indian tribes today are not sovereign, but they are trying to move down this path. Marge Anderson outlined a vision for sovereignty for the Mille Lacs Tribe that gives Indians the right to form their own government with the power to tax, regulate, and control a geographical area. This Indian government would have the ability to subject people to its laws and to enforce the law with military, police, or general citizen control.[2] In fact, this is close to reality on some reservations. Anderson believes there is support to continue pushing this envelope, noting, "People will work and fight and die to protect their sovereignty."[3] Precisely how far Indian sovereignty will distance tribes from American government is unclear. Erma Vizenor, a tribal official of the Minnesota White Earth Reservation, believes that tribal economic dependency on the federal government is an impediment to sovereignty. She believes that tribes can enhance their sovereignty by severing all economic ties with the government.[3]

A bigger underlying question is whether state and federal governments would "let" Indians secede from the United States in such a fashion. Similar attempts at defying U.S. government authority have been made by the likes of Montana Freemen and other separatist groups who would like to "wish away" all government not directly in their control. Ominously, however, Indians have already made significant progress to this ultimate goal, and have done so with the tacit and naïve approval of the American public. People believe actual balkanization of the United States would be impossible because the federal government wouldn't let that happen. It might surprise some, however, that government officials have let it happen in the past, and continue to do so today. At an Indian symposium in 1996, for example, Supreme Court Justice Sandra Day O'Connor identified three types of sovereign entities in the United States — the federal government, the states, and the Indian tribes — despite clear constitutional language to the contrary.

Such victories for greater Indian sovereignty spell bad news for America. Our past — indeed our present — has some ugly, abusive stories in it. But the United States still is one of the few countries that people are willing to risk their lives to reach, for the simple reason that it offers freedoms and opportunities for people of all races and cultures that are unmatched in the world. To gain better insight into the ills of ethnic separation, one needs to look only at the ethnic war that divided the former Yugoslavia into Bosnia, Serbia, Croatia, and Slovenia.

If that's too far away, or too ridiculous to contemplate in a superpower like the United States, just look north to Canada and the separatist movement afoot in Quebec that has been threatening to tear apart Canada for a generation. Concessions from the Canadian government over the last 20 years have given the province a distinct legal system and special powers to control immigration that make it possible to attract French-speaking newcomers. In a referendum held in Quebec in 1995, residents of the province voted against secession from Canada by a margin of just 1 percent.

French-speaking people of Quebec want to separate from Canada for the same reasons given by Indians in the United States: to preserve a unique culture and to control their own destiny. These are the same reasons, presumably, that motivated the Bosnians, Serbs, Croats, and Slovenians to violently separate the Balkans. Yet in the United States, all of these ethnic groups, with the exception of Indians, have comparatively little trouble integrating peacefully. Why? American citizens collectively share sovereignty, each holding it as an inherent individual right, instead of laying claim to it by right of ethnic privilege.

Three Scenarios

There are three possible scenarios for future U.S. policy toward Indians. First, all tribes could be given true sovereignty by allowing them to secede from the United States. This would, in all likelihood, be more traumatic for tribes than for the United States. All social services and other aid would be abruptly cut off, and tribes would have full financial responsibility for educating their youth, creating jobs, and providing basic municipal-type services like law enforcement and fire-fighting.

This would be *real* tribal sovereignty in the full legal sense. However, both Indians and the U.S. government are likely to fight such a scenario. In the long run, Indians might prosper under such a governance model. But in the short-term, they would no doubt experience chronic poverty by being cut off from government grants and other programs, that constitute a significant part of reservation revenue. While gaming revenues might offset some of the hardship, one has to remember that many Indians currently struggle with poverty, gaming revenues notwithstanding. Experts on gambling say that we have nearly reached the saturation point for gambling franchises, yet less than half of Indian reservations have casinos. Having little economic diversity, cutting off federal and state support would lay waste to the Indian economy. True

Indian sovereignty would also remove large amounts of energy and mineral resources from U.S. jurisdiction and Environmental Protection Agency monitoring, a situation that could cause serious problems in the future. In addition, it would likely displace large numbers of non-Indians who currently own land on reservations, or if they chose to stay these people would loose all rights guaranteed by the U.S. Constitution.

A second possibility is to continue tinkering with the current "quasi-sovereign" status of tribes, which has been the default position of U.S. Indian policy making for the last 200 years. There is no shortage of suggestions for nibbling at the policy margins regarding Indian affairs. But we should harbor no hopes that any changes would offer a long-term, productive solution for either side. It would likely benefit Indians in the short-term, as they would gain additional authority to govern themselves as well as non-Indians owning land on reservations, while maintaining the federal pipeline of financial support. However, it would fail, once again, to address the fundamental policy issue of tribal sovereignty.

Fergus Bordewich, in his book *Killing the White Man's Indian*, proposes an amendment to the Constitution that would clearly define tribes as self-governing and subject them to federal but not state laws. This would entail cutting and pasting parts of the U.S. Constitution on top of tribal constitutions, adding significantly to government bureaucracy while re-creating rights already guaranteed every American. What then would be the point of these quasi-sovereign enties?

Unfortunately, despite the fact that both Indians and non-Indians complain publicly about this quasi-sovereign strategy, it is an easy non-solution typical of government when it is faced with clear but opposing choices. Rather than ending this legal anomaly, bureaucrats perpetuate it by giving it newfound legitimacy through re-education. The Minnesota Department of Children, Families and Learning, for one, has established official curriculum on Native Americans that promotes Indian sovereignty. This curriculum is used to teach school children in grades kindergarten through twelve about Indian sovereignty and is part of the re-education plan Indian leaders envision to convince other Americans that Indian sovereignty is a legitimate right. Children who learn about Indian sovereignty in kindergarten are unlikely to question its validity later in life.

The third option, and in my view the best solution, is the elimination of Indian sovereignty in all its forms. This would put Indians on par with the rest of Americans, nothing more, and certainly nothing less. It would entail phasing out special financial support for Indians, while retaining basic access to social services based on need-not race. It would also entail the end of special hunting and fishing rights by way of eminent domain, which would include financial compensation for Indians. Reservations would become townships in a legal sense, governed by state and federal laws and the U.S. court system.

To many, this might sound harsh and authoritarian — a "punishment," if you will. One needs to take a step back to consider this proposal in its real light. First and foremost, it would provide Indians with the rights and legal protection that other Americans receive, rights widely admired and desired the world over. Admittedly, such a proposal does ask Indians to forfeit some existing rights and privileges, but only those which Indians enjoy at the expense and exclusion of all other Americans.

The typical argument against this strategy is that Indians will lose their culture and traditions, and ultimately their identity. This is an amazingly weak argument, one that pays the ultimate insult to the proud, deeply ingrained heritage of Indian culture. Such an argument assumes that Indian culture, by its very nature, is extremely fragile, non-adaptive, and offers its members only a tenuous attachment that is easily dislodged by superficial outside influences. Aside from Indians, no other race or culture is specifically targeted for "cultural protection" by U.S. law.

U.S. law does not preclude the collective gathering or geographic concentration of people of similar race or culture. It allows culture and tradition to be preserved *by choice* among its members, instead of by governmental edict. To say Indian culture could not — indeed, would not — survive is to underestimate the Indians' will to survive as a culture up to this point in American history, and to ignore the many distinct cultures that co-exist in American society today. Is there conflict in America among these different cultures? Of course, but arguably no more than the squabbles that would ensue in a collective Indian nation like that proposed by Ward Churchill.

Unfortunately, the Indian Reorganization Act of 1934 did a great deal to destroy Indian culture. Before tribal constitutions, Indian tribes were governed by traditional tribal leaders. Today, power within this constitutional framework is often concentrated in the hands of a few because tribal constitutions did not include such necessities as checks and balances of power. Over the years, people who advocated changes to the system have held out hope that Indian constitutions would eventually mirror the U.S. Constitution. The end result has been the creation of 550 new sets of laws, none of which created any rights that were not already guaranteed by the U.S. Constitution. Indeed, in many cases, tribal constitutions have impinged on the civil and property rights of Indians and non-Indians.

For this reason, I propose that tribal constitutions be abolished, and tribes be allowed to return to their traditional form of association with a council of elders if they so desire. These traditional Indian governments would fit into the American system of government without any conflicts with the U.S. or state constitutions. The Amish offer a perfect example of cultural preservation in the midst of a "modern" American society. Their dress, lifestyle and social structure are as different to today's mainstream culture as any Indian tribe.

A better question is whether today's Indian tribes really want to return to lifestyles of a bygone era. Certainly some do. One significant obstacle to returning to Indian life as it was 200 years ago is the practical elimination of hunting and gathering as a means of subsistence. This is not unique to America but has occurred virtually the world over. In a cultural sense, Indians today have every opportunity to practice the traditions and customs of their forefathers. Neither the U.S. government nor U.S. citizens stand in the way of this goal today, and all the sovereignty in the world will have little influence over whether Indians actually pursue this way of life.

As such, there are likely many layers of motivation behind the push for greater tribal sovereignty, with each layer satisfying the special interests of a different segment of the Indian population (not unlike our own system of governance, in fact). But continuing the policy of quasi-sovereignty makes a mockery of the U.S. Constitution and the integrity of the 550 Indian tribes in this country. The result will be continued disintegration of Indian tribes and the undermining of the fundamental rights of the American people.

In the United States we have popular sovereignty, also known as sovereignty of the people. Sovereignty by ethnic heritage, religion, or culture is illegal. In America, there are no Catholic governments, or Korean or Jewish or Polish governments. Indian governments are the one exception. The Civil War was fought to end ethnic sovereignty, and American federalism won. Now Indians are engaged in a struggle to re-invent ethnic segregation and race-based government. That struggle is the Second Civil War.

Chapter One Endnotes: My Unequal Family

1   I have changed the names of my relatives to protect their privacy.

2   D. J. Tice, "Ojibwe Aren't the Only Minnesotans Who Inherited 'Special' Property Rights," St. Paul *Pioneer Press*, March 19, 1997.

3   Steve Gilbert and Maureen Harrison, eds., *Abraham Lincoln: In His Own Words* (1994; New York: Barnes & Noble Books), p. 15.

4   Richard B. Morris and Jeffrey B. Morris, eds., 1996, *Encyclopedia of American History, Seventh Edition*, 1953, (New York: HarperCollins, 1996) p. 1201.

5   John William Sayer, *Ghost Dancing the Law: The Wounded Knee Trials* (Cambridge: Harvard University Press, 1997) p. 211.

Chapter Two Endnotes: Hunting and Gathering in the 21st Century

1   U.S. Dept. of Commerce, Bureau of the Census, *The American Almanac: 1996-97* (Washington: GPO, 1997) p. 8.

2   Paul Johnson, *Birth of the Modern: World Society 1815-1830* (New York: Harper Collins, 1991) pp. 222-224.

3   Charles Kappler, ed., *Indian Affairs, Laws and Treaties: Vol. 1* (Washington: GPO, 1903).

4   William Canby Jr., *American Indian Law in a Nutshell* (St. Paul: West Publishing Company, 1981) p. 80.

5   Stephen L. Prevar, *The Rights of Indians and Tribes: The Basic ACLU Guide to Indian Rights and Tribal Rights* (Carbondale: Southern Illinois University Press, 1992) p. 190.

6   Kappler.

7   Kappler.

8   Theodore Blegen, *Minnesota: A History of the State* (Minneapolis: University of Minnesota Press, 1963) pp. 159, 173.

9   Francis P. Prucha, *American Indian Treaties: A History of a Political Anomaly* (Los Angeles: University of California Press, 1994) p. 139.

10 Prucha, p. 184.

11 U.S. Court of Appeals, Eighth Circuit, *Mille Lacs Band of Chippewa Indians v. State of Minnesota, Minnesota Department of Natural Resources, and Rod Sando, Commissioner of Natural Resources*, Consolidated Appeal No. 97-1775, p. 9.

12 U.S. Court of Appeals, *Mille Lacs v. State of Minnesota*, p. 10.

13 U.S. Court of Appeals, *Mille Lacs v. State of Minnesota*, p. 11.

14 U.S. Court of Appeals, *Mille Lacs v. State of Minnesota*, p. 11.

15 Canby, p. 84.

16 Stephen G. Froehle and Randy V. Thompson, *On Petition for Writ of Certiorari to the United States Court of Appeals for the Eighth Circuit*, U.S. Supreme Court, October Term, 1997.

17 Froehle and Thompson, p. 52.

18 Froehle and Thompson, p. 51.

19 Prucha, p. 263.

20 Canby, p. 85.

21 Congress of the United States, *American Indian Policy Review Commission: Final Report* (Washington: GRO, 1977) p. 108.

22 U.S. Senate, *American Indian Policy Review Commission*, p. 523.

23 Fergus M. Bordewich, *Killing the White Man's Indian* (New York: Anchor Books
    Doubleday, 1996), p. 73.

24 Greg Gordon, "Former Justice Official Sentenced for Wrongly Representing Indians,"
    Minneapolis *StarTribune*, June 4, 1997.

25 "Star Tribune Indian Series Misses the Point," *Native American Press*, Nov. 7, 1997.

26 *The Resource*, June 1997, p. 2.

27 Pat Doyle, "The Casino Payoff: Gambling Creating Disparity of Wealth Among Tribes,"
    Minneapolis *StarTribune*, Nov. 4, 1997.

28 *StarTribune*, Nov. 4, 1997.

29 Jim Genia, Luncheon Presentation: Second Annual Indian Issues Symposium, St. Paul,
    Oct. 18, 1997.

Chapter Three Endnotes: To the Winner Go the Spoils

1   Information contained throughout this paragraph was taken from three Minneapolis
    StarTribune articles: Pat Doyle and Chris Ison, "Chippewa Leader Wadena Indicted,"
    Minneapolis *StarTribune*, Aug. 30, 1995; Pat Doyle, "Chip Wadena Trial Opens In St.
    Paul," May 14, 1996; Robert Franklin, "Conviction Unjustified, Court Told," Oct. 21, 1997.

2   *StarTribune* , Aug. 30, 1995; Oct. 21, 1997.

3   Pat Doyle, "The Casino Payoff: Tribal Spending Priorities Spark Debate," Minneapolis
    StarTribune, Nov. 3, 1997.

4   Pat Doyle, "Big Money Doesn't Impress Reservation Rife with Poverty," Minneapolis
    StarTribune, Oct. 22, 1995.

5   Lisa Grace Lednicer, "Theft Trial Begins for Trial Leader," St. Paul *Pioneer Press*,
    May 14, 1996

6   *StarTribune*, Oct. 22, 1995 (1989 interview quoted in article).

7   *StarTribune*, Oct. 22, 1995.

8   "Wadena Manipulated HUD Housing List, Paper Says," Minneapolis *StarTribune*,
    March 3, 1997.

9   *StarTribune*, March 3, 1997.

10 Lisa Grace Lednicer, "Wadena Guilty of Corruption," St. Paul *Pioneer Press*,
    June 25, 1996.

11 *StarTribune*, March 3, 1997.

12 *StarTribune*, Oct. 22, 1995.

13 *StarTribune*, May 19, 1996.

14 Lednicer, St. Paul *Pioneer Press*, May 14, 1996.

15 Information of the court trial taken from Minneapolis *StarTribune*, May 14, 1996;
    StarTribune, May 19, 1996; St. Paul *Pioneer Press*, May 14, 1996.

16 *StarTribune*, Aug. 30, 1995; *StarTribune*, Oct. 21, 1997; "Appeals Court Hears Argument
    in Wadena Corruption Conviction," St. Paul *Pioneer Press*, Oct. 21, 1997.

17 *StarTribune*, Oct. 21, 1997.

18 Fergus M. Bordewich, *Killing the White Man's Indian* (New York: Anchor Books
    Doubleday, 1996) p. 83.

19 Molly Guthrey, "Finn Gets 5 Years," St. Paul *Pioneer Press*, Sept. 6, 1996.

20 "Officials Seek Ways to Control Crime on Reservations," Minneapolis *StarTribune*, Aug. 29, 1997; "More Gang Activity Seen on Indian Reservations, Federal Officials Say," Minneapolis *StarTribune*, Sept. 18, 1997.

21 *StarTribune*, Aug. 29, 1997; *StarTribune*, Sept. 18, 1997.

22 *StarTribune*, Nov. 3, 1997.

23 *StarTribune*, Nov. 3, 1997.

24 "Tribal Officials Plan for Life Without Gaming Revenue," Minneapolis *StarTribune*, Oct. 22, 1995.

25 Pat Doyle, "The Casino Payoff: Tribes Struggling with Unemployment," Minneapolis *StarTribune*, Nov. 2, 1997; *StarTribune*, Nov. 3, 1997.

26 *Pioneer Press*, 1997

27 John R. Wunder, *Retained by the People: A History of American Indians and the Bill of Rights* (New York: Oxford University Press, 1994).

28 *StarTribune*, Nov. 2, 1997.

29 *StarTribune*, Nov. 2, 1997.

30 *StarTribune*, Nov. 3, 1997.

31 "Star Tribune Indian Series Misses the Point," *Native American Press*, Nov. 7, 1997.

32 "Indian Fisheries Association Cancels '97 Red Lake Season," Minneapolis *StarTribune*, April 22, 1997; Pat Doyle, "The Casino Payoff: Gambling Creating Disparity of Wealth Among Tribes," StarTribune, Nov. 4, 1997.

33 *Native American Press*, Nov. 7, 1997.

34 Gerald Vizenor, *Crossbloods: Bone Courts, Bingo, and Other Reports* (Minneapolis: University of Minnesota Press,1990) pp. 239, 240.

35 Bill Lawrence, telephone interview, Feb. 20, 1998.

36 Bordewich, p. 321

37 Bordewich, p. 320-322.

38 Vincent Hill, personal interview, Feb. 21, 1998.

39 "Fact Sheet," Mille Lacs Anishinabe People's Party (MAPP), Aug. 1995.

40 Hill, Feb. 21, 1998.

41 "Fact Sheet," MAPP, Aug. 1995, p. 2.

Chapter Four Endnotes: Indian Treaties and Racial Segregation

1   Francis P. Prucha, *American Indian Treaties: A History of a Political Anomaly* (Los Angeles: University of California Press, 1994) p. 1.

2   Prucha, pp. 23-27.

3   Prucha, pp. 36-37.

4   Prucha, p. 38. Parenthetical remark inserted by author for clarity.

5   Prucha, pp. 38-39, 65-66.

6   Minnesota Court of Appeals, Sylvia Cohen v. Little Six, Inc., d/b/a Mystic Lake Casino, Scott County District Court File No. C9501701, February 13, 1995, p. ??? (COLUMBUS QUOTES)

7   Minnesota Court of Appeals, *Cohen v. Little Six*, Inc., p. ????

8   Minnesota Court of Appeals, *Cohen v. Little Six*, *d/b/a Mystic Lake Casino*, Scott County Court File No. C9501701, February 13, 1995.

[9] Prucha, pp. 42, 66

[10] Prucha, p. 50.

[11] Prucha, p. 52. "Indian Nation" as used in Indian treaties is a matter of convention rather than one of reality. "Nation" was commonly used to refer to Indian tribes as an entity, while not conferring actual nation status to tribes as such.

[12] Prucha, p. 68.

[13] Prucha, p. 116.

[14] Prucha, pp. 118, 128, 119.

[15] Prucha, pp. 100, 101.

[16] Brian W. Dippie, *The Vanishing American: White Attitudes and U.S. Indian Policy* (Lawrence: University Press of Kansas, 1982) pp. 5, 6.

[17] Prucha, p. 153.

[18] Prucha, pp. 154, 155

[19] Dinesh D'Souza, *End of Racism: Principles for a Multicultural Society* (New York: The Free Press, 1995) pp. 75-76.

[20] Wilma Mankiller and Michael Wallis, *Mankiller: A Chief and Her People* (New York: St. Martin's Press, 1993), pp. 79-86.

[21] Richard B. Morris and Jeffrey B. Morris, eds., *Encyclopedia of American History, Seventh Edition*, 1953, (New York: HarperCollins, 1996) p. 192.

[22] Morris and Morris, p. 192.

[23] Prucha, p. 176, 177.

[24] Wilcomb E. Washington, *History of Indians-White Relations: Vol. 4, Handbook of North American Indians* Washington: Smithsonian Institute, 1988) p. 46.

[25] John Ehle, *Trail of Tears: The Rise and Fall of the Cherokee Nation* (New York: Anchor Books Doubleday, 1988) pp. 385, 390, 391

[26] Prucha, pp. 146, 147.

[27] Prucha, pp. 139, 171.

[28] Peter Farb, *Man Rise to Civilization: The Cultural Ascent of the Indians of North America* (New York: Penguin Books, 1991) p. 104.

[29] Prucha, p. 198.

[30] Theodore Blegen, *Minnesota: A History of the State* (Minneapolis: University of Minnesota Press, 1963) p. 159.

[31] Morris and Morris, pp. 218, 232.

[32] Prucha, pp. 235, 236.

[33] Morris and Morris, p. 626.

[34] Charles Kappler, ed., *Indian Affairs, Laws and Treaties Vol. 2* (Washington GPO, 1904).

[35] Judith Nies, *Native American History* (New York: Ballentine Books, 1996) p. 265.

[36] Mankiller and Wallis, pp. 121, 122.

[37] Ehle, p. 387.

[38] Mankiller and Wallis, p. 124.

[39] Nies, p. 265.

[40] Laurence M. Hauptman, *The Iroquois in the Civil War: From Battlefield to Reservation* (Syracuse: SyracuseUniversity Press, 1993), p. 91.

[41] Hauptman, p. 92.

[42] Prucha, p. 15.

[43] Hauptman, p. 92.

44 Hauptman, p. 96.
45 Annie Heloise Abel, *The American Indian and the End of the Confederacy, 1863-1866* (Lincoln: University of Nebraska Press, 1993) p. 345.
46 Mankiller and Wallis, p. 126.
47 Hauptman, pp. 11, 14, 39, 47, 49.
48 Ruth Maurry Underhill, *Red Man's America: A History of Indians in the United States* (Chicago: University of Chicago Press, 1971) p. 298.
49 Charles Kappler, ed., *Indian Affairs, Laws and Treaties: Vol. 2* (Washington: GPO, 1904).
50 Kappler, Vol. 2.
51 Kappler, Vol. 2.
52 Dippie, pp. 192, 193, 194, 200.
53 Wilcomb E. Washington, *History of Indians-White Relations: Vol. 4, Handbook of North American Indians* Washington: Smithsonian Institute, 1988) p. 58.
54 Wilcomb, p. 230.
55 Wilcomb, p. 230.
56 Congress of the United States, United States Senate, *Tribal Sovereign Immunity: Hearing Before the Committee on Indian Affairs* (Washington: GPO, 1996) p. 61.
57 Congress of the United States, United States Senate, *American Indian Policy Review Commission: Final Report* (Washington: GRO, 1977), p. 575.
58 Prucha, p. 1.
59 William W. Bishop, *International Law, Cases and Materials* (Boston: Little, Brown & Co., 1962) p. 199.
60 U.S. Senate, *American Indian Policy Review Commission*, p. 112.
61 Minnesota Court of Appeals, *Cohen v. Little Six, Inc.*
62 Minnesota Court of Appeals, *Cohen v. Little Six, Inc.*
63 Minnesota Court of Appeals, *Cohen v. Little Six, Inc.*
64 U.S. Senate, *American Indian Policy Review Commission*, p. 575.
65 Minnesota Court of Appeals, *Cohen v. Little Six, Inc.*
66 Vine Deloria, Jr. *Custer Died for Your Sins* (New York: Macmillan, 1969), p. 28.
67 Prucha, p. 18.
68 Prucha, p. 18.
69 Dippie, pp. 161-163.
70 Francis Paul Prucha, Americanizing the American Indians: Writings by the "Friends of the Indian" 1880-1900 (Cambridge: Harvard University Press, 1973) p. 80.
71 Dippie, p. 166.
72 Dippie, p. 164-166.
73 Dippie, p. 166.
74 Francis P. Prucha, *Documents of United States Indian Policy* (Lincoln: University of Nebraska Press, 1975) pp. 172-174.
75 Dippie, p 181.
76 Dippie, p 181
77 Dippie, p 179
78 Dippie, p 346
79 Prucha, *American Indian Treaties*, p. 373.
80 Dippie, pp. 277, 283.

[81] John R. Wunder, *Retained by the People: A History of American Indians and the Bill of Rights* (New York: Oxford University Press, 1994) p. 64.

[82] Wunder, p. ?? (DIRECT QUOTE)

[83] Wunder, pp. 64-66.

[84] Prucha, *Documents of United States Indian Policy*, pp. 222-224, 228.

[85] Prucha, *Documents of United States Indian Policy*, p. 227.

[86] Wunder, pp. 67, 68, 71.

[87] Wunder, p. 81.

[88] Wunder, pp. 82, 83.

[89] Wunder, pp. 88, 95.

[90] Alvin M. Josephy, *Red Power: The American Indians' Fight for Freedom* (New York: McGraw-Hill, 1971) pp. 17, 18.

[91] Josephy, pp. 21, 22.

[92] Josephy, p. 22.

[93] Stefan Kanfer, *The Last Empire: De Beers, Diamonds, and the World* (New York: Farrar Straus Giroux, 1993) pp. 187, 188, 217, 218.

[94] Dippie, p. 343.

[95] Dippie, pp. 336, 337.

[96] Dippie, p. 337.

[97] Prucha, *Documents of United States Indian Policy*, p. 233.

[98] Dippie, p. 338.

[99] Wunder, p. 99, 101.

[100] Dippie, p. 338.

[101] Wunder, p. 105.

[102] Dippie, p. 350.

[103] Wunder, p. 88, 106.

[104] SOURCE?? pp. 103, 104.

[105] Wunder, p. 100.

[106] REPORTER, "Article Headline," St. Paul *Pioneer Press*, 1977.

[107] Wunder, pp. 121, 122.

[108] U.S. Dept. of Commerce, Bureau of the Census, *The American Almanac: 1996-97* (Washington: GPO, 1997) p. 37.

[109] *Pioneer Press*, 1997

[110] Wunder, p. 106, 109.

Chapter Five Endnotes: 70s Activism

[1] Paul C. Smith and Robert A. Warrior, *Like a Hurricane: The Indian Movement from Alcatraz to Wounded Knee* (New York: The New Press, 1996) p. 39.

[2] Smith and Warrior, p. 41.

[3] Smith and Warrior, p. 42.

[4] Susan Hazen-Hammond, *Timelines of Native American History: Through the Centuries with Mother Earth and Father Sky* (New York: The Berkeley Publishing Group, 1977) p. 246.

[5] Smith and Warrior, p. 42.

[6] Smith and Warrior, pp. 42,45

7   Smith and Warrior, p. 55.

8   Smith and Warrior, p. 52.

9   Smith and Warrior, p. 54.

10 Smith and Warrior, p. 57.

11 Robert Warrior, *Tribal Secrets* (Minneapolis, University of Minnesota Press, 1995) p. 30-32.

12 Russell Means, *Where White Men Fear to Tread* (New York, St. Martin's Griffin, 1996), p. 105.

13 Vine Deloria, Jr. *Behind the Trail of Broken Treaties: An Indian Declaration of Independence* (Austin: University of Texas Press, 1974) p. 39.

14 Adam Fortunate Eagle, *Alcatraz! Alcatraz!: The Indian Occupation of 1969-1971* (Berkeley, Heydey Books, 1992) p. 15.

15 Smith and Warrior, pp. 9-12

16 Troy Johnson, *The Occupation of Alcatraz Island: Indian Self-Determination & The Rise of Indian Activism* (Urbana and Chicago, University of Illinois Press, 1996) p. 55.

17 Fortunate Eagle, p. 107, 109.

18 Johnson, p. 56-65.

19 Johnson, p. 74.

20 Smith and Warrior, p. 69.

21 Johnson, p. 53-55, 186.

22 Smith and Warrior, pp. 22, 25.

23 Smith and Warrior, p. 26.

24 Smith and Warrior, p. 74.

25 Smith and Warrior, p. 31.

26 Smith and Warrior, p. 34.

27 Johnson, p. 155-157.

28 Smith and Warrior, p. 75, 76.

29 Smith and Warrior, p. 63-65.

30 Johnson, p. 153-157.

31 Smith and Warrior, pp. 77, 60.

32 Smith and Warrior, pp. 100, 32.

33 Smith and Warrior, pp. 77-80.

34 Alvin M. Josephy, *Red Power: The American Indians' Fight for Freedom* (1971, Lincoln and London, University of Nebraska Press, 1985) p. 246, 247.

35 Smith and Warrior, p. 82.

36 Smith and Warrior, p. 93.

37 Smith and Warrior, p. 96.

38 S.L.A. Marshall, *The Crimsoned Prairie: The Indian Wars* (New York: Da Capo Press, 1972) pp. 230-234.

39 Josephy, p. 191.

40 Josephy, p. 193.

41 Josephy, p. 194.

42 Josephy, pp. 216, 217.

43 Josephy, p. 245.

44 Smith and Warrior, p. 103.

[45] Smith and Warrior, pp. 102, 103.

[46] Smith and Warrior, p. 104.

[47] Smith and Warrior, p. 127.

[48] Means, p. 163.

[49] Means, p. 151.

[50] Means, p. 160.

[51] Smith and Warrior, p 100

[52] Smith and Warrior, p112, 113

[53] Class notes, "Topics in American Indian Studies: Native Environmentalism at the Cusp of 2000." University of Minnesota, Fall, 1997,. Instructor: Winona LaDuke.

[54] Smith and Warrior, p. 112.

[55] Smith and Warrior, p. 114.

[56] Smith and Warrior, p. 115.

[57] Means, p. 196.

[58] Smith and Warrior, p. 115.

[59] Smith and Warrior, p. 54.

[60] Means, p. 198.

[61] Smith and Warrior, p. 116.

[62] Smith and Warrior, p 115,116

[63] Means, p. 164.

[64] Means, p. 207.

[65] Means, p. 220.

[66] Means, p. 204.

[67] Means, pp. 205, 206.

[68] Smith and Warrior, p. 120.

[69] Means, p. 223.

[70] Smith and Warrior, pp. 139-141.

[71] Smith and Warrior, p. 142

[72] Means, p. 223.

[73] Smith and Warrior, p. 151.

[74] Smith and Warrior, p. 143.

[75] Means, p. 227.

[76] Smith and Warrior, p. 143.

[77] Means, p. 225.

[78] Means, p. 227.

[79] Smith and Warrior, p. 144.

[80] Congress of the United States, United States Senate, *American Indian Policy Review Commission: Final Report* (Washington: GRO, 1977), p. 99.

[81] Means, pp. 228, 229

[82] Smith and Warrior, p. 174.

[83] Troy Johnson, Joane Nagel and Duane Champagne, eds., *American Indian Activism: Alcatraz to the Longest Walk* (Chicago: University of Chicago Press, 1997), p. 50.

[84] Francis P. Prucha, *American Indian Treaties: A History of a Political Anomaly* (Los Angeles: University of California Press, 1994) p. 413.

[85] Smith and Warrior, pp. 147, 149, 150.

[86] Smith and Warrior, pp. 145, 147.

[87] Smith and Warrior, p. 152.

[88] Smith and Warrior, p. 153.

[89] Smith and Warrior, pp. 146, 147, 153.

[90] Smith and Warrior, p. 154.

[91] Smith and Warrior, pp. 154, 155.

[92] Means, p. 231.

[93] Smith and Warrior, p. 156.

[94] Smith and Warrior, p. 156.

[95] Smith and Warrior, p. 157.

[96] Smith and Warrior, p. 161, 162.

[97] Deloria, *Trail of Broken Treaties*, p. 57.

[98] Smith and Warrior, p. 162.

[99] Means, pp. 233, 235.

[100] Means, pp. 233, 235.

[101] Prucha, *American Indian Treaties*, p. 414.

[102] Prucha, *American Indian Treaties*, p. 414.

[103] Smith and Warrior, p. 100.

[104] Smith and Warrior, p. 82.

[105] Smith and Warrior, p. 157.

[106] Josephy, p. 238.

[107] Dee Brown, *Bury My Heart at Wounded Knee: An Indian History of the American West* (New York: Henry Holt and Company, 1970) pp. 440-444.

[108] Marshall, p. 246.

[109] Evan S. Connell, *Son of Morning Star* (New York: Promontory Press, 1984) p. 383.

[110] Means, p. 265.

[111] Smith and Warrior, pp. 194, 196.

[112] Means, pp. 264, 266.

[113] Means, p. 267.

[114] Means, p. 267.

[115] Means, p. 281.

[116] John W. Sayer, *Ghost Dancing the Law: The Wounded Knee Trials* (Cambridge: Harvard University Press, 1997), p. 129.

[117] Sayer, p. 34.

[118] Means, p. 271.

[119] Means, p. 272, 273.

[120] Smith and Warrior, p. 203.

[121] Sayer, p. 35.

[122] Sayer, pp. 35, 36.

[123] U.S. Senate, *American Indian Policy Review Commission*, Vol. 2, p. 3.

[124] Sayer, p. 38.

[125] Sayer, pp. 45, 55.

[126] Sayer, pp. 45, 55, 42, 70.

[127] Sayer, pp. 186, 189, 194, 198, 132.

[128] Means, p. 319.

Chapter Six Endnotes: The Government Cave-in

1   Alvin M. Josephy, *Red Power: The American Indians' Fight for Freedom* (New York: McGraw-Hill, 1971) p. 96.

2   Josephy, pp. 191-194.

3   Francis P. Prucha, *Documents of United States Indian Policy* (Lincoln: University of Nebraska Press, 1975) p. 257.

4   Josephy, p. 215.

5   Josephy, pp. 216, 217.

6   Paul C. Smith and Robert A. Warrior, *Like a Hurricane: The Indian Movement from Alcatraz to Wounded Knee* (New York: The New Press, 1996) p. 258.

7   Smith and Warrior, p. 266.

8   Congress of the United States, United States Senate, *American Indian Policy Review Commission: Final Report, vol. 2* (Washington: GRO, 1977) p. 3.

9   American Indian Studies Center, *New Directions in Federal Indian Policy* (Los Angeles: University Press of California, 1979) p. 115.

10   Russell Means, *Where White Men Fear to Tread* (New York, St. Martin's Griffin, 1996) p. 137.

11   Means, p. 116.

12   Means, p. 139.

13   Means, p. 115.

14   Means, p. 166.

15   Means, p. 348.

16   U.S. Senate, *American Indian Policy Review Commission*, p. 571.

17   U.S. Senate, *American Indian Policy Review Commission*, p. 572.

18   U.S. Senate, *American Indian Policy Review Commission*, p. 573.

19   U.S. Senate, *American Indian Policy Review Commission*, p. 114.

20   U.S. Senate, *American Indian Policy Review Commission*, p. 573.

21   U.S. Senate, *American Indian Policy Review Commission*, p. 574.

22   Lisa Grace Ledener, "Wadena Guilty of Corruption," St. Paul *Pioneer Press*, June 25, 1996.

23   Pat Doyle and Chris Ison, "Chippewa Leader Wadena Indicted," Minneapolis *StarTribune*, Aug. 30, 1995.

24   Robert Franklin, "Wadena Conviction Unjustified, Court Told," Minneapolis *StarTribune*, Oct. 21, 1997.

25   U.S. Senate, *American Indian Policy Review Commission*, p. 575.

26   U.S. Senate, *American Indian Policy Review Commission*, p. 579.

27   U.S. Senate, *American Indian Policy Review Commission*, p. 581.

28   U.S. Senate, *American Indian Policy Review Commission*, p 605

29   Classnotes, "Topics in American Indian Studies: Native Environmentalism at the Cusp 2000," Instructor: Winona LaDuke. University of Minnesota, Fall, 1997.

30   U.S. Senate, *American Indian Policy Review Commission*, p. 595.

31   U.S. Senate, *American Indian Policy Review Commission*, p. 622.

32   Classnotes, "Topics in American Indian Studies: Native Environmentalism at the Cusp 2000," Instructor: Winona LaDuke. University of Minnesota, Fall, 1997; St. Paul *Pioneer Press*, 1997.

33   U.S. Senate, *American Indian Policy Review Commission*, p 586.

[34] U.S. Senate, *American Indian Policy Review Commission*, p. 1.

[35] Judith Nies, *Native American History* (New York: Ballentine Books, 1996) p. 279.

[36] U.S. Senate, *American Indian Policy Review Commission*, p. 143.

[37] U.S. Senate, *American Indian Policy Review Commission*, p. 99, 143.

[38] U.S. Senate, *American Indian Policy Review Commission*, p. 144.

[39] U.S. Senate, *American Indian Policy Review Commission*, p. 126.

[40] U.S. Senate, *American Indian Policy Review Commission*, p. 311.

[41] U.S. Senate,*American Indian Policy Review Commission*, p. 312.

[42] National Alliance policy statement

[43] The American Indian Research and Policy Institute, *The Road to Common Cause: The Threatened State of Tribal Sovereignty*, forum report from May 30-31, 1996.

[44] U.S. Senate, *American Indian Policy Review Commission*, p. 312.

[45] The American Indian Research and Policy Institute, *American Indians & Philanthrophy*, a summary report of the December 9, 1994 forum, p. ????.

[46] U.S. Senate, *American Indian Policy Review Commission*, p. 617.

[47] U.S. Senate, *American Indian Policy Review Commission*, p. 3.

[48] U.S. Senate, *American Indian Policy Review Commission*, p. 612.

[49] American Indian Studies Center, *New Directions in Federal Indian Policy: A Review of the American Indian Policy Review Commission* (Los Angeles 1979) p. 121.

[50] American Indian Studies Center, p. 120.

[51] U.S. Senate, *American Indian Policy Review Commission*, vol. 2, p. 11.

[52] American Indian Studies Center, p. 120.

[53] U.S. Senate, *American Indian Policy Review Commission*, vol. 4, p. 2.

Chapter Seven Endnotes: Examining the Indian Demand for Ethnic Sovereignty

[1] Congress of the United States, United States Senate, *Tribal Sovereign Immunity: Hearing Before the Committee on Indian Affairs* (Washington: GPO, 1996), p. 543.

[2] Minnesota Court of Appeals, *Sylvia Cohen v. Little Six, Inc., d/b/a Mystic Lake Casino*, Scott County District Court File No. C9501701, February 13, 1995.

[3] Amy Kubelbeck, "Legal Rights Fund Formed to Counter Tribal Immunity," *Native American Press*, Feb. 21, 1997.

[4] Steve Karnowski, "Appeals Court Decision: Ex-Employee Cannot Sue Little Six in State Courts," St. Paul *Pioneer Press*, July 11, 1995. GAVLE CASE

[5] Pat Doyle, "Sovereign and Immune: Tribes Often Can't be Touched in Court," Minneapolis *StarTribune*, July 24, 1995.

[6] Pat Doyle, "The Casino Payoff: Gambling Creating Disparity of Wealth Among Tribes," Minneapolis *StarTribune*, Nov. 4, 1997.

[7] Craig Greenberg (Gavle's lawyer), personal interview, May 1997.

[8] U.S. Senate, *Tribal Sovereign Immunity*, p. 2.

[9] U.S. Senate, *Tribal Sovereign Immunity*, p. 4.

[10] U.S. Senate, *Tribal Sovereign Immunity*, p. 565.

[11] U.S. Senate, *Tribal Sovereign Immunity*, p. 580.

[12] Fergus M. Bordewich, *Killing the White Man's Indian* (New York: Anchor Books Doubleday, 1996) pp. 110, 111.

[13] Bordewich, p. 73

14 U.S. Senate, *Tribal Sovereign Immunity.*

15 U.S. Senate, *Tribal Sovereign Immunity*, p. 622.

16 Bordewich, p. 110.

17 Bordewich, pp. 74, 109.

18 Bordewich, p. 114.

19 U.S. Senate, *Tribal Sovereign Immunity*, p. 625.

20 U.S. Senate, *Tribal Sovereign Immunity*, pp. 625, 626.

21 U.S. Senate, *Tribal Sovereign Immunity*, pp. 621, 625.

22 U.S. Senate, *Tribal Sovereign Immunity*, p. 628.

23 Bill Lynn, "Position Paper on the Designation of Trust Lands by Native American Tribes," City of Sault Ste. Marie, June 1, 1997.

24 Darrel Smith, *Indian Reservations: America's Model of Destruction, A Brief Expose of America's Disastrous Indian Policies* (Mobridge, South Dakota: Citizens Equal Rights Alliance, 1997).

25 U.S. Senate, *Tribal Sovereign Immunity*, p. 6.

26 Robert Whereatt, "Governor Joins Tribal Land Debate," Minneapolis *StarTribune*, Oct. 13, 1995.

27 "Scott County Accepts Tribe's Offer for Casino- related Costs," St. Paul *Pioneer Press*, June 19, 1997.

28 Minnesota Court of Appeals, *Granite Valley Hotel Limited Partnership, d/b/a Granite Valley Hotel vs. Jackpot Junction Bingo and Casino*, Red County Distric Court File No. C49614, February 18, 1997.

29 Attorney James M. Johnson, of Olympia, Washington, *Tribal Sovereign Immunity*, p. 337.

30 Minnesota Court of Appeals, *Granite Valley Hotel vs. Jackpot Junction.*

31 Minnesota Court of Appeals, *Granite Valley Hotel vs. Jackpot Junction.*

32 Minnesota Court of Appeals, *Granite Valley Hotel vs. Jackpot Junction.*

33 Minnesota Court of Appeals, *Granite Valley Hotel vs. Jackpot Junction.*

34 U.S. Senate, *Tribal Sovereign Immunity*, p. 544.

35 U.S. Senate, *Tribal Sovereign Immunity*, p. 545.

36 Minnesota Court of Appeals, *Granite Valley Hotel vs. Jackpot Junction.*

37 Minnesota Court of Appeals, *Granite Valley Hotel vs. Jackpot Junction.*

38 Minnesota Court of Appeals, *Cohen v. Little Six, Inc.*

39 Richard B. Morris and Jeffrey B. Morris, eds., *Encyclopedia of American History, Seventh Edition* (1953; New York: HarperCollins, 1996) p. 288, 654.

40 Morris and Morris, p. 661.

41 Rick Whaley and Walter Bressette, *Walleye Warriors* (Philadelphia: New Society Publishers, 1994) p. 31.

42 U.S. Senate, *Tribal Sovereign Immunity*, pp. 69, 70, 71.

43 U.S. Senate, *Tribal Sovereign Immunity*, p. 70.

44 U.S. Senate, *Tribal Sovereign Immunity*, p. 979.

45 U.S. Senate, *Tribal Sovereign Immunity*, p. 707.

46 Bordewich, p. 107.

47 U.S. Senate, *Tribal Sovereign Immunity*, p. 1089.

48 U.S. Senate, *Tribal Sovereign Immunity*, p. 37.

49 U.S. Senate, *Tribal Sovereign Immunity*, p. 1122.

50 U.S. Senate, *Tribal Sovereign Immunity*, p. 1115.
51 U.S. Senate, *Tribal Sovereign Immunity*, p. 1117.
52 U.S. Senate, *Tribal Sovereign Immunity*, pp. 1092, 1099, 1100.
53 U.S. Senate, *Tribal Sovereign Immunity*, p. 1117.
54 U.S. Senate, *Tribal Sovereign Immunity*, p. 903.
55 U.S. Senate, *Tribal Sovereign Immunity*, p. 1093.
56 U.S. Senate, *Tribal Sovereign Immunity*, p. 37.
57 U.S. Senate, *Tribal Sovereign Immunity*, p. 731.
58 U.S. Senate, *Tribal Sovereign Immunity*, p. 253.
59 Gene Bigey, Indian Symposium, Oct. 1997; Russell Means, *Where White Men Fear to Tread* (New York, St. Martin's Griffin, 1996).
60 U.S. Senate, *Tribal Sovereign Immunity*, p. 81.
61 U.S. Senate, *Tribal Sovereign Immunity*, pp. 96-97.
62 U.S. Senate, *Tribal Sovereign Immunity*, p. 96.
63 U.S. Senate, *Tribal Sovereign Immunity*, p. 97.
64 U.S. Senate, *Tribal Sovereign Immunity*. pp. 324, 325.
65 U.S. Senate, *Tribal Sovereign Immunity*, p. 78.
66 U.S. Senate, *Tribal Sovereign Immunity*, p. 61.
67 Means, pp. 370, 279.
68 Means, pp. 324, 325.
69 Means, pp. 365, 371.
70 *Cherokee Nation* cited in Minnesota Court of Appeals, *Cohen v. Little Six, Inc.*
71 Means, p. 543.

Chapter Eight Endnotes: Education and Propaganda

1 Vine Deloria, Jr. *Behind the Trail of Broken Treaties: An Indian Declaration of Independence* (Austin: University of Texas Press, 1974) p. 2.
2 Deloria, *Behind the Trail*, p. 3.
3 Vine Deloria, Jr. *Custer Died for Your Sins: An Indian Manifesto* (New York: Macmillan, 1969) p. 194.
4 Deloria, Custer, pp. 195-196.
5 Russell Means, *Where White Men Fear to Tread* (New York, St. Martin's Griffin, 1996) p. 234.
6 Means, p. 510.
7 Means, jacket quotes on inside cover.
8 Means, p. 546.
9 Means, p. 547.
10 Means, p. 552.
11 Means, p. 552.
12 Means, p. 234.
13 Means, p. 554.
14 Means, p. 542.
15 Means, p. 543.
16 Means, p. 519.

[17] Ake Hultkrantz, *The Religions of the American Indians* (Berkeley: University of California Press, 1979) p. 245.

[18] Dee Brown, *Bury My Heart at Wounded Knee: An Indian History of the American West* (New York, Henry Holt and Company, 1970) p. 444.

[19] Frederick Drimmer, ed. *Captured by the Indians: 15 Firsthand Accounts, 1950-1870* (New York: Dover Publications, Inc., 1961).

[20] Drimmer, p. 314.

[21] "Macalaster Academic Update," Macalaster College, Dept. of Anthropology, 1997.

[22] Jack Weatherford, *Indian Givers: How the Indians of the Americas Transformed the World* (New York: Fawcett Columbine, 1988) pp. 54, 55.

[23] Weatherford, p. 57.

[24] Will Durant, The Story of Civilization (New York: MJF Books, 1939).

[25] Weatherford, p. 43.

[26] Weatherford, p. 45.

[27] Weatherford, p. 215.

[28] Weatherford, p. 213.

[29] Weatherford, p. 214.

[30] Weatherford, p. 203.

[31] Lokihi pamphlet, *Proud Indigenous Peoples for Education*, Vol. 1 Issue 2

[32] Ward Churchill, *Indians Are Us: Culture and Genocide in Native North America* (Monroe, Maine: Common Courage Press, 1994) jacket cover.

[33] Ward Churchill, S*truggle for the Land: Indigenous Resistance to Genocide, Ecocide, and Expropriation in Contemporary North America* (Monroe, Maine: Common Courage Press, 1993) p. 3.

[34] Churchill, Struggle, p. 5.

[35] Churchill, Struggle, p. 5.

[36] Churchill, Struggle, p. 8.

[37] Churchill, Struggle, p. 26.

[38] Churchill, Struggle, p. 63.

[39] Churchill, Struggle, p. 415.

[40] Churchill, Struggle, p. 423.

[41] Churchill, Struggle, p. 425.

[42] Churchill, Struggle, p. 416.

[43] Churchill, Struggle, p. 425.

[44] Churchill, Struggle, p. 425.

[45] Churchill, Struggle, p. 427.

[46] Churchill, Struggle, p. 427.

[47] Churchill, Struggle, p. 428.

[48] Churchill, Struggle, p. 429.

[49] Churchill, Struggle, p. 439.

[50] Churchill, Struggle, p. 439.

[51] Churchill, Struggle, p. 441.

Chapter Nine Endnotes

[1] American Indian Research and Policy Institute, "Sovereignity Provides Framework for Understanding Tribal Governments," forum report on "The Threatened State of Tribal Sovereingity," May 30-31, 1996, p. 4.

[2] American Indian Research and Policy Institute, p. 4.

[3] American Indian Research and Policy Institute, "Tribal Governments: What Will They Look Like in the Year 2010, " keynote address in forum report, Nov. 15, 1996, p. 3.